it is what it is
writings on Dan Flavin
since 1964

Edited by
Paula Feldman and Karsten Schubert

Ridinghouse in association with

Thames & Hudson

First published in the United Kingdom in 2004 by Ridinghouse, 47 Lexington Street, London W1R 3LG in association with Thames & Hudson Ltd, 181A High Holborn, London WC1V 7QX.

www.thamesandhudson.com

© 2004 Paula Feldman and Karsten Schubert
For additional copyright credits see p. 294
Cover illustration © 2004, ARS, New York and DACS, London
Photograph: Cathy Carver, Courtesy Dia Center For the Arts, New York

British Library Cataloguing-in-Publication Data
A catalogue record for this book is available from the British Library
ISBN 0-500-976449

Designed by Herman Lelie and Stefania Bonelli, London

Printed and bound in the United Kingdom by Short-Run Press

Cover:

Dan Flavin, *Untitled ("monument" for V. Tatlin)* 1975 (left) and *Untitled ("monument" for V. Tatlin)*, 1975 (right). Collection Dia Center For the Arts, New York

Contents

Writings on Dan Flavin since 1964

Dan Flavin, space explorer

Looking at Dan Flavin's work one is always taken aback by the great discrepancy between means deployed and effect achieved. Even if we know what to anticipate, the reality of his work by far exceeds expectations. The use of the most basic light source and fittings (mass produced and standardized down to the colour range) paired with a layout code allowing little room for variant or digression, that such self-imposed strict limits could result in an art that is so varied, exuberant and alive, still awes. In a world where our response to images has become ritualized and blunted by repetition, to this day we have not quite got used to what Flavin is offering.

Considering Dan Flavin's fame and historical status as one of the great artists of his generation, it is surprising how seldom his work is exhibited, how rarely it is reproduced and how little it is written about. The reasons for this are manifold.

Flavin's works cannot be shown in rooms containing other artist's paintings or sculptures. Being neither painting nor sculpture, they commandeer space to the exclusion of all else. What Rosalind Krauss has termed the 'articulated spatial presence specific to Minimalism' Flavin took to its extreme. The light emitted leaves no room for anything else, and as a result his works are often relegated to a museum's lobby or other public areas, set aside from the main exhibition galleries. When I grew up in Berlin in the 1970s, the Nationalgalerie always displayed Flavin's work in the lower ground floor lobby. You saw it in passing on your way in and out.

The work is equally 'territorial' in a domestic context, and as a result only a few private collectors have had the stomach and dedication to integrate it into their homes.

It is virtually impossible to faithfully photograph Flavin's works in a way that conveys a truthful sense of their vibrant and extraordinary presence. The camera tends to turn emitted light either into a solid form surrounded by darkness or into a pale washed-out glow drowned in daylight. The optical lens is unable simultaneously to pick up artificial light and ambience (daylight) with any accuracy. Instead, one or the other always appears over-emphasised: in reproduction Flavin's work looks either loudly theatrical or plainly underwhelming. Compounding this, differently coloured fluorescent tubes, though appearing to the eye to have the same light output, in fact register as different intensities to the camera, making works seem to be in urgent need of maintenance. There is, to my knowledge, no photographic record that conveys any true sense of the reality of Flavin's art.

How does one write about work that is without precedent? Flavin posed a formidable challenge to writers because there was no already rehearsed discourse on which to fall back. No matter how difficult the work of Andre, Judd or Lewitt were, at a stretch at least they fitted into recognised notions of painting and sculpture. The work of one artist could be discussed with direct reference to the others. Flavin, on the other hand, offered no such short-cuts, and the curious status of his work – existing in a no-man's land between installation and sculpture – only added to the conundrum. The inexplicable gulf between cause and effect, the beguiling discrepancy between the economy of materials deployed and the simplicity of layouts on the one hand and the poetic effect achieved on the other, made matters again more puzzling and complicated.

A further aspect that is absolutely unique to Flavin's work is its particular temporality and (lack of) physicality: it is strangely without the look of history or the patina of age (the work knows no past-tense). Even the term 'work' seems to be indicative more of a process than an actual physical object; for his installations Flavin preferred the equally fluid term 'situation'.

Flavin's use of light is so unique and radical that many writers could only offer a frustrating tautology. In a way his work is a case study in art criticism without any cross-references: unable to appropriate from other discourses (contemporary or historic), writers had to start from scratch. They had to invent a terminology specifically applicable to a single artist and his body of work. Few critics were willing or able to go along with such an extreme demand. Looking at the first decade of writings assembled in this book the desperate struggle for words is fascinating, often touching, and sometimes funny.

By all accounts Flavin's personality hardly helped matters. Lacking Donald Judd's angry eloquence, his forte was, in the word of Marianne Stockebrand, a 'friendly, unrelenting passivity', an unsettling experience for those at the receiving end. Flavin rarely offered pointers or 'explained' his art. I believe he did not consider this part of his job as an artist.

The texts assembled in this volume document four decades of writings about the artist, from the initial tentative attempts at coming to terms with what Flavin was doing to Michael Govan's extensive essay of 1999, the first comprehensive overview of Flavin's career. In between lie reviews that are concerned with specific aspects of his work (Marianne Stockebrand) or particular exhibitions. Other texts paint a picture of Flavin as a protagonist of the art world (Hans Strelow), or attempt to place him in a wider, contemporaneous context.

From Judd's early, partisan praise to much calmer later appreciations, the sequence of texts shows much not so much a change of opinion but rather a shift from an instinctive to a more rational affirmation of Flavin's greatness. What most writers share is agreement about Flavin's extraordinary achievement, expressed, as time passes, with increasing eloquence.

Dan Flavin died prematurely at the end of 1996. His final decade was a difficult one, there were health problems, and his work was received lukewarm at best. I am sure he would be immensely cheered to learn about the progress made since. First there was the realisation of his long-awaited Marfa project in 2000. In the same year his survey exhibition at the Serpentine Gallery in London was received to great critical acclaim. In 2003 the Dia Foundation installed a large group of Flavin's work at its new outpost in Beacon, upstate New York, and finally there will be a much anticipated retrospective at the National Gallery of Art in Washington DC in the autumn of 2004.

Over the course of four decades the seeds for this new recognition of Flavin's achievement were laid by the many writers assembled in this volume. Their struggle to find words forms the foundation on which today's appreciation of Dan Flavin's singular achievement is based.

Karsten Schubert March 2004

Introduction

There is an implicit irony in assembling a collection of writings on the work of Dan Flavin. From the mid to late-1960s, polemical texts by Flavin appeared periodically in *Artforum* and *Studio International*. In lambasting critics, curators and dealers alike, his rhetoric was formidable. One discussion of the state of art criticism, for example, ended with the plea, 'Get the point at last; we who are artists and/or participants in art don't want you and the endless disservice of your self-conscious discursive "blight" on art.'[1] With the artist poised at his typewriter, it is a wonder anyone dared write about his work.

Of course, many did; the results are included in this anthology. It is by no means comprehensive, but offers instead an overview of responses to Flavin's art through the decades and across continents. Historical accounts of gallery and museum exhibitions accompany more speculative, offbeat pieces, such as Michael Gibson's investigation of 'the strange case' of the fluorescent tube. Among the authors in this anthology, the reflections of his artist contemporaries Donald Judd, Mel Bochner and Dan Graham contain some of the most astute assessments of his art. Just as the visual effects of Flavin's work defied the stringent categorisation of minimal art, this selection of essays attempts to extend the geographic and historical parameters of the discourse on his work.

Arranged chronologically, these writings begin with reviews of Flavin's exhibitions at Kaymar Gallery, New York, in May of 1964, which included both his 'icons' (reliefs with a light bulb or fluorescent tube) and fluorescent light pieces. Lucy R. Lippard, Kim Levin, and Judd counted among the critics to first take notice of Flavin's unusual application of light. By the autumn of that year, his exhibition at Green Gallery consisted entirely of these arrangements of fluorescent tubes. Writing for the *Village Voice*, David Bourdon observed that placement alone distinguished the Green exhibition from the window display of a midtown electrical company: 'The only thing that makes Flavin's tubes art is that they have been arranged and put into an art context.' One year later, Jacob Grossman in *Arts Magazine* recorded his impatient dismissal of the work, conceding, 'I cannot get beyond the object to the aesthetic involved'. Most acerbic of all was Hilton Kramer's 1967 declaration in *The New York Times* that Flavin was not an artist, but simply someone who had been given space in an art gallery.[2]

Outside New York, institutional exhibitions at the end of the decade unveiled Flavin's work to audiences often unfamiliar with contemporary art. Whitney Halstead's review of his first one-person show at the Museum of Contemporary Art, Chicago, in 1968 only hints at the controversy inspired by Flavin's radical approach, noting the exhibition's 'mixed reception'. Critics for Canadian newspapers such as Toronto's *Globe and Mail* and *The Vancouver Province* praised Flavin's National Gallery of Canada retrospective as a 'fantastically beautiful show.' The exhibition's transfer to the Jewish Museum in the spring of 1970 coincided with other shows, resulting in the simultaneous display of his work in five different New York venues.

Tracing these writings draws attention to the evolving responses of several critics to Flavin's art. Peter Plagens's discussion of Flavin's 1971 Ace Gallery exhibition, for example, reveals his dissatisfaction with the work. Two years later, the artist's substantial exhibition at the St. Louis Art Museum left him tongue-tied: 'When I was in the show I found, delightfully, I couldn't think like a critic; I couldn't make art-historical or art world connections, or glue any language to what I saw.' Watching the reactions of other museum visitors, Plagens concluded that the work succeeded in its appeal to both 'esoteric (art world)' and 'exoteric (public) audiences'.

Flavin himself might not have approved of some of the inclusions in this anthology, as in the case of the review of his first show at Galleria Sperone in Milan, an exhibition he chose not to recognise as one of his own.[3] Nonetheless, this piece, along with Hans Strelow's article in *Frankfurter Allgemeine Zeitung*, Pleynet's 'Lettres de Paris' in *Art International*, and Germano Celant's reviews in *Domus*, introduced his work to European readers. Strelow, for one, characterised Flavin as a mythical 'purist super-artist' who helped shape the 'artistic consciousness of the present time'. To Pleynet's knowledge, Flavin was 'the first to think like a sculptor in space', reconfiguring the definition of sculpture, 'a discipline that has been in need of renewal for a long time'. The early interest in Flavin's work in Europe is noteworthy, particularly in view of the precedent of European artistic experiments in light, which Frederik Leen explores.

By the late 1970s, this work was, to an extent, canonised. Evidence of this shift may be found in Graham's 1979 'Art in Relation to Architecture/ Architecture in Relation to Art', which discussed Flavin's pivotal role in creating installations dependent upon the surrounding architectural space. Graham later termed this the 'nasty criticality' of Flavin's art, subverting the gallery's existing light system and destroying 'all the other art on view in that space'.[4] At the same time, Flavin's exhibition at the Leo Castelli Gallery, New York, in 1980 resulted in reviews full of adjectives such as 'vintage' and 'classic'. For others, the work itself had 'lost its iconic presence'. Flavin, it seemed, had reached a stalemate, and to many observers his work appeared stagnant and repetitive.

Flavin's critical fortune changed in the mid-1990s, when his luminous installations once again inspired praise. With the controversy of thirty years behind them, these works elicited descriptions as ethereal, otherworldly spaces of coloured light. Flavin's exhibition at the Dia Center for the Arts, Pepe Karmel decided, was the closest one could come to 'finding inner peace' in New York City. Familiar historically and materially, the work had nonetheless evolved, both physically and in our perception of it, according to Richard Kalina. 'Its forms, means and associations seem to grow richer and more complex as time passes. New meanings accrue, the frame of reference widens'.

The renewed enthusiasm for his work, however, came at a point when Flavin's health began to dramatically deteriorate. He died in December 1996, just a few months after Kalina's feature appeared in *Art in America*. Roberta Smith's obituary in *The New York Times* eloquently testified to his legacy in producing 'an art brazenly radical...yet characterized by profound, even ecstatic beauty that was at once painterly and architectural'. As detailed by Tiffany Bell, the posthumous completion of two major projects in Milan and Marfa contributed to the expansion of his oeuvre until 2000.

Subsequent European exhibitions continued to bring Flavin's work to the fore. Following David Anfam's review of the 'literally eye-opening' Guggenheim Berlin show, Flavin's exhibition at the Serpentine Gallery, London in 2001 met with critical acclaim. Situated in the centre of Kensington Gardens, the gallery's windowed walls accentuated the work's relationship with the interior architectural space as well as its exterior surroundings. For Charles Darwent, the effect was that of a religious experience, recounted in quips about miracles, immaculacy, and transubstantiation. He suggested, 'If you're reading this on Sunday morning, my advice is to skip church and head to the Serpentine Gallery. You'll never get to heaven if you don't.' Similarly, Jonathan Jones described the gallery's 'chapels and cupolas of colour' resulting from art that 'drugged' one's senses.

Equally important to the critical reception is the art historical assessment of Flavin's work, which recently underwent a metamorphosis. Writing in 1990, Rosalind Krauss determined that a 'reprogramming' of this work in the context of late capitalist museums meant that a focus on space now replaced a focus on the object.[5] Or, as James Meyer has explained, 'Once the Flavin lamp surrounded the viewer in its glow...and became, of all things, a pleasurable experience, it could no longer be considered a critical work.' Indeed, the literature on Flavin's work from this date seems to affirm Krauss's prediction, from Karmel's suggestion of this art's zen-like qualities to Jones's association of 'an artificial paradise where we need never be in the dark'. Recent writing embraces the sensory pleasures of Flavin's work; words such as exuberant, beautiful and emotional supplant discussions of austerity, literalism, and the readymade. Perhaps what now stands is the notion of an 'aesthetic' Flavin alongside a 'critical Flavin'. In time, we have come to appreciate Flavin's art as a feat of installation, not objecthood, and, likewise, as a product of both conceptual and minimal origin.[6]

In his writing and in his art, particularly in his numerous 'dedications', Flavin pointed to a variety of sources for his work, from the philosophy of nominalism to the writings of James Joyce. The texts in this anthology identify all these sources except one. At a 2001 symposium at the Chinati Foundation, Michael Govan recounted that Flavin once cited Ralph Ellison's *Invisible Man* when asked by Carl Andre how he arrived at this particular form of light art.[7] As it turns out, Flavin first recorded this reference to Ellison in an artist's statement for two exhibition catalogues in the Hague and Turin during the spring of 1968. In these passages, he included an excerpt from the prologue of Ellison's novel.[8] Years later, at Documenta 11 in Kassel in 2002, Canadian artist Jeff Wall unveiled a transparency lightbox based upon this excerpt. Wall's *After "Invisible Man" by Ralph Ellison, the Preface*, 1999–2001, depicts the Invisible Man's basement hideaway, a 'hole...warm and full of light', the result from of ceiling wired with 1,369 filament lights. Wall's recreation of this scene illustrates the protagonist's claim: 'Light confirms my reality, gives birth to my form'.

Compared with Wall's literal re-staging of a scene from this text, Flavin's reference is undoubtedly more oblique, the connection more tenuous. Included as a supplementary citation, rather than figuring explicitly in his work, Flavin's quotation from the novel focuses on the protagonist's technical engagement with light. It also recalls a passage from his early autobiographical text, '...in daylight or cool white', which describes the dealer Dick Bellamy's visit to his Manhattan studio, at that time crammed with objects and knick-knacks. Bellamy delightedly announced his desire to transport the entire contents to his gallery. This surprised Flavin, who had never imagined that the way in which he 'wanted to live could become a saleable work of art'.[9] Soon after his move to Williamsburg, Flavin, like Ellison's protagonist, began to experiment with light bulbs in his 'icon' pieces. Flavin's nod to the *Invisible Man* reveals a certain identification with a character whose use of light, according to Ellison, amounted to an 'act of sabotage, you know. I've already begun to wire the wall... When I finish all four walls, then I'll start on the floor.' Unconcerned with the final outcome, he relied on 'a certain ingenuity'. The same could be said about Flavin.

Paula Feldman

1 Dan Flavin, 'some other comments... more pages from a spleenish journal', *Artforum*, Volume 6, Number 4, December 1967, pp. 2–25. In the same paragraph, Flavin placed a mock footnote to poke fun at the preponderance of footnotes, which he said 'encumbered' art writing.

2 Flavin responded by suggesting that Kramer print a blank space next to his name rather than appear 'a damned fool' who composed such 'drivel' in 'some other comments...more pages from a spleenish journal'.

3 Flavin stated in a letter to Brydon Smith that the show was prepared without his 'permission and conceptual administration'. See 'List of Exhibitions', Brydon Smith, ed., *fluorescent light, etc. from Dan Flavin*. Ottawa: National Gallery of Art, 1969.

4 Benjamin H.D. Buchloh and Dan Graham, 'Four Conversations: December 1999–May 2000', *Dan Graham Works 1965–2000*. Dusseldorf: Richter Verlag GmbH, 2001, p. 72.

5 Rosalind Krauss, 'The Cultural Logic of the Late Capitalist Museum', *October* 54, Fall 1990, pp. 3–17.

6 Anne Rorimer, 'From Minimal Origins to Conceptual Originality', Ann Goldstein, ed., *A Minimal Future? Art as Object 1958–1968*. Cambridge, Massachusetts: MIT Press, 2004, pp. 77–102.

7 Michael Govan, '...Electric Light Defining Space', *Light in Architecture and Art: The Work of Dan Flavin*. Marfa, Texas: The Chinati Foundation, 2001, pp. 83–84.

8 See *Minimal Art*, The Gemeentemuseum, The Hague, 1968, and *Dan Flavin*, Galleria Sperone, Turin, 1968.

9 Dan Flavin, '...in daylight or cool white', *Artforum*, Volume 4, Number 4, December 1965, p. 22.

Reviews and previews:
New names this month
Kim Levin

Dan Flavin [Kaymar; March 5-29] has shown his work in the recent
"Black, White and Grey" exhibition in Hartford and at the Green Gallery.
His color blocks, solid, smooth and impassive on the visible surfaces,
with light bulbs or fluorescent tubes at their edges, are elaborately
constructed from the inside. An acid green block, perhaps the best, has
one corner missing, with a red and green bulb protruding subversively
from that corner. Work drawings, like blueprints, accompany the
constructions, including one drawing of the positions of the screw
eyes on the back of a block. This infinite and elaborate deliberateness,
and the concern with structural possibilities are the work not of a
purist, but of a new austere kind of romantic spirit.

Art News, Volume 63, Number 1, March 1964, p. 14. [excerpt]

[Originally published under the author's initials]

In the Galleries
Donald Judd

Flavin's show is one of the most interesting I've seen this year. There are two kinds of work. Both kinds involve light. Along one wall there are six blocks, all measuring about two feet square and from a few inches to about a foot thick. The thinner ones are earlier and the thicker ones are later and are also better. Fluorescent tubes and incandescent bulbs are attached to the blocks, which are painted a single flat color, except for the one covered with terra-cotta linoleum. The lower right corner of a block painted cadmium green light is truncated. A dark green cylindrical light casing is mounted on this facet. Inside the green casing there is a small, flashing red bulb. The light is bluntly and awkwardly stuck on the square block; it protrudes awkwardly. The red in the green attached to a lighter green is odd as color, and as a sequence. The upper right corner of a block painted Mars black is truncated at an oblique angle. A short daylight-white fluorescent tube is mounted on the facet. The end of the tube sticks out slightly above the block. There are several interesting aspects to the pieces: they are things themselves; they are awkward; they are put together bluntly; the materials are considered bluntly – the paint is flat and the lights come that way; the lights are strong and specific. There are also several important negative aspects: the blocks are not paintings; they have none of painting's scheme of something framed; they are not composed in the ordinary sense; they don't involve illusionistic space; they don't have modulated surfaces; they don't play with parts of the world.

The second type of work that Flavin shows consists of parallel arrangements of fluorescent tubes. A red tube is flanked by two yellow ones in a four-foot vertical piece. Another work is an eight-foot cool-white tube placed on a diagonal. In another, four eight-foot tubes run side by side vertically. The two outside tubes are cool white and the inner ones are daylight white, which looks blue in this context. A line of light is thrown along each tube by the adjacent ones. The space between the two central tubes is blue, bluer than the bulbs. The two other tubes are less blue because of the white. The simple, unstressed, unconcluded placing of the adjacent lines relates to that kind of placing in Morris Louis's last paintings. The light is more particular and strong, though, and the lines are not within an area. Another piece is more complicated and is less related to Louis's work. Four cadmium-red-light tubes, four feet long, are parallel on a diagonal. An eight-foot yellow tube continues the diagonal. It adjoins the center of the end of the box supporting the red tubes. The box supporting the yellow tube stands out further from the wall than the first box. The change in the levels is interesting. The abrupt change of the diagonal from four short tubes to one long one is a disproportion or an awkwardness somewhat like that of the truncated corners of the blocks. The spaces between the red tubes are rose. The relation of the piece to the wall is odd; it is very open for one thing. The quality of the five long lines and their four-and-one relationship is strange, but I can't think of a way to describe it. (Kaymar, Mar. 4–28).

Arts Magazine, Volume 38, Number 7, April 1964, p. 31. [excerpt]

[Originally published under the author's initials]

New York
Lucy R. Lippard

Dan Flavin is not a sculptor and his medium is light rather than color. Half of this show consists of fluorescent fixtures hanging diagonally or vertically on the wall without further embellishment. In their shiny white metal settings, these lines of softly glowing white or colored luminosity become "paintings in light" rather than recognizable everyday objects. In a way they overtransform themselves. Four vertical white tubes – warmer bulbs on the outside and cooler within – create an extraordinarily sensuous and romantic pillar, far more reminiscent of theatrically illuminated classical architecture than of a Duchamp readymade. This and a single white diagonal are the two most successful pieces. When the lights are colored (red and yellow), they cross the borderline into decoration and become simply too beautiful.

The rest of the exhibition consists of hanging wall reliefs, or "icons" – solid colored boxes with lights in white porcelain settings attached to the sides. Here again the simpler is the better. A stark black box manages to balance the translucent white light, whereas the largest, *Conran's Broadway Flesh*, has sides lined with small pointed bulbs with sparkling filaments; the whole glitters like a jewel case. The disturbing thing about Flavin's work is this consistent tendency toward prettiness, despite the fact that the objects are strictly conceived. The dramatic qualities of light as a medium tend to obscure its initial clarity, but the idea is entirely justified in the statement of idealized purity made by the single white diagonal.

Artforum, Volume 2, Number 11, May 1964, p. 54. [excerpt]

[Originally published under the author's initials]

Art: Dan Flavin
David Bourdon

"There are certain caves in New Zealand where the ceilings are covered with thousands of glow-worms, each dangling a long luminescent thread. Any sudden noise causes the larvae to run off their lights, almost as one. After a brief wait, a few of the bolder insects will switch on, followed by a few more, and suddenly the cavern will again be aglow with an eerie light." (From the current issue of The Sciences, published by the New York Academy of Sciences.)

I want to go see those New Zealand caves now that I have seen Dan Flavin's eerie show of fluorescent light. At the Green Gallery (15 West 57th Street, through December 12) long fluorescent tubes hang not from the ceiling but on the wall – diagonally, vertically, horizontally – or they lie on the floor. Some of the tubes are colored: they are commercially available in red, pink, yellow, green, two shades of blues and several shades of white. (The only white Flavin has used is cool-white.)

Only Tubes

Flavin has been working with light for about four years. Until recently he constructed boxes, blocky wall-hangings about two feet square, around the edges and beveled corners of which he added colored incandescent bulbs or fluorescent tubes. He has exhausted his interest in that kind of construction and now works only with unadorned fluorescent tubes in his quest for a more rarefied purity of concept and means.

One of the earliest works in this direction, *the diagonal*, is still one of his best. A single eight-foot cool-white tube placed on a diagonal includes the wall as a work of art by casting light on it. Another amazing work is the one-two-three arrangement of vertically paralleled white tubes. One is a gold, blue, red, red-gold rectangle. On the floor lies a parallel arrangement of a two-foot yellow tube, a four-foot pink, a six-foot red, and an eight-foot red.

This art takes on a kind of biological luminescence. The works literally radiate energy, the emission of light becoming a major part of the art. (Turned off, they would not be interesting.) The light has an intangible fluidity that contrast sharply with the rigid contours of the tubes themselves. The colored lights affect each other. Looked at long enough, there are subtle changes of color and after-images. Adjacent tubes of contrasting color cast particular blends of color light. This art has instant turn-on.

These tubes probably owe as much to electrified marquees as they do to tiers of votive lights. They derive ultimately, I suppose, from Duchamp's first purchase in a hardware store. Flavin refrains from gimmicky or elaborate arrangements. His compositions are spare and purist. It would be hard to do less.

On the Avenue

After leaving the gallery, John Quinn and I walked over to a Greek cafeteria on 47th Street off Eighth Avenue. Coming out of the cafeteria, we were startled by the window display across the street of the Semi-craft Lighting Company (300 West 47th Street). A shop dealing in colored and fluorescent tubes, it looked like the Flavin show in the process of being dismantled. We crossed the street to study the windows. There was remarkable similarity. A white tube leaned at a diagonal against one wall. A pink tube stood in the corner. In contrast to the bare austerity of the Green Gallery, the Samicraft windows were cluttered with bulbs and tubes. The Samicraft people, after all, do not have their windows done by Dick Bellamy, nor do they think of their wares as art. The only thing that makes Flavin's tubes art is that they have been arranged and put into an art context.

It is easy to see things in an art context after an artist has pointed it out. Now anybody can put an eight-foot pink fluorescent tube in the corner of his living room an claim to have an artwork, if he is oblivious of the fact that it is only a stylish forgery.

The Village Voice, November 26, 1964, p. 11.

New York Letter
Jacob Grossberg

This is a "these are good things, but I wouldn't want to do them" kind of show. Flavin uses fluorescent light to create a geometry of light and position. There are seven pieces in the show. Fixtures are arranged in various sequences. They are of varying sizes, and have different-colored fluorescent tubes. The artist is asking too much of us, however. I cannot get beyond the object to the aesthetic involved. As geometry it is fine, but not new; as fluorescent fixtures, new, but not fine. Possibly I refuse to accept "something different" as a reason for activity, but I can find no other reason why these particular things should be of interest. (Green)

Arts Magazine, Volume 39, Number 4, January 1965, p. 54. [excerpt]

[Originally published under the author's initials]

Reviews and previews:
New names this Month
Jill Johnston

Dan Flavin [Green] took a giant Purist step with an arch and artful
arrangement of fluorescent tubes mounted on standard white fluorescent fixtures. The light tubes come in several colors, and white. The
light emitted and spreading a soft glow on the wall is the central issue
of the work. One of the most effective pieces was a long vertical pink
tube placed elegantly in a corner. It might seem inappropriate to call
the gentle suffusion of pink light from a matter-of-fact commercial
product "romantic," but if a pink-shot cloud in a fine sunset is to some
a romantic spectacle, Flavin's wall glow might be no less so to an
eye sensitized by his rarefied light. Of course Flavin's tube is hardly a
cloud and one curious effect of the work is the combined quality of
an intractably rigid cylinder and that incorporeal radiation that can't
be measured. The geometry of the tube is an absolute condition which
speaks for itself: yet the "arrangements" do intensify the "given" geometry. Variations on the theme include: the dynamic thrust of an 8-foot
white tube placed on a diagonal; three vertically paralleled white tubes;
a long horizontal work of red and green; a rectangular arrangement
of red, yellow, blue; a floor piece of four tubes in three colors.

Art News, Volume 63, Number 9, January 1965, p. 13. [excerpt]

[Originally published under the author's initials]

New York Letter
Lucy R. Lippard

Dan Flavin has been working with light for over a year now; his fluorescents at the Green Gallery, while challenging and occasionally satisfying, continue to raise the doubts I felt at his Kaymar show last year. They tend to overtransform themselves, becoming so theatrically attractive that the commercial origins and initial clarity of the idea are obscured, and are not replaced by a broader proposition. The idea is a fertile one and the artist is gifted enough to get more out of it, which makes the failures all the more irritating. By the act of arranging the "readymade" fluorescent tubes in their shiny white metal fixtures on the walls in simple groups or forms, Flavin makes them into reliefs or "paintings in light," leaving behind the found-object aesthetic and accepting the responsibility of creating fine art. But having made this decision, he has not yet succeeded in coming to terms with or adequately exploring the nature of fluorescent light and color, which is characteristically bland, sentimental and generally diluted in intensity. For this reason the pinks are truer and less "pretty" than the other colors. The reds and yellows are especially lacking in vitality, since these hues seem to demand a stronger or more direct statement, although not necessarily the satirical or optically vibrating ones suggested by contemporary trends. This is of course the manufacturer's fault rather than Flavin's, but once he has chosen to work with these materials he must resolve their particular limitations and discover their range. The conflict lies in the essentially classical or rigorous nature of the concept and medium, and the artist's inherent romanticism.

Art International, Volume 9, Number 1, February 1965, p. 37. [excerpt]

Excavating the Recent Past
Dore Ashton

The end of the season is a good time to do things not ordinarily possible, as the Kornblee Gallery proved in its exhibition of two works by two artists. All too rarely are we permitted to concentrate on a single work on a single wall.

In this case, Larry Zox is represented with a few tiny sketches leading up to the huge horizontal painting dominating an entire wall. And Dan Flavin has one neon construction and a miniscule sketch for it...

Flavin's neon-tube construction is composed of seven verticals, one of which descends almost twice the length of the others. Metrically, it would read ,,/,,,,. This final symmetry is in the orthodox constructivist tradition since the long right-hand side is balanced by the longer tube and its two left-hand companions. Balance is achieved through calculated asymmetry.

Having said this, it is important to take the medium into consideration. The glowing tube produces an irregular edge of light which then almost dissipates both symmetry and asymmetry in its effulgence. Rigour in basic form is erased by pulsating light, producing a strange and, in this case, compelling effect. The 'virtual volumes' discussed at length by the early constructivists are fully articulated here, but with a difference: where most constructivist sculpture was conceived in the round, or else in clear relief, this piece is neither three-dimensional nor in sharp relief. It hovers somewhere between the two and its virtuality is elusive. A cold icon or a lunar symbol? Whatever Flavin develops from this medium, I think it will be perplexing – one of the definition-eluding forms which seem to dominate the efforts of many younger artists.

Studio International, Volume 172, Number 880, August 1966, pp. 101 – 102. [excerpt]

Art in Process – Structures
Mel Bochner

Dan Flavin's *diagonal of May 25, 1963* is a 96-inch gold fluorescent lamp and fixture set at a 45-degree angle on the wall. The absoluteness of the angle and the primacy placed on arrangement in all his work are aspects that separate him from the other artists working with lights. Flavin does not use light. He abuses it. The light is almost secondary in an awareness of the objects. Of course, the fascination resulting from the gaseous fluorescent glow is undeniable. But any attempt to posit the objects with a transcendent nature is disarmed by the immediacy of their presence. They are themselves – which is enough and significant.

Arts Magazine, September – October 1966, Volume 40 Number 9, pp. 38 – 39. [excerpt]

Less is Less (for Dan Flavin)
Mel Bochner

Dan Flavin doesn't use light.
He abuses it.

'No more entities should be posited than are necessary.'
William of Ockham

'...the object had no being beyond phenomenon; it is not ambiguous, not allegorical, not even opaque, for opacity somehow implies a corresponding transparency, a dualism in nature. For him the object is no longer a common-room of correspondences, a welter of sensations and symbols, but merely the occasion of a certain optical resistance.'
Roland Barthes, 'Objective Literature: Alain Robbe-Grillet'

'I am working now on an enormous construct... in annoyingly monumental proportions done in dankish colours, overblown and frivolous, all of which may well earn me the name of the Michelangelo of the insipid.'
Eca de Queiroz (ca.1880), Letter to a friend.

'I know now that I can reiterate any part of my fluorescent light system as adequate. Elements of parts of that system simply alter in situation installation. They lack the look of history. I sense no stylistic or structural development of any significance within my proposal – only shifts in partitive emphasis – modifying and addable without intrinsic change.
    'All my diagrams, even the oldest, seem applicable again and continually. It is as though my system synonymises its past, present and future states without incurring a loss of relevance. It is curious to feel self-denied of a progressing development if only for a few years.'
June 16, 1966

'Electric light is just another instrument. I have no desire to contrive fantasies mediumistically – sociologically over it or beyond it. Future art, and the lack of that would surely reduce such squandered speculations to silly trivia anyhow. I do whatever I can whenever I can with whatever I have wherever I am.

'As a baseball player might put it, I am not a guess hitter, I simply try to stay loose at the plate to deliver hits in a league where the pitching is of no nonsense stuff.'

June 28, 1966. Dan Flavin, catalogue statement, *Kunst-Licht-Kunst*

'Dan Flavin has ruined electric lights for me, I'm going back to candles.'

Tom Doyle

'Usually he carried with him an old Gladstone bag filled with burned-out electric bulbs which it was his pleasure to throw unexpectedly, against the sides of houses and the walls of rooms. He loved the popping sound they made and the tinkling-sprinkle of fine glass that followed. He had an inordinate fondness for echoes.

'At the most inopportune times and inappropriate moments he would snap out frank four-letter words, such as when he was talking to a little child or the sister of a vicar. He had no reverence and no solicitude...

"Achievement" he used to say, "is the fools gold of idiots" ...He frequently threatened suicide...once he was fumbling around for some poison in the medicine chest when I ran in and pleaded with him, "You have so many things yet to do."

"Yes", he said, "and so many people yet to insult."'

James Thurber, 'Something to Say'

'"A fact in itself is nothing".
Claude Bernard
"Round numbers are always false".
Samuel Johnson
"Nothing artificial is really pleasing."
Saint Ambrose'

Dan Graham, 'Three Comments explaining an Earlier Untitled Poem'

'I feel nothing but immense and insatiable desires, an atrocious ennui and continuous yawns.'
Flaubert

'I look on the specious electrical light.
Blatant, mechanical, crawling and white,
Wickedly red or malignantly green
Like the beads of a young Senegambian queen.'
Vachel Lindsay

'"Current Art" came to Philadelphia last night – complete with blue-bloods and beatniks, neon tubes and bathroom light fixtures, several tons of sheet-metal and one bronzed apple.

"Illuminating, isn't it", quipped a well-dressed gent to his wife as they examined an 8-foot long naked fluorescent light fixture precariously leaning against a white wall.

Artist Dan Flavin, a 32-year-old New Yorker, created the work for the exhibition that opened last night at the University of Pennsylvania's Institute of Contemporary Art, at 34th St. above Spruce.

Some of us – not quite hip on "Pop art" – might think Flavin's work looks like a fluorescent fixture leaning against a wall, but "not so", says the artist. "It's a leaning diagonal – it bisects space – it's pure light not bogged down with colour or form".

"Oh", we said and moved on through the rest of the exhibit...'
Dick Aarons, *Philadelphia Daily News*

'You do not need to leave your room. Remain sitting at your table and listen. Do not even listen, simply wait. Do not even wait, be quite still and solitary. The world will freely offer itself to you to be unmasked, it has no choice, it will roll in ecstasy at your feet.'
Franz Kafka

'The largest display in the show was created by Ben Flaven, (sic) a tall, heavy man who wore a yellow necktie. The exhibit takes up half a room and consists of three small arrangements of white fluorescent tubes against a white background.

"It's integrated", said Flaven.

"Integrated?"

"I mean", he continued, "that the room, the surroundings are important. The lights are integrated with the spaces around them." This is not a new movement in the art world, Flaven said, because he does not believe in movements – in art, that is.'
John P. Corr, *The Philadelphia Inquirer*

'I am in the habit of shooting from time to time, and if I sometimes make mistakes at least I have shot.'
Hermann Goering

'With Flavin's work, if it isn't up it just doesn't exist.'
Jill Kornblee

'Things that exist exist, and everything is on their side. They're here which is pretty puzzling. Nothing can be said of things that don't exist. Things exist in the same way if that is all that is considered – which may be because we feel that or because that is what the word means or both. Everything is equal, just existing and the values and interests they have are only adventitious.'
Don Judd, 'Black, White and Grey'

'The monument and the scrapheap are historically reciprocal. History is the process of making one from the other.'
Robert Lepper

'The love of life is the kiss of death.'
Ad Reinhardt

'It is part of the Flaubertian genius to prefer an event's reflection in consciousness to the event itself, to prefer the dream of passion to real passion, to substitute for action the absence of action and for every presence the void. It is not the event which contracts under Flaubert's hands but what is between the events, those stagnant expanses where all movement is vibrationless and immobilised.'
Jean Rousset, 'Madame Bovary or the Book about Nothing'

'Today, one of the churches of Tlön platonically maintains that a certain pain, a certain greenish tint of yellow, a certain temperature, a certain sound are the only reality. All men, in the vertiginous moment of coitus are the same man. All men who repeat a line from Shakespeare are William Shakespeare.'
J.G. Borges Tlön, 'Ugbar, Orbis Tertius'

'Instead of causing us to remember the past like the old monuments, the new monuments seem to cause us to forget the future.'
Robert Smithson, 'Entropy and the New Monuments'

'I like everything about Dan's work except the lights.'
Sol LeWitt

'As opposed to the playfulness of camp, stoop is dead serious, it appreciates urban man and his droppings as they are: semiconscious, bigoted, ignoble, irrational, antilogical, humourless. The intellectual power elite is effete. Substitute for it the views that reflect public opinion of the majority; the stoop in the street. Majority as John Stuart Mill observed, breeds laxity, a laxity in which full consciousness can wither up and mercifully die.'

Lee Israel, 'Notes on Stoop'

'Beauty is the marking time, the stationary vibration, the feigned ecstasy of an arrested impulse unable to reach its natural end.'

T.E. Halme, *Speculations*

'Someday, all Art must come to light.'

Matisse

Art and Artists, Volume 1, Number 9, December 1966, pp. 24–27.

Art: More Aluminum, Less Symbolism
Hilton Kramer

Dan Flavin (Kornblee, 58 East 79th Street): The notion that Mr. Flavin is an artist is one that commands assent among knowledgeable people one respects. But on the basis of the current evidence – white fluorescent tubes arranged in vertical pairs (and that's all) – he seems to me no artist at all. He has simply been given space in an art gallery.

The New York Times, January 14, 1967, p. 26. [excerpt]

Reviews and previews:
New names this month
Elizabeth C. Baker

Dan Flavin [Kornblee; to Feb. 2] shows seven new fluorescent "proposals" all in cool white, chastely paired vertical lines of light at irregularly measured intervals around the gallery. All are recently executed, though some go back to idea-drawings of 1963. They are placed with calculated nicety, at uniform height, in relation to breaks in the shape of the room. This is subtle operation, though components of the group are so basic as to seem simple-minded. Each piece consists of standard, commercially available fixtures, one 8 feet long, the other, parallel and side-by-side, either the same size, 6 feet or 2 feet in length. The shorter tube is either centered alongside or flush with one end of the longer tube. Random variations within limited possibilities are presented offhandedly. More secret complexity appears in the two corner pieces, both paired 8-foot tubes: one set remains two distinct strips of light, with one fixture flat against the wall, one straddling the corner; the other piece, with the fixtures each flat to the wall and therefore perpendicular to each other, sets the glass tubes into actual contact with each other, fusing the bands of light, and also suddenly emphasizing the brittle fragility of the faintly-warm glass. In the only piece combining an 8-foot tube with two smaller ones, a 6-footer and a 2-footer placed end-to-end (where the sum of the parts is, inconveniently, *not* equal to the whole, but a little in excess) a teeth-on-edge irritation is produced. This could be, according to one's tastes, the best or the worst piece in the show: it has a jagged personality. At length, Flavin's show inspires silence, bathes one in soothing cool: one responds emotionally, though it may be outside the artist's intention. These new works, drawing back from recent effulgent color or daring structure, denote a renewed austerity, even a Puritanical self-denial: still, an insidious pull persists.

Art News, Volume 65, Number 10, February 1967, p. 13. [excerpt]

[Originally published under the author's initials]

Exhibitions in Milan
Tommaso Trini

Some neon tubes and nothing else. Nothing new, in Dan Flavin's show, judging from appearance, as all our ceilings, pavements and eyes are overflowing with those tubes which we use incandescent from evening to morning. In these compositions, however, they suddenly strike us, being cold and quite indifferent to our consumption. These daily commonplace objects have undergone no radical transformation, but were simply structured again according to a certain fashion. Flavin, though, acted in such a way as to render our expectation of a transformation or novelty quite vain – it is the American "cool" tendency...

Dan Flavin, Galleria Sperone

Flavin's structural compositions have been called "instantaneous monuments," which have only the forms and properties of the material produced by Radar Fluorescent Company, or by Philips.

Flavin does not transform his material, nor makes of it an image of light, warmth or color; he rather restores it to its origin: to the primary "warm white", "cold white", "gold, pink and blue fluorescent light" which define it as suitable for construction, thus eliminating the movement of creation and its very evolution.

Here we are confronted with monuments which do not recall the past, but neither call forth the future. They are confined to a fill a motionless space, where the time is according to Flavin an "inactive history."

Forms, just like matter, are likewise destitute of any analogic reference, being merely squares, triangles and segments, that is primary structures and objects which correspond most exactly in our minds to the meaning of "square," "triangle," or "segment."

Every obstacle existing between our look and the object seems to disappear, since no interpretation is possible. But it is not actually so.

If "Flavin's fluorescent lights" (as Robert Smithson noted) "are hampering a protracted observation: ultimately, there is nothing to see," the obstacle may lie in the fact that these structures give an opportunity to meditate. One of them bears the title: *monument 7 for V. Tatlin*. It is a homage to the founder of constructivism, as well as an acknowledgement of the fact that the insertion of Art in the matter-of-fact reality, to which Tatlin had sacrificed everything, has become true.

Domus, Number 446, February 1967, p. 32.

New York
Emily Wasserman

Once again Dan Flavin presents his unsentimental bars of fluorescence at the Kornblee Gallery. This year the whole show is green. All of the paired, eight-foot-long rods of light are set at diagonals onto the walls, extending from baseboards to door frames, moldings or corner angles. One is almost put off by the sheer intensity of the emerald glow when entering the room, but once inside, the color fades to an eerie pallor. The unrelenting light bleaches out shadows, dissolving even the silhouette of the glass tubes which contain it. Perhaps the most unintentionally dramatic effect is induced by this insistent green aura within the gallery: After a while, it can become a normality, making daylight or incandescence appear a startingly *unreal* pink/magenta in contrast.

Nevertheless, Flavin's yearly variations in color and placements – part of his a-historical "proposal" to shift emphases only slightly – seem to have become a dry exercise in technicalities by now. Although the initial impact of the green light does alter one's orientation to reality, the situation of the tilted light rods does not seem to affect actual space very radically (such as the flattening out of the angle, in installations where one tube occupied a corner). Other than the obvious use of the walls and room as an objectified field for the disposition of the tubes, there is not much spatial interest generated. Perhaps the simple frontal assault of linear sequences is all that is intended this time. Flavin, however, seems to have reached a stalemate here. If this present installation does really challenge accepted ways of seeing and perceiving, it is not particularly distinguished in doing so.

I am not convinced that what has been considered Flavin's "radicality" – the conceptual limit to which he pushes art-making, rather than the mass-produced form he uses to embody his interpretation of the process – does constitute an altogether significant esthetic innovation. I see Flavin's wholesale espousal of a commonplace commercial object – although he claims that it is "just another instrument" to be used as a vehicle for his sensibility – as a rather curiously *passive* acceptance of an available system. The question arises, whether or not this use of technical material truly does coincide with, or support Flavin's disavowal of fantasy or metaphysical allusion. In terms of visual phenomenon, the colored light set-up is, happily, *not* devoid of at least a nominal amount of "illusionism" or metaphoric connotation. The barely altered, ready-made light strips certainly do, however, sustain his disbelief in the need for "toil" to create art; but for all the optical rigors we are put to, the esthetic rewards of Flavin's demonstrations have become, unfortunately, as slight as his creative activities.

It is strange, with all the talk of a new "literalist" sensibility, few have suggested that although the actual formal results of such thinking may be appealing, the mentality represented bears some rather unsettling, even threatening implications. This is not to denigrate the whole movement towards literalness (there is a world of difference, for example, between the subtle craft in one of Larry Bell's mirror boxes, and Flavin's light tubes) but simply to point out the weakness in Flavin's brand of this feeling about reality. In effect, it asks us to go beyond the mere use of industrial terms and materials as the artist's tools, to condition ourselves to the "beauty" or pure objective "reality" of the mechanized. It is a kind of "1984" passivity, a lyricizing of basically uninventive, unprofound forms. Besides, where did Flavin get the idea that fluorescent tubes *are* real (more so than paint and canvas) just because they have become a common part of our environmental reality? He has himself pointed to a future condition of "no-art," but at a time like the present, this attitude and its assumptions should be questioned and countered, rather than simply encouraged as a wholly valid new convention or direction.

Artforum, Volume 6, Number 4, December 1967, p. 59. [excerpt]

Chicago
Whitney Halstead

The second major exhibition at the Museum of Contemporary Art was Dan Flavin's *Pink and "Gold."* The reception which it received in this city was a mixed one and in this respect it paralleled the varied and mixed attitudes which have greeted the new museum and its program.

Flavin's show epitomized the paradoxical – a quality which has not always found favor in art. The placing of fluorescent tubes in an arithmetical progression (one which contradicted the illusion of visual perspective) was impersonal, cool (as "cool" as the light which they radiated) and yet it became a uniquely personal idea. Although completely matter-of-fact in the use of commercially available light tubes and the hardware which held them, the arrangement created – or more correctly allowed – an evanescent, almost mystical event to occur. The impersonal mode including the selection and use of readymade materials is of course reminiscent of Duchamp and because of this, one speculates about the importance of Flavin's idea itself for the future.

Finally, the catalogue described the exhibition as a "broad, bright, gaudy, vulgar system" which it admittedly was; but the paradox or at least the contradiction was that it was hardly a "system" and it was "vulgar" only by the associations which the viewer brought to it. True, it seemed to conform to the expectations we might have regarding one of those large movie theatre foyers (the Balaban and Katz "palaces" out of the 1930s) and it might be what we would see if the wall panels were to be removed, thus showing lights and their fixtures. Whereas the vulgar, gross, gaudy movie house is historically matrixed by a host of sentimental associations – making it in the '60s a superb example of camp – Flavin's proposition strips this away and in doing so achieved its greatest value. This was particularly apt for Chicago and it may help to explain some of the reservations that greeted the show.

Artforum, Volume 7, Number 8, April 1968, pp. 66–67. [excerpt]

Art
John Perrault

Dan Flavin's new fluorescent light fixture arrangements (fluorescent lamp: "an electric discharge lamp in which light is produced by passage of electricity through a metallic vapor or gas enclosed in a tube or bulb.") now at the Dwan Gallery makes me want to take back every gratuitous pun I have employed in the past when "discussing" his works. In short, the new works are terrific, and I have seen the light. My doubts have not been illuminated, they have been eliminated.

Flavin's five new works are tough, elegant, and quite beautiful. Of all the artists working with light, he is the best and the most serious. We are not bombarded with flicker-tricks or entertained with flashing cubes better suited to discotheques or department stores at Christmas. Usually light is used to spotlight other things, but Flavin forces us to look at the light itself.

There are three works in the small office to your left as you come off the elevator to enter the gallery. Each of them is composed of one blue fluorescent light and a smaller ultra-violet one. By themselves, the found-forms (ready-made length) are beautiful. Turned on (ready-made light), they change all other light – the desk lamp light in the room, for instance – into circular zones of orange.

In the main room of the gallery, Flavin has created a rectangular frame of lights against one corner. By framing, it calls attention to the corner but it also dissolves the corner in light. The two horizontal fluorescents are white and face outward. The vertical lamps are pink and gold and face toward the corner and they stain the wall with color. Inside the square the colors blend at the center to create a fleshy, peachy, orange haze.

The back room of the gallery is barred by nine vertical lamps facing into the room. An empty room. An empty room full of light.

The Village Voice, November 14, 1968, p. 18. [excerpt]

The Flavin Case
Philip Leider

Dan Flavin's current show at the Dwan Gallery is his sixth one-man
in New York since 1961; he has also appeared in almost every group
exhibition of consequence during the past half-decade. During most
of this period he has worked exclusively with fluorescent light tubes,
unadorned and untransformed, quite as they might be seen in any
hardware store. In spite of this extensive exhibition history, Flavin's
work has proven difficult to place critically, or even to engage serious
critical interest. The current exhibition – one of Flavin's strongest –
seems not only to increase the need to distinguish his efforts from
what has been called "novelty art," but even to establish his work in
some minds as art at all.

Periodically in the history of modern art the notion that "painting
is finished" has produced innovations of considerable freshness and
importance. Flavin's work is often associated with two contemporary
sets of ideas which have in common only the conviction that conventional painting is an exhausted medium. The first, the so-called
"literalist" ideas most closely identified with Flavin's friend, Don
Judd, proceed into three-dimensional works not easily classifiable as
"sculpture" out of the conviction that modern painting, especially after
Stella, had rendered any form of "illusionism" unbearable. Flavin's
first "proposals" – groups of fluorescent tubes arranged on gallery
walls and often called "icons" – seemed to conform to this mode of
the thinking, save for the fact that Flavin seemed to make no effort to
rid the works of a rich romanticism with religious and atmospheric
overtones quite out of keeping with these ideas. The second set of ideas
is associated with the various light and kinetics movements, and are
based on the proposition that conventional painting and sculpture simply cannot retain conviction and remain a sort of quaint anachronism

in a technological age. But Flavin's consistent refusal to sophisticate his medium or to complicate it with the technological extensions that are undoubtedly available to him make his presence more and more embarrassing in an exhibition of gyrating sculpture or rainbow-hued, complexly programmed "light art."

The current show at Dwan continues to reveal Flavin's approach as unique. The first of the two works in the show is installed catercorner in the gallery's main showroom, the only object in the room. It is composed entirely of eight-foot-long fluorescent tubes (mounted on their customary pans) arranged to form a square. The vertical sides of the square consist of two tubes on each side, one pink and one yellow. These tubes face the corner, while the backs of the pans face the viewer. The two horizontal sides of the square are made of white tubes, and these face outward, toward the viewer. It is a splendid work.

The piece functions like a painting, and from this comes much of the humor as well as the seriousness of the work; it does not, as does much of Flavin's work, including the second piece in the show, make the space of the room an intrinsic part of the work. Functioning "like" a painting, the work permits Flavin the freedom of reference to other paintings which is so much a part of advanced art in our time, a freedom he uses mostly playfully. Less playful, however, is the piece's testing of the question of what *is* a painting, or, more to the heart of the matter, what *counts* as a painting. Thus, the corner of the room that is both enclosed and colored by the fluorescent square is washed with the light of the combined pink and yellow tubes which face into it, creating a kind of orange/salmon strikingly reminiscent of the impudent and delightful palette of Willem de Kooning, which so stirred the art world two decades ago. The instantaneous evocation of "de Kooning's color" orients us quickly to the general "painterly" frame of reference of the work. We soon note that the corner has been dissolved, visually, as a corner. One sees it as a plane, "sprayed" with light much – and with much the same effect – as Jules Olitski sprays a canvas plane with paint. The depth of the colored field, as in Olitski, varies before one's eyes from appearing very shallow to appearing very deep.

It is a completely successful effect, achieved with materials so matter of fact, and in so plainly self-evident a manner, that we are quite disarmed, and give ourselves to the work wholly. The matter of Flavin's "medium" simply dissolves before the success of the work: one can't question whether art can be made from plain, store-bought fluorescent light tubes if one has already, in fact, responded so pleasurably to just such a work.

Flavin's second work is less successful only because of the unavoidable Surrealist overtones which the installation creates. This work is located in the narrow doorway between the gallery's two rooms. Nine white fluorescent tubes are installed vertically in the doorway, reaching from lintel to floor, completely blocking passage. The light faces the empty room; the backs of the pans face the viewer and prevent his entrance. The light in the room is visible from between the tubes. The effect is striking enough, but too many of its properties are wholly owned by Surrealism; the empty room and its mysteries, the irrationally blocked doorway, even the flat, enigmatic quality of the light that one perceives in the room as one peers through the prison-like bars. The work involves a rearrangement of perception which is of itself absorbing: one must adjust to the paradox of a work of art with, so to speak, its back to the viewer, "directed" not at him but at an empty room. In so doing, he becomes aware of the room in a different way, and aware of himself in the strange situation in which the artist has placed him. That the work cannot manage this particular rearrangement without evoking the spirit of Surrealism seems to me its weakness, for what is fresh and ingenious in Flavin seems compromised by the evocation of what is stale and tiresome in Surrealism.

Taken together, the works beautifully enrich one another, each emphasizing the salient features of the other. The one is open, feminine, the other hermetic, masculine; one is severe, monastic, otherworldly, the other gaudy, playful, secular; one takes sole possession of the space it dominates, the other expansively returns it to the viewer. The show allows one to evoke, and indulge, many moods.

It would seem that this exhibition must confirm Dan Flavin's position as a special case. He persists in being his own man, unassimilable to any category or movement, and achieving, with considerable frequency, works which one confronts with the standards one brings only to the best work being done.

The New York Times, November 24, 1968, p. D27, D29.

In the Galleries
Stephen A. Kurtz

Dan Flavin [Dwan] showed four earlier light sculptures and two recent works that qualify more as situations than as entities. *Untitled (to the "innovator" of Wheeling Peachblow)*, in which four pink and gold vertical members face the wall, and two blue-white horizontal members face the spectator, establishes an esthetic phenomenon of a corner in the gallery's largest space. The reflected light undergoes delicate modulations in color and intensity, softening the corner, and making it a unique *place*, as opposed to the coldly lit, non-specific *space* elsewhere in the room. *Untitled (to Dorothy and Roy Lichtenstein on not seeing anyone in the room)* consists of nine spaced blue-white units, simultaneously illuminating a room and barring its entrance. The contradiction is disturbing, not without ironic humor, and again creates an esthetic place of a given, nondescript environment. The earlier pieces, which variously combine a short ultraviolet tube with a longer blue-white light, retain their object status and seem, therefore, less intriguing.

Art News, Volume 67, Number 8, December 1968, p. 16. [excerpt]

[Originally published under the author's initials]

Dan Flavin
Ira Licht

For the skeptical, who may not yet see the art beyond the fluorescent fixtures, let it be established from the outset that simulation of light has ever been the goal of painters. Indeed, it is the prerequisite of vision and because forms are only visible through light, it was but the logical (if bold) step for Flavin to construct objects of light. The fluorescent tube is his medium.

The unchanged hardware lacks of the look of art history and the dead weight of tradition; it escapes metaphor and symbolism, Light thus neatly "prepackaged" serves the artist's esthetics of instant comprehensibility and non-hierarchical relationships. It lends itself to simple and clear arrangements which bear no traces of the act, or psychology, or emotions. No skill is necessary or desirable with these parts; no craft intervenes between concept and information.

Flavin's early fluorescent works were sparely linear or clustered images, forthrightly proclaiming the directness and clarity or the power and energy of light. They were separate pieces but implicit in their conception and installation was a tendency toward a more encompassing spatial involvement. The 1964 *monuments to V. Tatlin* were individual works, effective singly but intended primarily as a serial unit. Other pieces of the same year engaged the floor, the door jambs and the corners of the room, presaging the artist's current environmental concerns.

A notebook entry from the summer of 1961, the time of Flavin's *icons*, his earliest works with light – usually incandescent bulbs mounted on painted constructions, and considerably anterior to the fluorescent structures – expresses this involvement with the entire room:

"When we bring people to a room we must involve them plastically with that room. I do not want works or theatrical activities placed between them and the room. Visitors should not be so put out. I want them warmly involved. I want clarify not mystification."

The attitudes expressed then can be observed, with interesting modifications, in five recent major exhibitions: Flavin's rooms at the Hague *Minimal Art* survey and at *Documenta* and his one man shows at the Chicago Museum of Contemporary Art, Pennsylvania State University and the Dwan Gallery, New York. *An artificial barrier of blue, red, and blue fluorescent light (to Flavin Starbuck Judd)* continues earlier pieces which reached down physically from the wall to capture a part of the floor, and paces more than 55 feet across the space of the Hague Gemeentemuseum galleries in modular units derived from the standard lengths and colours of fluorescent tubes.

Another system was used for *alternating pink and "gold."* Here, the entire interior space of the Chicago museum was ordered through serial progression and the interplay of coloured light, shadows and reflections. For *Documenta*, and its more illusionistic variation at Penn State, Flavin eschewed the "gaudy" colours and mural-like solution of Chicago, placing ultra-violet lamps modestly along the floors and up the corners, less to illuminate the environment than to define its limits. He utilized the reticence of ultra-violet (its visible glow extends mere inches beyond the source) not so much for the image of the lights as for the transforming quality of the light. The invisible rays activated the blackness of the room whenever a white shirt passed or a paper was dropped. Visual interest was transferred from the self-effacing art work to the effect of a charged atmosphere and the spectators who became, involuntarily, participants.

Flavin approached a similar situation rather differently in his most recent exhibition, at the Dwan Gallery in November. Continuing the investigation of illumination itself instead of illuminated art, he had removed from the smaller room of the gallery all movable objects, then barred the entrance with nine 8 foot fixtures. Through the interstices one could not see the lamps, only the empty room – its space filled with light and each detail: glossy white formica shelves and cabinets, matte white walls, cream plastic blinds, sharply distinguished by the particularizing character of cool white fluorescent light. Only one work occupied the larger room, an 8 x 8 foot square the effaced the corner across which it was set by a suffusion of peach-pink splendor. An approximation of the "Peachblow" art glass of which the artist is a collector, the light was created by combining pink and "gold" lamps turned into the corner, and modified by daylight lamps shining outward. It may be Flavin's finest example yet of colour-light mixture – in which he is still to be challenged.

Unquestioned mastery of the resources of coloured light is, however, of secondary importance in appraising Flavin's pre-eminent stature among "light artists." The fact is Flavin is a major artist, a leader of the so-called "Minimal" artists, who works with light and is quite distinct from "light artists" who are usually identifiable by their lack of formal inventiveness. Flavin understands and exploits the qualities of light. He scorns as irrelevant light as projected, reflected or twisted into decorative patterns. He treats his medium both as form and phenomenon always with a firm control of structure, ambience and idea. Flavin challenges and explores a number of artistic concepts, not only about light. With his work, self-proclaiming and self-contained, needing nothing brought to it and offering all, and in which form, image, colour and light become a single entity, Flavin supersedes humanistic values and traditional definitions to investigate fresh directions in spatial experience and control as well as new realms of perception.

Artscanada, Number 124/127, December 1968, pp. 62–64.

New York
Rosalind Krauss

The four years of Dan Flavin's exploration with the fluorescent tube as "image-object" sets up inescapable parallels with those fantastically patient teaching manuals that came out of the Bauhaus during the 1920s. I am especially reminded of Klee's *Pedagogical Sketchbook*, where a point set in motion becomes a line, and then...and then...until the page resounds with the full orchestration of graphic illusionism. Flavin seems to be doing it all over again only this time mindful of the admonition about there being no line to be found in nature. As Flavin deploys it, the fluorescent tube is clearly a graphic device. It possesses both the figurative density of a line, and the inherent ambiguity of its position in space. It can build images, the interiors of which are different in quality from the space outside them; it can differentiate or divide space either along a frontal surface or in depth. Finally, it can produce stable illusions, as when corners of rooms are eradicated by even lighting, or skewed by contradictory cast shadows.

But unlike a drawn line, which is itself an edge or boundary, Flavin's instrument *produces* an edge at some level of remove or disjunction from the fluorescent tube. For edges in the wall-hung works appear as the unilluminated sides of the pans carrying the tubes, and the shadows they cast. Modeling is as important to Flavin as it ever was in traditional drawing – for it is the changing value of luminous diffusion which produces the effects of Flavin's images: their floating appearance, their contradiction of the known structure of the space they inhabit – and modeling too is made the *product* of the physical line rather than something which line itself carries or incarnates. It is as though Flavin's tube, in its various combinations, were dramatizing again and again the mysterious capacity of line itself to reproduce the visual conditions and was asking where *in the line* this power resides. That he thinks of this power as secreted somewhere at its core, like a kind of essence which one can never arrive at no matter how fine one makes the line, no matter how carefully one dissects a substance, is suggested to me by his initial choice of the fluorescent tube. For the tube literalizes the notion of essence by means of a stream of electrons which is in fact contained at the line's core. In the two large images set up by Flavin in his latest gallery show this whole drama was extended by turning the tubes away from the viewer so that the cause of the visible effects was even further masked behind the opaque barriers of the metal pans.

The first image was an eight-foot square spanning across one corner of the gallery. The top and bottom edges were established with white light, while each side was composed of two abutting units – the interior ones pink, the exterior yellow. The even suffusion of pink light into the corner of the room almost obliterated it, by canceling the distinction in value between the two wall planes. Unlike his earlier proposals for the corner-frame image, Flavin set the bottom edge of this version directly on the floor instead of suspending it at some distance above the ground. The intrusion of the floor area into the visual field of the image appeared like a pictorial device – almost a collage element – to disrupt the illusion by reasserting the actual shape of the room.

The other large-scale image – a sequence of nine vertical, eight-foot tubes, spaced at about equal intervals in the doorway between the two gallery rooms and completely barring access to the luminous space of the room beyond them – seemed equally to gesture toward the pictorial. It particular reference for me was the simultaneous depth and physical inaccessibility of illustionistic space. But, of course, the space "in the room beyond" is not illusionistic. It is real; and as such it cannot be brought to bear on the conventions of painting. It can only be juxtaposed with them, to an end that I see as being as conceptually trivial as Flavin's declarations about line. All of this of course imputes to Flavin intentions which may not have been his. However, the pictorialism is there; and along with it the gothic sense of hiddenness and mystery.

Artforum, Volume 7, Number 5, January 1969, pp. 53–54. [excerpt]

Dan Flavin
Germano Celant

On entering the various galleries giving one-man exhibits of Dan Flavin's neon tubes – Kornblee in New York, the Chicago Museum, and Sperone in Turin – one gets the impression of being faced with a visual imperative. The informational datum is the presence of the light, the attention is only attracted by this presence.

The news, then, is the light, not its image. The only purpose is to put the spectator before the object light – commonly considered an instrument – in order to give him a chance to grasp it directly. Initially, light lived through an "example" which was more elementary, less informative and rich, the neon tube. The arrangement was always geometrical according to the size of the tubes – a corner, a square, or a series of combined elements. The tubes live autonomously as non-sign elements, the only sign begin the light they give out. In fact, the informational importance depends on the discovery of the light as information in the pure state (McLuhan). All Flavin's work, then, consists in this initial "discovery" and in having developed a system of diagrams for the arrangement of luminous elements. The variations are numberless and the possible geometrical and chromatic combinations vary infinitely. Flavin belongs to the post-ideological world of Anders, the events taking place on the level of the organization of information in the pure state, thus each arrangement "merely awaits coordination again and again. Sometimes, adjustment or new variants are employed. Then, and only then, do I think to move my pencil once more. I am delighted by this understanding" (Flavin).

Flavin's recent work has been enriched by an almost provocatory didactic component, the use of neon containers.

The light, which technology has reduced from the primogenitary element that it was to an instrument, also lives through the medium of superimposed elements such as the containers. The defeat of the technological rationale is thus complete. The plastic containers are completely annulled by the incisive and concentrated action of the light, which no longer functions as a source, but as a visual lava. Consequently, also the work carried out by means of square containers can exist autonomously as light-forms, compositions become more complex and at times fill up an entire room, creating spaces made with light. Light is no longer content with a side role but invades the scene of life: light takes command. The element light lives with the element man as an equal. Flavin manages to make clear for us all our alienation towards an element which originally must have had a powerful influence on life and which technology has now reduced to cold light. What we want then is deconditioning, the recovery of the vital use of light, the recovery of its constructive and formal element, and the negation of the formalistic superimpositions of design. The problem is no longer the mediation of light, the problem of the lamp or of the source, but the use of light, and it is not merely an artistic problem, but a concrete, vital matter influencing our grasp of reality.

The misinformation of light continues deforming our perception of everyday reality, and the problem is to re-analyze the source of light, to restudy natural light, its origins outside our shell of walls, and perhaps to seek to create the natural situations with which, in the daytime, light gives body and perspective to things and to space, to turn the problem inside out so that the only possible design becomes the form of the form of the window.

Casabella, Number 332, January 1969, pp. 54–55.

Aspects of Flavin's Work
Don Judd

Three main aspects of Flavin's work are the fluorescent tubes as the source of light, the light diffused throughout the surrounding space or cast upon nearby surfaces, and the arrangement together or placement upon surfaces of the fixtures and tubes. The lit tubes are intense and very definite. They are very much a particular visible state, a phenomenon. The singleness or isolation of phenomena is new to art and highly interesting. Irwin and Bell and a couple of others in Los Angeles are also interested in developing single phenomena. The dominance as an aspect of the fluorescent tubes is not as great as that of a single phenomena in Bell's and Irwin's work. Most art, including mine, involves several things at once, none developed toward exclusivity. Art is generally more specific than it used to be; its visible aspects are more important; but usually there is a comparative balance between the few main aspects. The dominance of one phenomenon, what the presently balanced would call imbalance, is a particularity of one thing. It's very different from a particularity which is the sum of several things. I want a particular, definite object. I think Flavin wants, at least first or primarily, a particular phenomenon. The even, confined glow of the tubes, which is intense but not so much so as that of the incandescent bulbs, is standard and not much changed by the different colours. The uniformity of the phenomenon and also of the length of the fixtures may be the coexisting situation for the considerable freedom in the disposition of the lights. The pieces vary a lot. There's a nice looseness to the work as a whole and often to individual pieces, the room at the Kornblee Gallery for example.

It's obvious that colour as material and colour as light are extremely different. Colour almost always seems applied, except for raw materials and they're seldom bright. Since the tubes are sources of light their colours seem given and unchangeable, and since as light the colours are much more visible than are material colours, their differences are conspicuous. Two juxtaposed painted whites are subtle; two juxtaposed white tubes are pretty obvious. There isn't any difference between the light and the colour; it's one phenomenon.

The light is interrupted by the edges of the white fixture the tube is mounted on, causing a shadow which outlines the face of the fixture. If the fixture is on a wall the light dims gradually outward from the fluorescent tube. In a rectangle shown recently which spanned a corner, light cast from pink tubes and light from gold ones intermingled. The cast light was an important part of the piece. In the show at the Kornblee Gallery all of the tubes were green, giving the whole room green light. After a while natural light seen through the window seemed rose and the green seemed fairly normal. This diffuse or pervasive light isn't the same as the cast light. I was impressed at the Kornblee show by the power and complexity of the combination of the three main aspects.

Some of Flavin's pieces are as discrete as any painting or sculpture, requiring only a wall or a floor. Most use part of a room. The show at Kornblee was one piece involving the whole room; the show at The Museum of Contemporary Art in Chicago was one piece involving the whole space of the main floor of the museum. Both shows are among the best things I've seen. In both the rectangular space was articulated by the lights. These weren't discrete. They were interior articulation but not interior structure; they made an interior exoskeleton. The room at Kornblee, once a living-room, was articulated according to its two doors, a narrow window and a fireplace centred on one wall. The tubes were slanted on either side of the doors, for example, and flanked one long empty wall. The piece used a mediocre specific place. The museum piece was different. The space is mainly a very large room with two central walls enclosing some functional areas and so is a vague and general standard exhibition space. The eight-foot fluorescent tubes, all vertical, were disposed in a scheme upon all of the walls regardless of their position or length. The scheme was devised for the variability of the walls. In the centre of each wall were adjacent pink and gold tubes, the pink to the left. Two feet to the left was a gold tube and two feet to the right was a pink one. Four feet to the left of the gold tube was a pink one and so on. The distance increases two feet each time and the colours alternate. Except for the two centred tubes the cast colour was just the basic area of a tube.

fluorescent lights, etc. from Dan Flavin, National Gallery of Canada, Ottawa, 1969.

Fluorescent tubes:
the pigments on his palette
Kay Kritzwiser

Brydon Smith, who organized Dan Flavin's show at the National Gallery of Canada, kept saying: "This guy's just so great!" The young curator of contemporary art searched for amplifying words, then repeated: "He's just so GREAT!"

Obviously, then, this day must be a search for a quality of greatness in the 36-year-old New Yorker whose show is on two floors of the Capital's National Gallery.

At 11 a.m., the odds are against Flavin. He's tense, remote and an aura of "Don't monkey with the buzz saw" flickers like lightning around his head. The afternoon before, a television crew had monkeyed and left, binding wounded egos. The press, this morning, is getting short shrift. "He has no use for art critics," Brydon warns.

So the waiting, the watching, the keeping of one's cool (and the keeping out of Flavin's hair) begins.

Flavin is a light artist, working with fluorescent tubes. So what's great about a fluorescent tube? The same kind of fluorescent tube The Globe and Mail maintenance men sometimes bounce off one's desk?

The tubes, laced with colored wires, are strewn on the floor. Flavin calls this art? Hanging three fluorescent tubes side by side in Canada's home of the masterpiece? That hostile father of the 4-year-old who paints better pictures with his fingers than the professionals is just going to have a fit.

But wait: there's a lot more to all this than meets the eye.

Smith carefully seals down the plexiglass cover on the early (1957) Flavin drawings, arranged on tilted tables in the first gallery of this carefully plotted retrospective show.

"The danger of a retrospective show," he says, "is that it tends to try to recreate history, instead of showing by what slow degrees of thought and research a man like Dan arrives at his present work."

Around this room, Flavin's motivating ideas become his autobiography, which he later confirms. The *Act of Love* drawings are heavily Hans Hofmann, because Flavin studied at Hofmann's school in 1956.

His handwritten excerpts from James Joyce's writings are encased in cloudy swirls of color. (Flavin reads Joyce – without a guide. His 7-year-old Stephen is named for Stephen Daedalus.)

Flavin's 1959 sculptures, named for 13th-Century philosopher Saint Thomas Aquinas and for William of Ockham, the 14th-Century scholastic rebel, are clues to Flavin's art heresies.

Into the gallery comes Flavin, a big, un-athletic, clean shaven man. A gentle handshake, but no words wasted. Later, he leans against a gallery wall. "I'm lazy. My wife says if it weren't mandatory to breathe, I wouldn't.") But now he is coil-springed over the lack of 8-foot white fluorescent tubes and 6-foot red ones. Smith soothes him. The gallery has tracked some down in Halifax and Oakville. They're on their way.

Smith puts a label on a pencil sketch from 1963, *the diagonal of personal ecstasy*. That's how it all began. That sketch was Flavin's first surety that a bar of cool fluorescent light was an entity.

It's the clue to his eventual rebellion against physical painting; the key to the means he finds now to articulate space with the use of a luminous line of light.

Time to leave the drawings for Flavin's sculptures with electric-light bulbs. They are witty (*mini-white for Barbara Rose*. That's for the New York art critic, Barbara Rose. But Flavin has bracketed it with the sly companion, *de-flowered abstract antidote to the Barbara Roses*.)

They are irreverent in the way an Irish Catholic seminary-trained student has a right to be irreverent.

In the next room you can see how he rejects his box constructions. Why should he be limited by a preconceived construction? Why should he not make the whole room his box? Why not use cold light columns to contradict dimensions of a specific space?

A gallery electrician obligingly switches on lights and Flavin's understanding of how to make a strip of light in a cold tube work with the same properties of a tube of paint becomes astonishingly clear.

Flavin manipulates primary colors (Mondrian colors of red, yellow, blue) so that they become reflected and directed lights in juxtaposition, affecting and changing each other.

One room is transformed into a long bridge of color, with the neon-lit angular arches of light flung along a corridor with shimmering authority. Turn from the corridor and you face Flavin's vertical tubes in a corner. They out-Noland Kenneth Noland; for the colors hang there, a source of light, the way Noland's paint colors cannot.

Smith switches on the lights in the ultraviolet room, and the triangular walls are disclaimed immediately by the long slim rods of purple light.

In the room to Dorothy and Roy Lichtenstein (1968), a jumpsuited electrician is at work behind the vertical bars of fluorescent tubes which are intended to change the space from a room into a simple accumulation of light. But no matter that this room isn't ready; the green room is.

Here a waist-high barrier, composed of parallel segments of an infinite line, floods white light into the room. But it changes slowly to such a pervasive green that you feel you are in the centre of a buoyant act of light, and as close to a mystical experience as you ever want to come.

By contrast, the austerity of the monuments to V. Tatlin, the final works and Flavin's most recent, are single and cold, stripped of unnecessary fact. They are as separate an entity as any William of Ockham axiom. ("Entities are not to be multiplied," Ockham reasoned in the 14th Century).

The Arc Room is left. The electricians are working overtime. Flavin, tired but at ease, kids Heiner Friedrich, his Munich dealer. Heiner's long pale hair falls over his face, and he groans over a mistaken measurement which is throwing the whole arc out.

"Look at Heiner, making like a movie Erich von Stroheim," Flavin laughs. He's able to shrug off the morning's irritations, to talk about art.

He has no use for the artist with notions of grandeur about his personality or ability: "I'm a utility." He has worked in museum. He knows when to make a fuss, when to lean against a wall and appreciate his helpers.

He suspects artist who claim they are originals. He hates the big-star gesture. Has contempt for the whole celebrity syndrome typified by the Les Levines and the Andy Warhols; has no use for switchers – the abstract expressionists of this week who are the pop art men of the next.

He has disdain for worshippers of the New York art critic Clement Greenberg. He chuckles: "He doesn't recognize me, either. I'm only a footnote with Judd." (Donald Judd, New York artist, wrote the catalogue essay, "Aspects of Flavin's Work.")

"They've made Greenberg the Pope. Well, I won't kiss his ring. Let the others do it."

Flavin is impatient with art education as such: "I put myself through the whole education bit to find out what it's all about. No Man's Land. All those people who think of art as the search for the Holy Grail!"

Art schools are all right, he allows, providing they don't try to teach art. "Art education is useless. You can't tell people what to think. There's no substitution for personal thinking."

He understands the little Victorian lady worker over her sampler better than the art educationists who cram controlled ideas into people's heads. "Some things people still have to do by themselves. We can't be controllably art-conscious any more than we can be controllably happy."

Smith estimates 480 fluorescent tubes have been used for Flavin's exhibition: "We get the material and labor on a cost basis. It's an extremely cheap show to install compared with most National Gallery major shows. Compare it with the shipping costs of the Jordaens. And the insurance for this is nothing."

Smith is elated over the National Gallery's purchase of a Flavin's *the nominal three (to William of Ockham)* 1963–64. In 1966, you could get a Flavin for $450. Now? Smith clammed up. "Today they could be in the thousands. The guy's really so great."

He may be right. Flavin, in his cool, unemotional search for the shape of light is on the edge of exploration and in this Moon Age.

The Globe and Mail, September 13, 1969, p. 30.

Flavin's 'mystical' aura
Joan Lowndes

Fluorescent light, etc., from Dan Flavin at the Vancouver Art Gallery is a
fantastically beautiful show by one of the most original artists now
working on the American scene.

At 36 he is in complete command of his chosen medium, fully
justifying Brydon Smith's decision to give him such a comprehensive
12-year retrospective.

To define what he is doing is not easy. He has taken standard lengths
and colors of fluorescent lamps and, using them as found objects,
made from them sculptures, environments, paintings (as in the work
dedicated to Jean Boggs) and most importantly, architectural spaces.

He positions them against the walls, on the floor, across corners,
on the ceiling, playing at will with the volume of the room.

With startling directness – he has said the medium bears the artist –
he often turns them so that their supporting pans face out toward
the spectator to form a square framework, while the light from their
tubes is directed into a corner or into a room.

In this way he effects a plastic revolution: The disintegration of
structure and the redefinition of interior space. This is what his art
is really about: the articulation of space through light.

Just as *Madame Bovary* can be termed a book about nothing in which
the most eloquent parts are the voids between events, so the spaces
between Flavin's acts of light become "blank magic."

In photographs these blanks read as emptiness; in actual fact they
are openness. The Renaissance artist, proud of the piazzas and magnificent buildings of his era, took delight in perspective. Flavin, in our
age of cosmic exploration, gives us the experience of space.

As one progresses through the exhibition, which should be viewed
chronologically beginning from the left, one notes how the concepts

of this acute and subtle mind broaden until, in the last works created especially for these twin exhibitions at the National Gallery and the VAG, he gives proof of that thrust of energy, that nerviness which has carried American artists to the forefront in the contemporary field.

A prime example is our illustration: *untitled (to S.M.)*, in its 64-foot corridor. Modified from the Ottawa version and possibly improved, its units are placed not as triangles on the floor, but suspended as squares from the ceiling.

People walked under it slowly at the opening, watching the reflected light scoop vaults overhead, overcome as they were by the work in general.

Other large scale works, which use an entire room as their container, are the romantic *alternating pink and yellow* and *an artificial barrier of green fluorescent light*. In the former, in which two-foot lamps are placed around the baseboard of the room, casting reflections up the walls and down onto the floor, one experiences a euphoric expansion of space.

Passing then into the green room, one's flesh looks ghastly and one is confronted by the frustration of the barrier. This same hint of sadism appears earlier in the exhibition in the contrasting rooms flanking the rotunda.

A peculiarity of the barrier room is that the atmosphere seems pervaded by pale bright green light.

Although Flavin is classed as a minimalist because of his simplicity of means and the concrete "thereness" of his work, it is also highly charged with emotion.

Vancouver Province, November 17, 1969, p. 29.

A Dan Flavin Retrospective in Ottawa
Jack Burnham

A few years ago a retrospective exhibition implied that an artist of stature had about summed up his career; perhaps he would do more, but it would be in the general stylistic vein of his most established work. Thus is it doubly significant that some of the most original talents of this decade have already had their retrospectives? Whatever the implications, Dan Flavin's at the National Gallery of Canada in Ottawa served two purposes: it was a spectacular experience in a period of lethargic museum going, and for the first time Flavin's innate complexities began to unravel themselves. My only regret is that this showing was so brief (September 13 to October 19), for it is doubtful that another museum will readily duplicate its care and completeness. The National Gallery of Canada is a renovated office building in the Miesian tradition of exposed steel frame and massive glass fenestration. Its low-ceilinged interior spaces are stark and unpretentious, a perfect complement to Flavin's strengths. Much of the credit for the exhibition belongs to the museum's Curator of Contemporary Art, Brydon Smith.

At first it may seem that this retrospective suffers from a certain preciousness and overattention to incidental early works. The viewer is tempted to go straight to the fluorescent arrangements, bypassing everything before as so much biography. However, for an artist as subject to misinterpretation as Flavin, this would be a mistake. As Brydon Smith insists, Flavin is as uncompromising about himself as he is about others. If he had unnecessarily exposed himself in these tentative beginnings, he has given us the opportunity to learn a great deal from them.

Typical are a series of watercolor, calligraphic paintings (1959), each a variation of a single poem from James Joyce's early *Chamber Music*. These own their decorative effects to the Abstract Expressionism of the day – as do a folding book of illustrated Irish poems dedicated to Joyce and one of his secretaries James Johnson Sweeney. Flavin's obvious veneration of Joyce and identification with the novelist's early years are crucial to understanding his relationship to art.

A broken family life and partial disengagement from the Catholic faith became the foundations for Joyce's salvation through art in his early biographical novel, *A Portrait of the Artist as a Young Man*. Elements of these also appear in Flavin's autobiographical sketch (revised for the catalog from the December, 1965, *Artforum*). Irony, arrogance, and uncommon literary skill mark both efforts. Yet it is a truism of Joycean scholarship that inseparable from Joyce the Catholic renegade, is Joyce the uncompromising Jesuit mind. As a human being Joyce transcended the closed-minded logic and intolerance that at one time identified the Jesuitical use of Scholasticism – unfortunately Flavin has not. After the trauma of rejecting the priesthood, Joyce's Stephen Dedalus began the process of evolving a new faith. Stephen, in a famous conversation with his friend Lynch, expressed the foundations of Joyce's early ideas in esthetics:

> I thought he (Thomas Aquinas) might mean that *claritas* was the artistic discovery and representation of the divine purpose in anything or a force of generalization which would make the esthetic image a universal one...But that is literary talk. When you apprehend that basket as one thing and have then analysed it according to its form and have apprehended it as a thing you make the only synthesis which is logically and esthetically permissible. You see that it is that thing which it is and no other thing. The radiance of which he speaks in the scholastic *quidditas*, the *whatness* of a thing.[1]

And then, further on, Stephen explains:

The personality of the artist, at first a cry or a cadence or a mood and then a fluid and lambent narrative, finally refines itself out of existence, impersonalises itself, so to speak...The artist, like the God of the creation, remains within or behind or beyond or above his handiwork, invisible, refined out of existence, indifferent, paring his fingernails.[2]

Paring his fingernails or not, Flavin could write in 1966: "I have succeeded in developing no concern for art as labor. Work is finished for me. Now, it is left to electricians and engineers, etc."[3] However, it would be the shallowest interpretation to see this as a rejection of artisanship or craft – Flavin labors like the rest of us. Rather, as for Joyce, it is the creation of a seemingly omniscient psychology, or in the Mallarmean sense: the most perfect poem is that conceived but permitting no necessity to be committed to paper.

Prior to the first fluorescent arrangement, Flavin made a series of "to be and would be" icons. These are mainly rather small masonite box-forms mounted with incandescent lamps or fluorescent fixtures. Nearly all have their lights mounted off the face of the icon. Each of the mute forms might be interpreted as a *tabula rasa*. His notes of 1962 compare them to a Russian icon: "But my icons differ from a Byzantine Christ held in majesty; they are dumb – anonymous and inglorious. They are as mute and undistinguished as the run of our architecture. My icons do not raise up the Blessed savior in elaborate cathedrals. They are constructed concentrations celebrating barren rooms. They bring a limited light."[4] *icon VI (Ireland dying) (to Louis Sullivan)* and *icon VIII (the dead niggers icon) (to Blind Lemon Jefferson)* have flashers attached to their lights – a sin for which Flavin has not failed to chastise other "light" artists.

The diagonal of May 25, 1963 is a seminal work, the first placement by the artist of an 8-foot cool white fluorescent light on his Brooklyn loft wall. Subsequently, this first placement was reverified by a small yellow grease pencil drawing on cardboard, *the gold diagonal*. Ever since, the juxtaposition of fluorescent fixtures (standard sizes: 2, 4, 6, and 8-foot lengths) has been almost the exclusive consideration of the artist.

But what is more amazing, if not unique, is the journalistic cauterization which Flavin, unaided, has performed upon the body of his own art. His reputation is that of giving out considerably more punishment than received. In a press-dominated art world critics tend to think twice about bandying with Flavin. Better to ignore than to invoke such charitable suggestions as: "If I were you, I would not bother to vie for the infamous bit part of a tawdry, clownish, expedient-expendable middleman type dupe, having blabbed, blustered and bawled publicly for too long about..."[5]

But the strategy employed by Flavin is philosophically more interesting than this particular piece of heavy information would seem to indicate – the reason being that, by Minimalist-Systemic esthetics, criticism is not really critical or supplementary, rather it is reinforcement of the existence and phenomenal implications of the object itself. For instance, Flavin has been exposed to three levels of criticism: comic relief dominates; but Flavin easily dismisses dullards and provincials because they make exceptionally fat targets, forgetting as Baudelaire admonished, "To insult the mob is to degrade oneself." Occasionally, competent critics have looked at Flavin's work, but unless they belong to a favored circle who abide by Flavin's rules, they may as well move on to a more compliant quarry. When such critics write about the sculptural nature of Flavin's proposals, or his connections with the Constructivists, or his "environments," or make comparisons to various technologically-oriented colleagues, Flavin or his friends insist with some validity that these are irrelevancies. Who then qualifies to write about Flavin? For this third mode of criticism, Mel Bochner has spelled out the ground rules:

> Criticism has traditionally consisted of one of three approaches: 'impressionistic' criticism which has concerned itself with the effects of the work of art on the observer – individual

responses; 'historical' criticism which has dealt with an *a posteriori* evolution of forms and techniques – what is between works; 'metaphorical' criticism which has contrived numerous analogies – most recently to scientism. What has generally been neglected is a concern with the object of art in terms of its own material individuality – the thing itself.

Two criteria are important if such an attempt is to be made. First, the consideration should be concrete (deal with the facts of the thing itself). Second, they should be simplificatory (provide an intellectually economic structure for the group of facts obtained). The latter is necessary because description alone can never adequately locate things. In fact, it very often confers upon them an enigmatic position. Nonetheless it offers more interesting possibilities than the impressionistic, historic or metaphoric approach.[6]

Don Judd appears to be the most obvious candidate for the production of such enigmata. To say that his strictly critical writings lack style and value judgements is to ignore the *raison d'être* of criticism, namely *exposure*. Protracted descriptions signify approving recognition, as demonstrated by Judd's review of Flavin's Kaymar Gallery show in 1964:

The second type of work that Flavin shows consists of parallel arrangements of fluorescent tubes. A red tube is flanked by two yellow ones in a four-foot vertical piece. Another work is an eight-foot cool-white tube placed on a diagonal. In another, four eight-foot tubes run side by side vertically. The two outside tubes are cool white and the inner ones are daylight white, which looks blue in this context. A line of light is thrown along each tube by the adjacent ones. The space between the two central tubes is blue, bluer than the bulbs. The two other spaces are less blue because of the white.[7]

This is not criticism in any responsive sense, but rather a kind of flat-footed literality which is essentially Flavin's work reduced to words. It should be no cause for surprise then that Judd wrote the introductory essay for the artist's retrospective exhibition. The prose is succinct but parts are extremely odd, a cross between one of the French post-psychological novelists and specification writing for a missile support system:

> Art is generally more specific than it used to be; its visible aspects are more important; but usually there is a comparative balance between the few main aspects. The dominance of one phenomena, what the presently balanced would call imbalance, is a particularity of one thing. It's very different from a particularity which is the sum of several things. I want a particular, definite object. I think Flavin wants, at least first or primarily, a particular phenomenon.[8]

These quotes are chosen not to criticize the ideas or established methods contained therein, but to suggest that they sustain a certain philosophical consistency with the artist's mature work. In fact, when Flavin insists that the art of his work is only marginally concerned with the physicality of his lighting systems, or with luminosity, or the making of "environments," or the creation of objects, one is simply led up a *cul-de-sac*. More precisely, Flavin's vituperative letters and essays, his use of humor as an instructional device, his refusal to acknowledge interpretation except through minute description, his rejection of schools and movements and art history – even the physical blockage caused by some of his arrangements – are all *deflectional devices*, deflecting away from the methodological comprehension of his work. Though Flavin celebrates almost unending variations with which his serial arrangements can be installed, he is scornful of those attempts to duplicate his work without his permission and assistance. Moreover, if a certain critic becomes fascinated with the illusional qualities of his arrangements, Flavin is there to remind him that, after all, these are merely stock fixtures purchasable in any hardware store. As a dialectical device these strategies have their correspondences with Stéphane Mallarmé's doctrine of beauty in nothingness, where all secrets are hidden from the mob by the syntactical complexities of mere words, barriers to the empty but eminently worthwhile space within:

> For just as we have the right to elicit emptiness from ourselves (hampered as we may be by reality too solidly, too preponderantly enthroned in us), so do we act that a sublime attraction may lovingly deliver us from that reality – and yet be filled with it and shed glittering lights upon it through empty space and in wilful, solitary celebrations.[9]

Poets and novelists by their art possess the advantage of creating deflections directly, for example by the progressive stratifications of meanings and syntax used by Joyce. But the Thomastic training of Joyce – evidenced in his early esthetics – is also an experience shared by Flavin. The question arises then, how does a Catholic youth exposed to Scholasticism see God, and that same God later transmuted to beauty and art? To answer, God is the unadulterated act of existing, the coming together of essence and existence. In Thomistic terms, no human intellect can penetrate the implications of such a fusion. And since God is absolute perfection, we can only share negative knowledge of his qualities and effects, one of these being creativity. Yet for man the act of creation remains partial since God's wholeness and perfection cannot be divided. Joyce makes this clear through Stephen Dedalus:

> But temporal or spatial, the esthetic image is first luminously apprehended as selfbounded and selfcontained upon the immeasurable background of space or time which is not it. You apprehend it as one thing. You see it as a whole.[10]

It would be misleading to overestimate Flavin's preoccupation with churchly doctrine, but there are two early works that support it. One is a watercolor collage mounted on masonite, upon which has been affixed a very crushed tin can, its shining surfaces substituting for the robes of the portly Dominican monk, *Thomas Aquinas Doctor of Canon Law* (1959). The other is *East New York Shrine* (1962/63), one of three upright icons in the exhibition. A tiny glowing statuette of Mary is enshrined in an Aerolux Lite bulb, and set upon an empty tomato can – "Pope Brand." What appear to be black rosary beads and a black tassel extend from a pull chain. An inscription around the base of the can reads "HOLY MOTHER LOADED WITH GRACE PLEASE HELP PLUNK SONJA–DAN FLAVIN–1963," referring to the excellent artist and humorist, Ed Plunkett.

One of the seminal arrangements produced by Flavin is his *the nominal three (to William of Ockham)* (1963/64), first shown in the 1964 Green Gallery exhibition. Here the basis for other serial works can be found. It begins with two 8-foot fluorescent lamps centered upon a wall; extended to the left and right at equal distances are a single lamp and three lamps butted together. In the original installation of 1964 the groups of lamps are spaced only a few feet apart; for the National Gallery of Canada installation they are positioned on a 24-foot wall so that the two outer groups line up with the extremities of the partition. On the left side the single lamp touches the open end of a partition, on the right side the group of three butts against a corner so that its illumination casts a brilliant reflection onto the adjoining wall. The more spatial setting at the National Gallery not only alludes to Barnett Newman and other field painters, it calls into question the running battle between the Minimalists and various formalist critics. Obviously Flavin is a formalist and one who has extended the viability of Formalism in not wholly accepted ways. His dematerialization of painterly space takes into consideration room dimensions, reflectivity of surfaces, ambient conditions, and juxtaposed art works in a way that no painter ever dreamed of doing. *the nominal three* alludes to William of Ockham and that scholastic's famous device for testing the irreducibility of logical premises. The nominalism which Flavin asserts is a double-edged logic. On one hand he denies universals (the painter's field and its inherent illusions) by simply setting up three groups of fixtures—no more, no less; concurrently Flavin creates not only a two-dimensional surface, but a series of hodological spaces within and beyond the work itself. This posits the indivisibility of esthetic experience, not by means of abstractions and universals, but through the immediate experience of concrete objects. Of course the two are contradictory and Flavin is faced with the same dilemma as Ockham, namely how does one intuit a nonexistent thing (unified esthetic experience and/or God) if it is assumed that all knowledge must be based upon intuition gained by direct experience with real objects?

The exhibition's catalog, *fluorescent light, etc. from Dan Flavin*, is a useful guide. Among the artist's idiosyncrasies is an obsession for precise documentation – certainly no small virtue for future scholars. Yet nearly two-thirds of the listed works are not directly connected with the fluorescent arrangements which are, in fact, the only reason for the artist's reputation. This imbalance is augmented by the fact that seven works, six of them room-size, have been omitted from the catalog. For many visitors these represent the heart of the show, yet they have been described only in a Xerox supplement. In fairness it must be added that neither Flavin nor Brydon Smith was responsible for this oversight, but rather the National Gallery of Canada. One might only wish that another edition of the catalog would contain the missing works.

While Flavin eschews the term "sculptural" applied to his arrangements, I am hard-pressed to think of a better word for *monument 4 for those who have been killed in ambush (to P.K. who reminded me about death)*. First seen in the Jewish Museum in 1966, *monument 4* consists of four 8-foot fluorescent fixtures wedged into a corner some inches above eye level, transforming that quadrant of the room into a penetrating reddish glow. If one is at a loss to explain why Flavin has so outdistanced his rivals using light, workmanship is one clue. There are a number of tailor-made boxes that fit into any expensive New York condominium, but that is not workmanship, it's good business. "Truth to material" has something to do with workmanship, but more than that it is turning liabilities into esthetic advantages. I was told by Brydon Smith that Flavin feels the electrician at the National Gallery is the best with whom he has ever worked, and I can believe it. There is virtually not one electric cord or connection in sight. The fixtures have been joined together by hollow threaded connectors, on each side of which a wing nut is fastened. Electrical wires run through the connectors, and all outlets are flush connections inside the wall, leaving no visible plugs or receptacles. The effect is incredibly clean. Once taken off the wall, Flavin uses the deflecting properties of his sheet-metal box supports with equal authority. In contrast to the direct intensity of adjacent fluorescent tubes, fixtures turned away from the spectator produce, not blackness, but patches of nonlight. The light from the fluorescent sources has three consistencies: there is the light of the tube itself, reflectivity from the fixtures and walls directly around the sources, and the ambient "environmental" glow which in subtlety and effect depends upon the strengths of the colors used. Strong colors produce more presence than admixtures approaching white light, although some of Flavin's more successful effects are with variations of pale colors and white. Again, it is the ambiguous quality of this "trinity" of devices and the seen-not-seen presence of the fixtures themselves that, at least in the artist's mind, makes the adjective "sculptural," with all of its connotations, of doubtful value.

One of the most interesting smaller works was made specifically for the exhibition, *untitled (to Jean Boggs)*. It consists of four vertical 8-foot fluorescent lamps, a green, blue, yellow, and red. The lamps are clustered into a 45-degree corner so that the blue, yellow and red tubes directly confront the viewer. However they are angled so that slight changes in position produce different changes among the primaries – these being the result of the green lamp which is located behind the front three. A hint of green is seen below and above the front cluster of blue, yellow and red, but the primary action of the green is a strange washing effect which it has on the three dominant colors. To my mind this piece, which superficially resembles one of the vertical striped canvases of Morris Louis, is superior to the illusional effects of *untitled (to the "innovator" of Wheeling Peachblow)* (1966/68), shown last year at the artist's Dwan Gallery exhibition. One of Flavin's major strengths is preserving the integrity, the "thingness" of his light sources. *Wheeling Peachblow* is a framed picture, producing the kind of diorama stage effect popular in the last century. Its washed colors and illusionism are enchanting but they lean toward devices of painters far less gifted than Flavin.

In an exhibition which uses light with unequal mastery it may be carping to touch upon weaknesses, either Flavin's or mine, in confronting his work. Some of Flavin's environments far transcend anything comparable, while some do not. I might as well dispense with the latter.

Untitled (to Jane and Brydon Smith) (1969) is a grouped series of eight arrangements using cool white, daylight and blue fluorescent light. There are two vertical and two horizontal arrangements positioned near the center of each side of an open well-shaped area running through the two floors of the exhibition. There are derived from the artist's sketches for *monument to V. Tatlin*. It is doubtful that Flavin seeks any direct link with the Constructivists (although it is certainly there, but rather he obviously admires Tatlin's handling of ordinary materials and turn toward functional art projects. Each of the corners of the room contains an identical work, a cruciform shape in blue and white repeated with modules of 2, 4, 6, and 8-foot fixtures. Standing in the room, one looks at the top white fluorescent tubes, while the blue lights face the wall. As stated in the catalog, "The total area effect of this area, which could be viewed from above and below, was one of maximum discretion based on careful positioning of the eight installations and subtle differences between the blue and daylight fluorescent light in the spatially open corner pieces above and the cool white of the closely packed confronting Tatlin monuments below."[11]

I feel that the cold white light of these eight pieces provides little of the atmospheric unity which often contributes to Flavin's other room-sized efforts. The light is hard and the pieces remain by themselves, rather like a good Antonakoses.

Somewhat different comments are in order for a room entitled *three tangential arcs in daylight and cool white (to Jenny and Ira Licht)* (1969). Here arcs of 2-foot fluorescent units cover the floor, thus blocking entry into the room. Complementary arcs with reversed daylight and cool white tubes cover the two side walls. Some years ago Flavin wrote: "I believe that art is shedding its vaunted mystery for a common sense of keenly realized decoration."[12] Flavin, however, is rarely guilty of decoration in the trivial sense – but this piece may qualify. In the catalog supplement the reversed order of the daylight and cool white arcs on the left and right sides of the room, particularly when seen from opposite ends of the gallery space, are described as "optical complication(s)." I feel Flavin has created such effects with considerably more economy, without employing well over 100 lighting units. To repeat a maxim dear to Flavin, "Ockham's Razor": "principles (entities) should not be multiplied unnecessarily." What has made Flavin's installations stand out from similar art is the fact that his arrangements rarely ignore the space in which they are contained. But while these arcs are flaccidly imposed upon the room's dimensions, they do suggest an interesting phenomenon. The floor configurations and the lower arcs stop just short of intersection. Optically they nearly succeed in destroying the corners of a rectilinear space.

Untitled (to S.M. with all the admiration and love which I can sense and summon) (1969), is another blocked space. Here 8-foot lengths of red, yellow, pink, and blue fluorescent light are composed into a series of four double triangular sections, similar to simple bridge trusses. Each adjoining section (top horizontal members) provides a mixture of two different colors. From one end of the passageway, these effects are considerably cooler than when viewed from the other end. While these admixtures are interesting, it is doubtful in my eyes that the basic colors and their ensemble hold together. Originally one of the attractions of emitted light was the range and quality of colors available for use. There are approximately three times as many neon colors as there are standard fluorescent hues; using gels or other masking devices, the color range runs much higher. One of Flavin's consistent strengths has been that he has drawn upon a necessarily limited palette, and used it with great insight. One thinks back to the days when Flavin was not above exhibiting with all kinds of artists using light; the singularity of his contributions was their muted, untheatrical simplicity – a disturbing feature in a gallery of carnival effects. However, this passageway piece is questionable.

As far as I am concerned, Flavin's four other rooms are unmitigated successes. The artist's *untitled (to Dorothy and Roy Lichtenstein) on not seeing anyone in the room)* (1968), appeared last year in the Dwan show. The dedication alludes to an early painting by Lichtenstein of a peephole with the caption: "I can see the whole room...and there's nobody in it." While the joke is semantic in the Lichtenstein painting, in Flavin's piece the viewer is virtually denied entrance to a small room by the vertical positioning of the fluorescent fixtures. Surely if one wanted to make a case for the artist's deflection of the spectator from intimate contact with the art, it is in this overt example. Flavin's decision not to acknowledge any interpretation of his work except through literal description is the counterpart of his reluctance not to "place" the work of art, such as is the self-defined nature of nearly all *light sculpture*. We see this in Sartre's little known essay on the sculptor David Hare: "Each figure will have secreted its own shell, a living and personal space which will protect it from our space."[13] For Mallarmé this space was suicide, rejection, and creative failure – those acts that destroy a being and therefore cause the world to be haunted by its absence. In several instances Sartre has made the observation that he cannot tell you who he is, but only who he is not. Since the artist is acutely dependent upon his future becoming, descriptions of self can only be made in terms of negations. Sartre also takes up the epistemological implication of hodological space in his chapter on the human body in *Being and Nothingness*:

> The point of view of pure knowledge is contradictory; there is only the point of view of *engaged* knowledge. This amounts to saying that knowledge and action are only two abstract aspects of an original, concrete relation. The real space of the world is what Lewin calls 'hodological.' A pure knowledge in fact would be a knowledge without a point of view; therefore a knowledge of the world but on principle located outside the world. But this makes no sense; the knowing being would be only knowledge since he would be defined by his object and since his object would disappear and since his object would disappear in the total indistinction of reciprocal relations.[14]

Such ambiguity might account for Flavin's reluctance to use the word "environment," or at least as its reputation has been established in the art world. One has come to believe that environments are engaging, that somehow they produce opportunities for sensual involvement that are otherwise absent from art. Flavin's best rooms place us in a situation where all normal activity is inappropriate or irrelevant. For instance, I watched the reaction of a guard when children sat down on the floor in *alternating pink and yellow (to Josef Halmy)* (1967/69). He told them to get up, because "that isn't allowed in here." Well, the problem is that the room is not suited to gallery behavior, such as focused contemplation or adjusting to a point of view. The children had the only reasonable approach, namely that they were going to become a part of the work by forgetting about it.

The room itself consisted of seven walls; at the base of each lay alternating units of pink and yellow fluorescent fixtures. The fixtures were butted together so that about a foot space was left at each corner. This gap defined the room as a series of rectilinear jogs, very much like the open walls that Louis Kahn employed beginning in the early 1950s. This punctuation had the effect of "measuring" the wall lengths, while the orange ambient light above dissolved the topology of the walls and ceiling. I consider this installation somewhat superior to Flavin's final plan for his *alternating pink and "gold"* layout for the Museum of Contemporary Art in Chicago. While the Ottawa room had originally been planned for Chicago in 1967, it was felt that the citizens of Chicago might have trouble digesting such a "minimal" offering; probably so, since they had no little problem with the alternate exhibition which did appear there. Moreover, the layout of the main floor of the Chicago museum with its central partitions would have obscured the relational function of the border lights.

Adjacent to the *pink and yellow* setting is a final room entitled *an artificial barrier of green fluorescent light (to Trudie and Enno Develing)* (1968/69). This consists of overlapped square units of 4-foot fluorescent lights formed literally into a barrier for nearly the entire length of the space. One is permitted to get to the other side by going behind a narrow partition that acts as a kind of false wall Antecedents for this room include Flavin's *greens crossing greens* at the Stedelijk van Abbemuseum in Eindhoven, Holland; and his 1968 red and blue barrier for the Minimal art exhibition at the Gemeentemuseum, The Hague. The catalog explanation of this room is basically optical: the room is saturated with a pale green light, so that the fluorescent tubes appear uncolored or white. This pervasive green acts symbiotically with the previous *pink and yellow* room so that on returning to that room, the atmosphere has changed from orange-yellow to a "rich rose red."

An artificial barrier of green fluorescent light relates in concept to the artist's installed but never exhibited work at the Whitney Museum last year. Flavin ostensibly withdrew from that exhibition because he felt that noise from another display interfered with his own installation. It is also implied that he had substantial doubts about showing with the other invited artists. Both versions are reasonable. But what is most interesting is the way Flavin has in practice defined the word "environment." For the systems engineer, systems are always embedded in an environment, the environment being that area which is not under the control of the system – but which may affect the system. For the engineer, systems boundaries involve a trade-off: namely, how small can one make a system (small meaning size, cost and complexity) so that one has sufficient control over its essential parameters – *without* excluding important aspects of the environment from the system? This in a nutshell is what the best formalists have been doing for a decade: making more and more of the environment *their system*. So, in effect, the environments are not what the artist is concerned with. What we now call "environmental" *used* to be the environment for the artist. Evidently, Flavin and the Whitney do not share the same definition of *environment* – in the long run, I suspect, that will be the Whitney's problem.

With the *barrier of green* we begin to see why Flavin objects to the term "sculpture" applied to his arrangements. On entering the room the viewer looks down on the overlapping squares so that they appear as a heavy skewed line. This compares to many common environmental experiences. The "walk-in, walk-out" tag which Flavin has given some environments is not a device of depreciation; but rather it applies to what Sartre has insisted about himself: *descriptions of self can only be made in terms of negations*. Negations do not have to be studied or analyzed in any rational way, but merely felt instantaneously to be effective. Doubtless Flavin could fill the same space with just as much green light – and do it with no visible means – but to do so would release the irony of employing those very ordinary and unhandsome fixtures. We have the example of what happened when an unsupervised exhibition was made of the artist's work at the Galleria Sperone in Turin, 1968. Special plastic faces were put over all the fluorescent fixtures; immediately the installation began to smell of "light art" and artifice.

Special mention should be made of *untitled (to Heiner Friedrich)* (1969). The room is a partitioned corner on the upper floor of the exhibition. It is triangular, painted to reflect no light, and illuminated with 2-foot fixtures of ultraviolet fluorescent light. Lines of fixtures are arranged diagonally from lower right to upper left across each wall. The effect is more disconcerting than one might expect. Last year at the Kassel Documenta, Flavin devised a situation in a tall room where UV fixtures lined all the corners up to but excluding the ceiling. The shape of the space was thus defined by light sources which emit almost no ambient light. This is even truer of the Ottawa installation. One enters a nearly pitch black room expecting to "redefine" its boundaries and rectilinear corners. This proves impossible and gradually one acclimates to the triangular space – but not before the effort is made to "flatten it out." This sounds very optical, but it is not so in any overt sense, mainly because there is no contrivance or effort to fool the eye. I was misled by my own casual acceptance of all rectilinear room spaces. These simple means are Flavin at his best.

All attempts to "analyze" – whether psychologically or methodologically – an artist such as Flavin are perforce doomed to rejection. And probably a good thing too. It has been said that Flavin has assumed Ad Reinhardt's duties as "conscience of the art world." If Reinhardt lampooned his colleagues it was with a level of esthetic insight and nonviciousness that Flavin has always lacked. What has impelled Flavin to gratuitously insult other artists and institutions is more than likely a profound insecurity unwisely assuaged by the media. The "hardware" quality of his proposals and the sentimentality of his titles are again ramifications of a double-edged logic, a view that sees the world in terms of friends and enemies, very good artists and very bad artists. Literary tantrums are a way of destroying much of the good faith generated by his brilliant art, and at the same time, knowing that the art cannot be rejected by his peers. In psychology there are terms for such a syndrome. Can we take his rejection of art history, of other art movements, and particularly of artists seriously? Well, yes and no. The polemics point to symptoms and malfunctions in the system, but never reveal the underlying conditions provoking them. Only new ideas destroy the status quo, never diatribes. If the artist survives by realizing new negations, the critic sustains himself by negating old ones.

1   Joyce, James (1916) *A Portrait of the Artist as Young Man* (New York: The Modern Library Inc., 1928) pp. 249–250.

2   *Ibid*, p. 252.

3   Flavin, Dan (December 1966) "Some Remarks" *Artforum*, p. 27.

4   *Ibid*, p. 28.

5   Flavin, Dan (December 1967) "Some Other Comments..." *Artforum*, pp. 24–25.

6   Bochner, Mel (Summer, 1967) "Serial Art Systems: Solipsism" *Arts Magazine*, p. 40.

7   Judd, Donald (April 1964) (Review) *Arts Magazine*, p. 31.

8   Judd, Donald (September 13–October 19, 1969) "Aspects of Flavin's Work" in *fluorescent light, etc. from Dan Flavin* exhibition catalogue (Ottawa: The National Gallery of Canada) p. 27.

9   Mallarmé, Stéphane (1956) "Music and Literature" in *Mallarmé: Selected Prose Poems, Essays & Letters* (Baltimore: The Johns Hopkins Press) p. 48.

10   Joyce, James, *op. cit.*, p. 249.

11   Flavin, Dan and Smith, Brydon (September 13–October 19, 1969) *fluorescent light, etc. from Dan Flavin* exhibition catalogue supplement (Ottawa: The National Gallery of Canada) no page numbers.

12   Flavin, Dan (December 1966) "Some Remarks" *Artforum*, p. 28.

13   Sartre, Jean-Paul (October 1947) "Sculpture a 'n' dimensions" in *Derrière le Miroir*, unnumbered insert.

14   Sartre, Jean-Paul (1943) *Being and Nothingness: An Essay on Phenomenological Ontology* (Translated by Hazel E. Barnes) (New York: Philosophical Library, 1956) p. 308.

Artforum, Volume 8, Number 4, December 1969, pp. 49–55.

Art: Jewish Museum Retrospective for Artist of 36
John Canaday

Some friends of mine with children of kindergarten age reported
to me recently that their 5-year-old son, Play School class of '69, was
graduated last June in full academic regalia. The idea behind the
ceremony seems to have been that with things going the way they
are in universities, this might be the last chance the boy would have
to wear a cap and gown.

I feel much the same way about artists like Dan Flavin when they
are given something called a retrospective exhibition, as the Jewish
Museum is doing for Mr. Flavin right now. "Ars longa, vita brevis" is
no longer true, for although life is as fleeting as ever, art fads are
even more so. Thus, "Let's get in there with a retrospective while the
getting's good" has become an activating principle of art salesmanship.

Mr. Flavin will turn 37 this year and the earliest works in his retrospective, which goes back 12 years, serve only to show that he was
formerly an extremely immature and even amateurish painter who
wisely gave up the brush. What he gave it up for, quite recently, was
fluorescent tubing – neon, I call it – and the Jewish Museum has given
all three floors to this celebration of Mr. Flavin's having achieved the
status of maestro.

It is not at all a crowded exhibition, since a great deal of open space
is required to accommodate compositions such as Mr. Flavin's short-
length tubes of alternate colors lined up in regular horizontal sequence
around the baseboard of a large room. There are also, however, some
more compact arrangements, say about 6 or 8 feet high, where half a
dozen tubes of different lengths may be lined up vertically.

As a matter of fact I enjoyed Mr. Flavin's show rather more than I
expected to, but for a reason having little to do with his work. By the
damnedest coincidence in the world I happened to drop in on it last

Thursday, which turns out to have been St. Agnes's Day, which I have always thought of as the coldest day of the year ever since reading John Keats's opening lines of his poem about it:

> St. Agnes' Eve – Ah bitter chill
> 　it was!
> The owl, for all his feathers, was
> 　a-cold;
> The hare limped trembling
> 　through the frozen grass
> And silent was the flock in
> 　woolly fold.

Things have been every bit that bad on Fifth Avenue this week and it was good to get into a nice warm museum. And because I was reluctant to go out again, I spent a long time examining Mr. Flavin's tubes. They did not grow on me. As boutique decoration, acceptable although obvious. As works of art to be taken seriously – no go.

The New York Times, January 24, 1970, p. 25.

Dan Flavin: Fiat Lux
William S. Wilson

A distinction which throws some light on Flavin's art is that some electric lights are made to see by, others are made to be seen. Neon is made to be seen, as in signs, so that the use of neon by Watts, Chryssa, Antonakos and Nauman has a tinge of advertising display about it. Neon art contains the ironic feeling that goes with the elevation of esthetically valueless materials to fine art. With the irony goes the freedom from good form enjoyed by advertising. The Pop Art irony may recede in time, as it has in Rosenquist's *Tumbleweed*, and it is reduced in recent works which are direct and autotelic. Whereas Bob Watts imitated the signatures of Picasso and Matisse in neon, Bruce Nauman imitates his own; Chryssa's *Gates to Times Square* must refer to the actual signs of Times Square, but Joseph Kosuth's *Neon*, the word *neon* spelled out in neon, refers to itself. But even Kosuth's *Neon* alludes to neon as used in signs, and therefore it has a double focus, on the physical fact, and on the idea. Ben Bern's tensile lyricism in neon avoids the referential content, and achieves a directness and sweet univocation by using material which is meant to be looked *at* and looked *through*, in a way so that it can only be looked *at*. Now that candles are obsolete for seeing by, even they are to be seen in the art of Richard Serra and John van Saun. The sun itself is to see by, not to look at directly, and has long symbolized reason. The moon, which can be looked at, and which sheds a light which conceals as much as it reveals, has long symbolized the imagination.

Dan Flavin has shown incandescent bulbs and fluorescent tubes which are not ordinarily meant to be looked at. As the light bulbs occur in the early construction – *For Barbara Roses, East New York Shrine* – they have some of the irony and freedom from good form implicit in the use of commercially valuable but esthetically valueless objects as fine art. Some irony remains in later fluroescent work, when considered in the context of European-American art history, with hardware store appliances offered as equivalent to the art of the museums. But more important than the irony in the raw use of commercial or industrial materials is the shift in focus from the fluorescent light as subsidiary to sight to the object of sight. Flavin's work belongs with that of Kelly, Morris and Lichtenstein, among many others, who have shifted focus from a whole precious work of art to the material conditions and technical operations which underlie the making of walls, buildings and paintings. The subsidiary parts of the traditional whole esthetic experience are accepted as sufficient because they are more physically real than that elusive and ambiguous whole, and because those parts relate to the whole of human culture, not just an esthetic overlay. Not art history – painting, sculpture and some vases – leads up to Flavin, but a history of learning to draw straight lines, to shape rectangles and to make decisions based on accurate information about a situation.

Not even the history of the use of actual light in art leads up to Flavin; he has written that he "...knew nothing of the Moholy-Nagy sculpture or, for that matter, all of the output of the European solo systems and groupings like *Zero* which were introduced to New York relatively recently or not at all."[1] The background which one chooses for his art will depend upon the meaning found in it. Willoughby Sharp, in an otherwise useful essay, "Luminism and Kineticism," writes that Flavin uses light as a *found object*.[2] This phrase brings up Dada and Surrealism and some inaccurate implications. Duchamp was already there with the necessary distinction: "to separate the *mass-produced readymade* from the *readyfound* – The separation is an operation." The difference is essential. Neon, because of advertising, is closer to the readyfound. The found object descends from the Surrealist proposition that things in the world are real when they echo images in the mind. The world is the dream of a larger consciousness; so when Breton finds a wooden spoon, and Giacometti a mask, each has found an image in the dream of the world that matches an image in his own dream.

Flavin's fluorescent units belong instead with the *mass-produced ready-made* which has controlled implications, not a mysterious suggestiveness. A cup rack or a fluorescent fixture emerges from industrial and technological operations which are esthetically unselfconscious or anesthetized, and they are metaphorically sterile. The readymade dispels the mystery of creativity because it is already made, and it resists irrational symbolism because the manufacturer can have had no symbolist purposes. The hardware emerges from the operations of manufacturing shaped by the esthetics of technology, with its criteria of simplicity, efficiency and commercial success. These operations also help to shape the meaning contained in the objects if they are used as art.

Ira Licht has written of Flavin's work: "The unchanged hardware lacks the look of art history and the dead weight of tradition; it escapes metaphor and symbolism."[3] But metaphor and symbolism are not escaped so easily, either as a part of the work or as a resonance of the whole work. The elimination of particular metaphors in recent art is for the sake of revealing the identity of the object. When A is compared with B, A loses some of its reality. It may become emotionally accessible, or intellectually available, but it has been assimilated into someone's impressions or interpretations of A, and is the less A for that – its self-contained physical identity lessened by the intrusion of a non-physical nonfact of resemblance. Poets have always criticized metaphors – "Shall I compare thee to a summer's day?" – and in this century have criticized metaphor itself. Northrop Frye in his essay "The Myth of Light" quotes the right lines:

Trace the gold sun about the whitened sky
Without evasion by a single metaphor.[4]

But there is still the question of the whole object, art or not, as a metaphor. Both Mel Bochner and Dan Graham have quoted Roland

Barthes on Robbe-Grillet in relation to Flavin's work: "...the object has no being beyond phenomenon; it is not ambiguous, not allegorical, not even opaque, for opacity somehow implies a corresponding transparency, a dualism in nature. For him the object is no longer a common-room of correspondences, a welter of sensations and symbols, but merely the occasion of a certain optical resistance."[5] Notice that this definition of objects is a fiat by Robbe-Grillet, not a proof. The appropriate response is not a refutation but an equally clear fiat of one's own. My approach to Flavin's work makes the physical things figure forth an interior process, which makes them metaphors, or which makes explicit the metaphor in the title of a work, *daylight and cool white (to Sol LeWitt)*, 1964 as well as of an autobiographical sketch, "...in daylight or cool white."

Ira Licht is right that the work "lacks the look of art history." Let that dispose of the theory that art derives from art, and that such meaning as it has derives from formal interrelations standing in a critical relation to other formal interrelations – that art can be no more than an edgy and attenuated revival of Cubism. Thinking about art in relation to art can be a way of thinking about reality, but that is an impoverished reality, and that is certainly not Flavin's way of thinking: "I like thinking here and now without sententious alibis." There must be a sense in which the work of this man who likes thinking represents the work of conscious mental operations. What remains is to understand the relation of the materials, fluorescent tubes, to such a meaning.

Titles of early assemblages – *East New York Shrine, icon IV* – have uncontrolled religious implications, and Flavin is quoted as having written in a journal, August 19, 1962, "I can take the ordinary lamp out of use and into a magic that touches ancient mysteries."[6] Flavin's perception of his own work has changed from mystery to factuality: "In the beginning, and for some time thereafter, I, too, was taken with easy, almost exclusive recognitions of fluorescent light as image. Now I know that the physical fluorescent light tube has never dissolved or disappeared by entering the physical field of its own light as you have stated. At first sight, it appeared to do that, especially when massed tightly with reciprocal glass reflections resulting as within 'the nominal three,' but then, with a harder look, one saw that each tube maintained steady and distinct contours despite its internal act of ultraviolet light which caused the inner fluorescent coating of its glass container to emit the visible light. The physical fact of the tube as object in place prevailed whether switched on or off."[7]

The later titles avoid inneundo for sharply inflected descriptions: "White around a corner." The question remains, when the fuzzy edges of allusion are trimmed, whether or not, as Flavin says, "Symbolism is dwindling." It *is* if symbolizing means the trick of representing one thing by another; so it must when it is realized that symbolizing undermines identity, and that anything can represent anything else if a code is available. Also dwindling is the sense of a symbol as a way of knowing something which can't be known in any other way. This symbolizing re-enforces mystery, and suggests unverifiable profundity. Certainly the works of Flavin do not belong with the palpable obscure. They are symbolic, but they turn symbolizing inside out by symbolizing clarity. Clarity as a value is suggested in his writings: "Clarity obtains my mind, after all." "I aim constantly for clarity and distinction first in the pattern of the tubes and then with that of the supporting pan."[8]

Flavin's many statements against obscurity point to the meaning of this clarity. Each work represents his clear decision – what he calls his *proposal* – and his work as an artist is the work of deciding what to put where. As a maker, what he makes are clear decisions. Flavin has isolated his work from art history, so that it cannot be explained reductively by influence or development; he has isolated it from kinetic works and other light art, those two great disappointments of the last decade, by not transforming the materials; and he has made it unyielding to formalist criticism. This independence shows in the work as the look of self-reliant decision. Each configuration represents a decision and delineates a border between uncertainty and certainty. So Flavin's statement that art is shedding its mystery is true for his work in that it is an expression of clear, radiant and sometimes arrogant decision, made within the elisions of experience. "Before becoming seven," he wrote in "...in daylight or cool white," "I attempted to run away from home but was apprehended by a fear of the unknown in sunlight just two blocks from our house." [9] Now the unknown has more to fear from him.

Many of the qualities that inhere in Flavin's work have been defined by him in the essays, which are models of disconnected and potentially endless prose, without falsifying transitions or sham coherence. Some works have been described by Elizabeth C. Baker ("The Light Brigade," ARTnews, March, 1967), Barbara Reise ("Untitled 1969," *Studio International*, April, 1969), and by Dan Flavin and Brydon Smith ("fluorescent light, etc....," *artscanada*, October 1969). Not to contradict but to supplement these, I would describe the effect of the light on the room in terms chosen to suggest that the light is to the room as decision is to consciousness. An obvious function of light is to dispel darkness. "A light bulb in the dark," wrote Robert Rauschenberg, "cannot show itself without showing you something else too." [10] A light introduces visual clarity, and this is simultaneously intellectual clarity and often emotional clarity. With the introduction of Flavin's lights, solid walls are pulled forward or pushed back as the light defines its own space against the resistance of the readymade place. The solid floors sometimes immaterialize as the reflections open up planes and make the light look real, the floor somewhat illusory. My strongest impression is not of light dispelling darkness, but of light dispelling, or dominating, other *light*. The effect occurred tellingly in the Kornblee Gallery when the green lights made the daylight outside look rose. Looking at fluorescent light makes us see things differently. So does deciding.

I am interpreting the meaning of the arrangements of standard fluorescent units installed in gallery and museum spaces. My fiat is that we experience meaning, and that the name of the meaning we experience in Flavin's work is *decision*. Decision as such, which is isolated in these works, bears a relation to light, albeit metaphorically, as when I say that decision is the ability to overcome darkness. *Light* is the name of the meaning we experience in decision. At this stage, the *decision is the light*. Flavin displays his decisions in what he calls proposals or propositions. A proposal puts forward something which can be accepted or rejected, and Flavin can sound quite benign: "Friends, when as its artist I write about proposal for fluorescent light I develop a continuity of suggestive speculation but please understand that I do not wish to enforce conclusions against your individual participation with it." But what looks like *proposal* to him looks like fiat to me. The decision could be shown in a diagram for an installation, but as Jill Kornblee said, "When Flavin's work isn't up, it just doesn't exist." Hence, *the fiat is the light*. The standard fluorescent fixtures are made to see by; when they are shown to be seen, looking at them is like looking at our fiats. Flavin has created a rational image of man's decisive and active consciousness as the illumination of his world.

1 "some other comments," *Artforum* VI, December, 1967, p.21.

2 In *Minimal Art*, edited by Gregory Battcock, New York, 1968.

3 "Dan Flavin," *artscanada* XXV, December, 1968, p.62.

4 *artscanada* XXV, December, 1968, p.8, quoting Wallace Stevens.

5 Mel Bochner, "Less is Less," *Art and Artists*, December, 1966, p.25 and Dan Graham, "Dan Flavin: Pink and Gold," the catalogue of the Museum of Contemporary Art, Chicago, December, 1967.

6 Quoted by Barbara Rose, "ABC Art," in *Minimal Art*, p.295.

7 "some remarks...," *Artforum* V, December, 1966, p.28.

8 *Artforum*, December, 1967, p.21.

9 "...in daylight or cool white," *Dan Flavin, fluorescent light, etc.*, The National Gallery of Canada, Ottawa, 1969, p.8.

10 "Random Order," *Location* I, Spring, 1963, p.29.

Art News, Volume 68, Number 9, January 1970, pp. 48–51.

Flavin's Proposal
Dan Graham

There is no projected core of inner vision, only the literal projection
of each fixture and tube from the ground of the wall...The lights are
simultaneously the sign and the thing specified and the medium for
in-forming them both. Fluorescent light objects in place are re-placeable
in various contingently determined, independent relations with specific
environmental situations and are also re-placeable from their fixtures
and in having a limited existence.[1] The components of a particular
exhibition upon its termination are re-placed in another situation –
perhaps put to a non-art use as part of a different future. Individual
units possess no intrinsic significance beyond their concrete utility. It
is difficult either to project into them extraneous qualities – a spurious
in-sight – or for them to be appropriated for fulfillment of personal
"inner" needs. (Much modern art, after Jasper Johns, dispenses with
symbolic load.) The lights are untransformed; there are no symbolic,
transcendental or monetary (redeeming) added values present. Light
is immediately present in all places; the sensation is optical and singular.[2] The lights and fixtures are aggregated side by side;[3] the medium
is transparently outside the conventional pictorial linear perspective
where the eye, from a fixed viewing position, penetrates the frame
continuously to reach a contained central "vanishing" point. Light
short-circuits process; there is no extended process of seeing. Generation and decay are not embodied in a succession of different forms
of the same subject. (Flavin's proposal is not part of some platonically
substantial body of work or process.) The use of fluorescent light
available in any hardware store disenburdens the work of the weight
of personal or historically generated (evolutionary) determination...

1   DAN FLAVIN: "I sense no stylistic or structural development of any significance within my proposal, only shifts on partitive emphasis modifying and addable without intrinsic change. The system does not proceed; it is simply applied. All my diagrams, even the oldest, seem applicable again and continually. It is as though my stem synonymizes its past, present, and future states without incurring a loss of relevance. This differs greatly from the former sense of development, piece by piece."

2   NICHOLAS OF AUTRECOURT (13th century Nominalist, burnt publicly in Paris, 1247): "Things exist by virtue of themselves and nothing else; everything outside of the mind is by that fact individual."

3   DON JUDD: "Things that exist exist and everything is on their side."

Arts Magazine, Volume 44, Number 4. February 1970, pp. 44–45.

Art: A Different Light
John Perrault

The fluorescent light constructions, arrangements, and situations –
"situations" rather than environments – by Dan Flavin, now at the
Jewish Museum, are clean, cool, elegant, intelligent, and beautiful.
This retrospective show originated at the National Gallery of Canada,
Ottawa, and we are lucky to have it here in New York even if, as the
Canadian catalog seems to indicate, it has been slightly abridged.

Flavin's constructions are composed of standard size fluorescent
lights. Duchamp once said that one could find all the art materials
one needed in any hardware store. Flavin's works, however, are not
examples of found art. Although the fixtures and the tubes are important, the light emitted is probably more important, as are the
arrangements of the various readymade sizes and tube colors that
Flavin selects and combines. The works emit light and rather than
passively reflecting light, the works are the light. They are not sculpture in any traditional sense. Because light reflected off the wall is
an important aspect of the works and because colors – often merely
different degrees of white – are also important, the works relate as
much to painting as to sculpture. Saying that they fall somewhere
between painting and sculpture would only be half true because it
does not imply the architectural concerns of the works. They are
unique works of art that are beyond traditional categories.

The fact that a particular piece is varied each time it is set up in a
new space indicates that the works are to some degree what I should
like to call "situational." By "situational" I mean that the visible part
of the work is in some way at least partially determined by the situation, the locale, the setting, and, in Flavin's case in particular, the
architecture of each exhibition space. But his works are also, to use
the opposite term, "impositional." They impose another order or

another statement upon a particular space. New work that interests me is invariably a combination of these extremes. A purely situational work – if there can be such a thing – adjusts totally to the context and, if not invisible, approaches invisibility and therefore becomes an aesthetic, if not metaphysical, game of hide-and-seek. An impositional work is more traditional. Most modern art is impositional. Its presence takes no account of the environment, but its presence inflects or changes the environment, often by chance placement or interior decorator whim. New art, as opposed to "modern" art, more often than not takes the context or the architecture or the setting into account. In fact, it is often directly inspired by these factors. The Jewish Museum show allows us for the first time to see a great number of Flavin's works all at once, and although his pieces are often derived from particular spaces, more often than not they are set up to destroy or alter our perceptions of those spaces. Fluorescent lights are set up in corners, effectively destroying those corners, or are arranged along the floor corners to cast reflections that destroy the literal space and replaces it with a perceptual or an aesthetic space.

I have two minor criticisms of the show. One is that some of the pieces have been ineptly transferred. There are too many false rooms constructed in the actual space in an effort to mimic what I can only assume was the architecture of the National Gallery of Canada. The other criticism – and this is difficult for me to express with any kind of clarity – is that I question the value of including so many inferior early works. Flavin's attempts at imitating de Kooning, Kline, and Johns, although interesting, are on the whole depressing. His draftsmanship, even including rough sketches of current arrangements, is abominable and serves only to cloud his real value as an artist. Even his first light works ("icon," as he calls them) are of questionable value. His *Barbara Roses* piece is merely campy. On the other hand, these pre-fluorescent pieces indicate that suddenly Flavin became inspired and became an artist with something to say. Given the fact of Flavin's intensely Catholic background, I do not hesitate to suggest the possibility that he was the victim of "grace," for in my mind there is no doubt that his fluorescent pieces and the concepts behind them make him, in spite of the early junk, a major artist.

In terms of the fluorescent pieces – the only ones worth considering – the key word has to be "opposition." There are many oppositions going on at once in any of these pieces. I mean by this and what follows to indicate the complexity of Flavin's fluorescent works, a complexity that may not be readily perceivable, but is nevertheless there and is what makes him such an important artist, in all the best senses of that word.

There are oppositions between the fluorescent lights and the walls upon which they are mounted or the spaces that they transect. There are oppositions between natural light and artificial light, reflected light and direct light; between history and style. There are oppositions between the cold arrangements and the sentimental dedication titles and a submerged religious content. It is undeniable that the works are contemplative. Nevertheless one cannot help but see fluorescent lights in a different light after viewing Flavin's masterful manipulations.

The Village Voice, February 5, 1970, p. 16.

Art
Lawrence Alloway

With Dan Flavin, the Jewish Museum revives the kind of show that has been strongest in its program: retrospectives by artists under 40. The precedents are two exhibitions arranged by Alan Solomon, when he was director: the Robert Rauschenberg show in 1963, when the artist was 38, and the Jasper Johns show in 1964, when the artist was 34. The Flavin show is arranged by Brydon Smith, who two years ago arranged the James Rosenquist exhibition, when the artist was 35. That show and the Flavin were not originated in New York but by the National Gallery of Canada where Smith is a curator. The Rosenquist never came to New York but fortunately the Flavin did. Flavin is 37 and his work occupies three floors of the Jewish Museum.

The museum has seldom looked better. It is not that Flavin's glowing light pieces should be regarded in terms of decor and, thus, as enhancements of the galleries. The relationship is more ambiguous and rewarding than that, but it is true that the works, as they emit visible energy, illumine the space they occupy, which is architectural. The works do have a diagrammatic architectural character, resembling at times pilasters and arcades, fences and gates. These are the works that consist of regularly repeated units. The single, compact pieces often have an obelisk- or urn-like symmetry. The room becomes a container of light and it is the cast light, no less than the formal display of the tubes, that is beautiful. The long pergola-like structure with four colors, for example, is totally changed by the light-order, depending on which end you enter.

The catalogue is full of detailed information, not the sort that a curator digs up but the sort that an artist thrusts on him. He has a (fantasied?) memory of toilet-training at the age of 2 weeks. The catalogue includes the information that his mother, "a stupid, fleshy tyrant of a woman," destroyed his childhood drawings and that he had a Latin teacher who blushed when reprimanding teen-age Flavin. Such detail wins away from Robert Indiana's catalogue of his 1968 retrospective the prize for overexposure in recent art documentation. Flavin's self-regard and punctiliousness are evident also in the show's balance. Although his mature style does not start until 1963, the drawing of his first fluorescent light piece is No. 73 in the chronological catalogue.

His early work, though overshown, provides information about New York in the early sixties and it expresses awkwardly qualities that are embodied subtly in his later pieces. In 1958–61 he drew in an Abstract Expressionist style, but interpolated long quotations from James Joyce's early poems and *The Song of Songs*. The words, sentimental and exalted respectively, are tangled in a dirty snarl of ink and water color. This sense of art as an exalted text survives in his mature work which, significantly, he calls icons. And it is true that the Fun House flicker of much light art is miles away from the steady glow of his fluorescent gases. He is more like a Keeper of the Flame than a Coney Island technologist.

In 1960 Flavin used found objects, especially flattened cans, the crinkled blobs of which he attached to panels, adding paint. These works have the rusty and grimy texture of much Downtown art of the period (seen, also, in the early work of Jim Dine, Claes Oldenburg and Lucas Samaras, among others). When he shifted from junk to newly purchased and functioning objects, he did as other artists were doing, moved from an expressionistic urbanism to a more highly structured style. But though Flavin's style changed, two constants remained. He moved from found objects to new objects, but preserved his interest in ready-mades. Also, he preserved his custom of dedication – to friends, to artists, to victims; a persistent memorial intention suffuses his work, in contradistinction to the new age/new media slogans of some light artists.

The first work in Flavin's characteristic style is *the diagonal of personal ecstasy*, originally dedicated to Brancusi, because of Brancusi's *Endless Column*, at once serial in form and archaic in content. Now it is dedicated to Robert Rosenblum, who owns an early Flavin drawing and some of whose lectures on Ingres Flavin attended. All this information comes from the catalogue, as does the artist's description of the work as "a common eight-foot strip with fluorescent light of any commercially available color."

The number of ways that Flavin has deployed standard light fixtures since 1963 is impressive. In the following year he grouped four tubes in two colors vertically and many of his best works have been in this position. Sometimes they are seen in progression along a wall or round a room, sometimes in a series of stepped forms (as with the Tatlin monument). Since 1966, by various stages, he has complicated his work, beyond diagonal or vertical groups, moving from an art of placement to one of construction. He has overlapped strips and angled them at various gradients, thus introducing design as a shadowy linear structure at the core of his glowing light. In the past few years he has sometimes been tricky in a way that is far removed from his beginning, as with the piece that you look through from behind the reflectors that carry the strips; they illuminate a room from which you are excluded.

Flavin has produced an abundance of remarkable work, but the course of his development raises a problem. There is a perceptible drift from economical forms with a maximum of released light to greater complexity and coloristic nuance. Initially he condensed his early diffuse interests, with a brilliant intuition, into his single bar of light. He did it, moreover, without losing his sense of art's sacredness. Later the problem arises – as it has for others who have clenched their art into one thing – how to keep on working. Often this has meant relaxing and a gradual return to a traditional canon of complexity. A successful retrospective, as it presents a contour of a life's work up to date, raises such questions. I wonder if Flavin, as his pieces get more fancy and multicolored, is not starting to suffer from the limits of his ready-made materials. It may be time for him to consider custom-made fluorescent lights as a means of expansion.

The Nation, February 9, 1970, pp. 155–156.

Dan Flavin's self-sufficient light
Christopher Andreae

An untitled poem (pencil on paper, 11 inches by 8½ inches) written (or drawn?) in 1961 by Dan Flavin reads: "fluorescent / poles / shimmer / shiver / flick / out / dim / monuments / of / on / and / off / art." The note in the catalog for the Flavin exhibition held at the end of last year in Ottawa, observes: "This is Flavin's only poem about fluorescent light."

It may be his only poem on the subject, but fluorescent light, presented as art, has become virtually synonymous with his name. Now he has installed an exhibition of fluorescent lights throughout the Jewish Museum. I've been to see it twice, and find I have no real desire to write much about it – not, I should add, because I am uninterested by Mr. Flavin's art, but because it is noncommunicable, nonverbal, perfectly self-sufficient, and has to be experienced.

You can coldly observe facts about it: the presentation of light as object; the shedding and diffusion of light; its role as source; the lighting and coloring of a whole enclosed environment; reflections in shiny floors; the casting of shadows along the sides of fixtures, and of light on the wall-surface; the fierce glare of the tubes themselves; the tidiness of the installation (no wires showing); the visual disruption of the wall or room structure by the placement and strength of the lights – and so on.

Taking it personally
Or you can translate it into personal sensations: a consciousness of the iconic nature of the fluorescent tubes, and of the "religious" aura that attaches to them (supported by an awareness of Mr. Flavin's Roman Catholic background and by the titles he applied to some of the first pieces in which he used electric light); or a kind of aesthetic dismay at the calm acceptance and use of untransformed industrial products to make art – or rather, as art. (Actually I don't find this particularly

strange; it seems easy enough to admit that these are "Flavins" quite as much as they are "readymades.") Or they can stir up some completely subjective response or memory, like the intense delight you took as a child in the unique brightness and Christmas-tree excitement of colored lights, or some weird, scarcely rememberable action or place connected with ultraviolet light (a possible reaction to one of the pieces shown here).

Mr. Flavin's own aesthetic seems to fall somewhere between the personal and factual approaches.

"I know now that I can reiterate any part of my fluorescent light system as adequate," he has written. "Elements or parts of that system simply alter in situation installation. They lack the look of history..."

Ancient mysteries

On the one hand his art seems self-denying and formal in the extreme: strict drawings in fluorescent light installed and arranged without personal touch – formalized phenomenon-art. On the other hand, and almost because his means are so commonplace, his art seems as though it has or must have potent overtones of mystique.

He has described his *diagonal of personal ecstasy* (an eight-foot strip of fluorescent light placed diagonally on the wall) as having "potential for becoming a modern technological fetish." And he wrote in a journal entry in 1962: "I can take the ordinary lamp out of use and into a magic that touches ancient mysteries. And yet it is still a lamp that burns to death like any other of its kind. In time the whole electrical system will pass into inactive history. My lamps will no longer be operative; but it must be remembered that they once gave light."

The otherwise uninteresting nonfluorescent bits and pieces in the exhibition do tend to underline the personal nature of Mr. Flavin's attitudes: jotty drawing, notes, illustrated poems ("I am afraid at times I have painted so as to thoroughly overwhelm the text"), the rather dreadful earlier "icons," the surrealist-silliness called *Barbara Roses* (after the critic).

But if his use of fluorescent tubes does have a discernible history, it is in a move away from the unitary and iconic, to something more purely physical and environmental. This "on-and-off art" makes the unnoticed just not noticeable but worthy of notice. And this is true of the surrounding space quite as much as the lights themselves.

The Christian Science Monitor, February 14, 1970, p. 14.

New York
Jean-Louis Bourgeois

A major new realm, vast and stunningly beautiful, is opening in art. It is the art of light, of radiance, literally of glory. Till very recently, it was practiced largely by prisms, Roman candles, and saints. Now artists have begun to practice it too. Dan Flavin has been a pioneer. His first pieces using lights date from 1963. Earlier this month the New York art world saluted Flavin on a scale which surpasses its celebration of any other American artist since World War II, including Pollock and de Kooning. Five exhibitions of Flavin's work ran simultaneously, including an important retrospective (previously seen in Ottawa) at the Jewish Museum. The Metropolitan's *1940–70* and the Museum of Modern Art's *Spaces* shows each gave Flavin a full room; the Dwan and Castelli Galleries each gave him several. So Flavin, earlier this month, achieved all that the New York art world has to bestow – temporary majesty.

Flavin is revolutionary in that he is the first high- (as opposed to vernacular) art artist to make a source of light his working material. There have been a few exceptions, such as stained glass windows and chandelier tear-dropping/prism-ing, but generally the materials of fine arts till now have been restricted to surfaces like canvas, bronze, and marble, which receive light instead of emitting it. To be a "master of light" meant, till Flavin, light depicted, e.g. De la Tour, Rembrandt, Monet, or of the play of natural light and shadow, as in the deep eaves of Frank Lloyd Wright's hailed Robie House (1909) or in the deep colonnade of Etienne Boullée's visionary temple façade.

It is only since Dada, and till recently only in a marginal way, that mirrors, which show light its own image, have been accepted as a "legitimate" material in high art. (For a particularly fine recent example, see Robert Smithson's "Flash" poster for the Jewish Museum.)

And now the time for the legitimation of artificial light – both the appliance and the radiance – has arrived.

Widening one's conception of art from surface alone to include light as an aspect of art isn't something done casually. When I first saw Flavins, convinced that what was important was the surface of his art, I studied his lamps as objects. For example, diligent in looking at *daylight and cool white* (*to Sol LeWitt*), 1964, a piece using four very bright, closely-set parallel fluorescent tubes, I thought hard about "Flavin as an electric color-band painter," and counted nineteen parallel bands in the "composition" of the tubes (first bulb, reflection of next bulb on first bulb, mounting, reflection of first bulb on next bulb, next bulb, etc., all brilliantly lit). That night, for my bull-headedly traditional efforts I suffered a terrible headache. Except possibly as needlessly masochist pain trips, brighter Flavins are not about surface – at least not the surfaces of the light source itself.

Instead, they are about radiance itself, and its many moods. This is a great jump from art as immediate surface, but there are stepping-stones. One of these is Flavin's artful use of reflections. On a wall at the entrance to the Jewish Museum show, Flavin deliberately set up a long fluorescent diagonal in such a way that along with its own reflection in the tile floor, the piece became a large "V" visually inviting the spectator into the show. Throughout the various shows, floor and even ceiling reflections abound – so much so that it becomes clear that installing a Flavin in a carpeted room may literally mean eclipsing one third of the piece. But important as the stepping-stones are (another is the halo), what is most important is the whole journey – each of the fluorescent pieces experienced as a situation, an environment, impromptu architecture, a stage. The white, bright *monuments for V. Tatlin 1964–69* at Castelli cast a harsher mood; but the color pieces at Dwan make their spaces lush, lyrical, intimate. Watching a gallery of Flavins come on, light up, is a breathtaking show, a genuine electric circus; the pieces burst into life, seizing the space around them like giant instant dyes. Mr. Russell Woeltz has suggested that a Flavin show calls for cameras, still and movie, to take shots not just of the lamps themselves but of the people and objects they can so strikingly dramatize.

If every light has a mood, the mood of white light is rigidly vacuous. True, incandescent white is a little warmer than fluorescent, but generally puritan sterility is the norm – in public places, in homes, in offices – an almost universal asceticism, strange when such abundant beauty is within easy reach. The notion of Flavins as proxy suns is more than just gaudy metaphor. If "ecology" can refer to our everyday urban experience as much as to distant wilderness, then electric light is as crucial a man-made resource as water and sunlight are natural ones. We all spend a large part of our waking lives in light conditions which Flavin's mastery of the genre now reveals to be sterile and ugly. Flavin himself is in the best possible position to dramatize this fact. ("For myself, I would not resist 'public service.'")

What if Flavin applied his light artistry to the lighting of important public spaces – for example Grand Central Station's vast Information Hall? Once famed for its starred canopy, the hall is now so lavishly encrudded with electric ads that the ceiling is nearly invisible; the ads desecrate an official public landmark. Given the practical authority, Flavin could recast the hall in terms as lyrical or noble as he chose, even programming many or changing moods in which to bring back the stars.

If Flavin the Sun-King of Grand Central sounds appealing, imagine Flavin king of our avenues, bedrooms, classrooms, and offices – no temporary art-world luminary, but his basic insight immortalized by constant use. This would be permanent – not merely temporary – majesty, perhaps even enshrined in the language. Till now Flavin has made capital-F Flavins with lamps bought direct from commercial suppliers; he has made no secret of this. In the future, perhaps people by the thousands, as well as public authorities, might install and enjoy small-f "flavins" bought from the same source. Flavin's lamps are found objects of a rare kind in art – manufactured, generally available, and, given the richness of light and mood they yield, not expensive. Flavin is in a unique position to use his high-art status to further the ecology of all our eyes, thus helping to start a genuinely democratic art of the rainbow.

Artforum, Volume 8, Number 8, April 1970, pp. 81–82. [excerpt]

The Power of Colour Light: Dan Flavin – Success and Myth of an American Artist
Hans Strelow

Dan Flavin is one of the best known and appreciated post-Pop American artists in Germany and on the European contemporary art scene. Rudolph Zwirner introduced Flavin in 1966 in a show in his Cologne gallery. At the same time, Flavin showed in the exhibition *Kunst-Licht-Kunst* (*Art-Light-Art*) in Eindhoven, the exhibition *Kompass III*, again in Eindhoven and at the Frankfurt Kunstverein, *Minimal Art* in Den Haag, the Kunsthalle Düsseldorf, and the Berlin Academy of Fine Arts. The touring exhibition of the collection Ströher, Documenta IV and solo exhibitions at Heiner Friedrich in Munich and Konrad Fischer in Düsseldorf followed.

Flavin's spaces, which are defined by the light of neon tube compositions, became a steady presence on the art scene. Yet, they cannot easily be related to any, in fact to none, of the existing tendencies. Could one think of it as light art; light art hitherto defined in relation to kinetic art? The clear object-based character of the tubes and metal supports cancel this out. Minimal art? The bright light cannot be reconciled with the typical aspects of Minimal Art. Environment? The often serial and geometrical composition of the neon tubes make Flavin's work transportable and flexible and gives it autonomy. Maybe it is the impossibility to clearly categorise Flavin's work that makes him an ever up-to-date part of the contemporary art scene for the last five years. This time period is long enough to either forget an artist, or to make him a 'young classic', which means to brand him, classify him and 'fix' him once and forever, which happened to the leading American pop artists.

Instead, the myth of a purist super-artist, the artistic consciousness of the present time is being built around Flavin, which he supports with his often-polemical manifestos. Flavin has acknowledged fans who surround him constantly; especially when he travels from his home in Lake Valhalla, Cold Springs to Manhattan in order to enjoy the hectic New York art buzz and attend to his manifold interests (Flavin is known as an excellent connoisseur and collector of early American glass). Not long ago, for one weekend Flavin made the improbable come true through temporal overlaps: he showed simultaneously in five different prominent locations in New York. The show at Dwan Gallery, Flavin's sole gallery agent for years, opened at the same time as that as the Castelli Gallery, now sharing Flavin's work with Dwan since recently. This double exhibition was celebrated with a wedding-like dinner for the *haute volée* of the New York art world in an elegant art nouveau setting at Lüchow's German restaurant. Flavin's work was also included in the exhibitions *New York Painting and Sculpture 1900–1970* at the Metropolitan Museum and *Spaces* at MoMA. And coming from Canada, Flavin's retrospective just opened at the Jewish Museum.

The response of New York's only remaining decent newspaper, the *Times*, was ridicule ending with the following sentences: "Acceptable as boutique decoration, although obvious. As an art work to be taken seriously – come on." It seems to be the rule now that the most original avant-garde artists very often get a beating from the *New York Times*. Or they become ridiculed in a more or less intelligent way whilst other often mediocre artists come off well and are praised graciously. With regard to things which one does not understand or which one does not bother to deal with, it is a common – and generally highly developed – attitude in New York to evade the issue and instead switch to a frivolous chatty tone and derision. It is indicative of the state of affairs that the National Gallery of Canada in Ottawa gave Flavin the opportunity of a retrospective, which went on to Vancouver and then in a reduced form to New York's Jewish Museum.

The exhibition in Ottawa was organised by the curator for contemporary art at the National Gallery, Brydon Smith, and was accompanied by an extraordinarily well-documented catalogue. It showed an artist who solved a problem in contemporary art by means of a method comparable to the one which once helped Columbus put the famous egg on its feet: Flavin found an element which was ideal for his intention to work with light without depending on technology. Flavin uses the light of the neon tubes, whose form and length are industrially fixed, as colour. Like the constructivists, he draws on colour in geometrical basic patterns, preferably squares and rectangles. With Flavin, however, the form and colour of the body of light are pre-fabricated. Hence, the artistic act lies in the choice and composition of the bright elements, which finally build the 'Gestalt' of the work. This reduction to the act of invention, dispensing with crafty efforts is a crucial concept in modern art. It provides the basis for its idea of autonomy.

Flavin enjoys a strong reputation within future-oriented artists' circles. Without any doubt this is due to the stroke of genius the now 37-year-old artist carried out in 1963. Only relying on the act of invention, he realised *the diagonal of May 25, 1963 (for Robert Rosenblum)*, a 2.44 meter long neon tube, which Flavin installed on a wall in an angle of 45 degree to the floor. And from this discovery Flavin developed one of the most powerful plastic languages in contemporary art.

The show in Ottawa provided Flavin with the kind of space that suits his work best – the National Gallery is based in an anonymous former office building. There are numerous white rooms without windows; individual character is given by their different measures. It became clear in this show that Flavin's neon tubes always relate to one another within a space, they never relate to the room itself. So it was the interrelation of the individual works to one another in a series of rooms, which made the Ottawa show so impressive.

This effect was most striking in the two rooms with the works *alternating pink and yellow (to Josef Halmy)* of 1967/69 and *an artificial barrier of green neon light (for Trudie and Enno Develing)* of 1968/69. When one comes out of the room with the green neon light barrier, which consists of overlapping squares of 90cm long tubes, the adjacent room, with its alternating pink and yellow tubes laid out in the angle of floor and wall, which had just seemed orange, now appears bright red. When one goes back into the green room and gets used to the green light, which here as well as in all the other rooms seems to be part of the atmosphere, the neon tubes themselves look white.

The decisive fact is not so much this optical effect, but the ensemble of light and its given form. Flavin refers to the fact that we generally perceive colour only through light. He defines his use of neon light in his work in terms of a intensification of colour. The form of the individual element, the light tube and its support of enamelled steel is given, whereas the 'overall form' of the composition following the system of the series stems from the artist.

The amount of the light is so great, that the space in which Flavin's works are installed often looses its optically perceptible material existence completely; the walls, floor and ceiling are drown into obscurity or, in the case of ultraviolet light, into complete darkness.

The New York Castelli Gallery exhibition showed the strictest, most homogenous group of work, which was even better installed than in the Ottawa show: four *monuments for V. Tatlin* (1964/69). Groups of vertical neon tubes are placed in the centre of each wall in the square main space of the gallery. Their light is a cold white. The parallel arrangement of seven tubes of four different lengths make possible a strict constellation of different variations within one system. The association these arrangements of tubes evoke are tower, skyscraper, monument, hence the dedication to Vladimir Tatlin, the Russian constructivist, who in 1920 designed the *The Monument to the Third International*. Flavin's bow to Tatlin is not to be understood in a stylistic way. The constructivists aimed for a non-figurative art and used geometry as a vehicle – by the way, it has to be said that Tatlin distanced himself from them by proclaiming this art "machine art". Flavin's works, however, are light systems, a pure realisation of thought art equals colour equals light.

"Die Macht des Farblichts: Dan Flavin – erfolg und Mythos eines amerikanischen Kunstlers," *Frankfurter Allgemeine Zeitung*, 4 April 1970, p. 9.

Translation from German: Maxa Holler.

Letter from Paris
Marcelin Pleynet

So many careers are built on the strength of a single idea, that one cannot be insensitive to an exhibition which, under the signature of one artist, proposes to bring together three or four. Dan Flavin, who is showing four pieces today at Galerie Sonnabend, belongs to that generation of American painters who had to seriously take into account the work of their illustrious predecessors. In fact, Flavin makes no secret about it: "To start with," he writes in "...in daylight or cool white", an introduction to his exhibition catalogue, "I fanatically studied the work of all the others: Guston, Motherwell, Klein, Gorky, Pollock, Rothko, Jasper Johns and other practitioners of the new art." Indeed, these painters offer the viewer the opportunity to become passionate, and the passion they ignite is definitely worthwhile. They also play, to a varying extent, key roles in the contemporary pictorial debates and most of them have contributed to updating the problem posed by the evolution of a post-Cubist space. It is unquestionably from these painters that Flavin takes his concern with spatial transformation and, I would say, pun intended or not, his light. Arguably, Flavin's approach to this problem is very different from that of his predecessors – it is more abstract, i.e. it transports to a real space what was until then only posed within the context of pictorial knowledge. Above all, it means that Flavin is, as far as I know, the first to think like a sculptor in space what his predecessors created from the limitations of surface.

When Flavin notices that a fluorescent neon tube, lit in the angle of a room, transforms space, he does not discover light in the same way that Mr. Jourdain discovered prose; he discovers a discipline that has been in need of renewal for a long time: sculpture. Sculpture, contrary to what is sadly commonly believed, does not lie in the transformation of some solid, but in the transformation of space by the luminous presence (in light) of that solid. Therefore, the comparison made by Flavin between his tubes and Brancusi's *Endless Column* deserves to be taken into consideration and discussed: "Brancusi's *Endless Column* and my diagonal both had an elementary and uniform visual nature, but both sought to transcend their obvious length limitations as well as their apparent simplicity. *Endless Column* was a sort of imposing mythological totem rising toward the sky. As far as the diagonal was concerned, it played the role of a modern technological fetish due to its use by everyone and anyone as an ordinary light source." In both cases, they are sculptures whose very irrational effects can obviously be compared, but the means used to acquire those effects are different, if not opposed. Without any ambiguity, the Brancusi piece transforms the space where it lies, whereas Flavin's tube, once lit, emphasises an ambiguous, undefined space – it is there, even, that its quality lies. Moreover, Flavin admits this freely: "This kind of installation doesn't allow much 'artistic shaping'" – but then, is this all about an "artistic shaping"? Unquestionably, one cannot ignore the limitations specific to the material used in the creation of any sculpted piece; what distinguishes Brancusi's and Flavin's material *in the first place* is precisely the difference that separates artistic materials from industrial materials. This is in a way what has always in the past, and again today, limited Flavin's production – Flavin who, however his career may evolve, still remains today a sort of primitive forerunner of modern sculpture's possibilities. This formal limitation is entirely technological, and the artist will most certainly fail to go past it by telling stories of "fetish", setting itself apart by, on the one hand, the rigidity of its material and, on the other hand, the repetitive aspect of its organisation. This surely does not come as news to Flavin, because it is precisely due to these factors that his evolution as well as the great complexity of his latest pieces are defined. He goes past the repetitive aspect of the materials' structural possibilities thanks to the addition of colour tubes, while the rigidity is put into question in the construction of a few pieces, by his use of tubes whose indirect light is diffused from the back of their metallic supports, only then visible. However efficient, this approach does not altogether cancel out the technological limitations of the enterprise – limitations that are expressed again in the range and quality of the colours that Flavin uses. But it is credit to the exhibition presented at the Galerie Sonnabend that it poses some progressive questions in the context of modern art research – is it not the only one in Paris today?

Art International, Volume 1, Number 10, Christmas 1970, p. 62. [excerpt]

Translation from French: Carolyn Vermalle

New York
Kenneth Baker

Dan Flavin acknowledged the death of Barnett Newman with a modest show at Castelli in which one piece was specifically dedicated to the late master. There is something vaguely offensive about dedicating pieces of visual art to the deceased; it is perhaps like sending candy rather than flowers to a funeral. (And Flavin has just done it again in the Whitney Annual.) Anyway, one looks closely for formal justification for such a dedication. Flavin's untitled piece was a frame arrangement from floor to ceiling with blue and red verticals facing into a corner and a pair of yellow horizontals facing into the room. Aside from the use of the primaries there seemed to be almost nothing to connect this piece with the enterprise of Newman's painting. There is, however, a certain quality of the fluorescent tubes that finds a parallel in Newman's painting, namely, the sense that the lighted tube, like a Newman stripe, is exactly there, where it says it is, and not in some illusive zone. But this is the sense that Flavin lost by turning the red and blue lights into the corner, for the sake, I guess, of having color soften the corner by bending the space. The combination of the primaries in fluorescent light seems to pose nothing like the problem that it posed for Newman, perhaps because Flavin has so seldom been able to make color function in accord with the structure of his works. This show was a reminder that Flavin lives.

Artforum, Volume 9, Number 6, February 1971, pp. 79–80. [excerpt]

2-Part Show: Flavin's Works of Light
David L. Shirley

It is easy to frown upon the light constructions of Dan Flavin, who is having a two-part exhibition at the John Weber Gallery, 420 West Broadway, and the Castelli Gallery, 4 East 77th Street. The constructions don't seem to command much thinking, nor do they seem to require much talent in their composition or craftsmanship. Made out of commercial fluorescent fixtures, they appear in the work of art unchanged, with their nuts, bolts and tubing exposed, much as they would appear in any neon salesman's showcase. But the constructions deserve more serious critical attention than that. Mr. Flavin is, in fact, one of the best light artists.

Mr. Flavin has been making the same light constructions since he had his first New York exhibition in 1961. In his investigations of "real" light, he does not seem to have made much progress. The exhibitions have been tediously similar. But repetition does not necessarily invalidate the experimental or esthetic value of his investigations with light. Despite the raw, untouched presentation of the fixtures, Mr. Flavin has attempted to translate the problems of "simulated" light that have fascinated artists for the last century. At times he engenders an encompassing romantic atmosphere.

Each construction is made out of four fixtures, each eight feet long. The fixtures are joined into a square and placed onto a wall corner, the tubing exposed on the top and the bottom of the work and the fixture pans facing out on the sides. The fluorescent colors are pink, yellow, blue, green and white. The constructions at Weber are monochromatic and the ones at Castelli are of three colors each.

Mr. Flavin's experiments with light and its action and interaction prompt color compositions that engage the construction itself, the wall behind the construction and the surrounding room. They are, in a way, stabs at uniting "painting," sculpture and architecture. This ambitious fusion of the arts does not always hit its mark.

Yet the atmospheric effects, such as those produced in the Weber Gallery, where there are two constructions in one room, one of pink and one of red, produce a handsome environment of lavender, punctuated with warm glows at the light source. The constructions at Castelli combine into more defined compositions and work more as "paintings" than as environmental pieces. Even if Mr. Flavin does not advance in his experimentation with real light, he will nonetheless have made a contribution in that direction.

The New York Times, October 30, 1971, p. 27.

Los Angeles
Peter Plagens

...the business of great artists has always been to transcend, for interior not exterior reasons, what they've been esthetically "born" into. It's going to be awfully tough for the next great sculptor.

Perhaps Dan Flavin is he, but a) he doesn't call his work sculpture and b) I don't know that Flavin will be anywhere near understood. Not that he hasn't tried to explain himself; somebody gave me a catalog of the Canadian retrospective Flavin was awarded two years ago, and it's chock-full of revelations, not the least of which is a whiny, lyrical, confessional autobiography through which Flavin injects, *ex post facto*, a first novelist's drama into what appears as a cuddly, crisis-free, middle-class upbringing:

> I continued to draw, to doodle somewhat privately in class, in the margins of my textbooks. Now there were battered profiles of bloodied boxers, with broken noses and Dido's pyre on a wall in Carthage, its passionate smoke piercing 'pious' Aeneas' faithless heart outbound in the harbour below.
>
> Young Father Fogarty, my second year Latin professor, was unimpressed with such demonstrations of talent, especially as they evolved in his class against the daily lesson plan. He often censured, even ridiculed, me. Nevertheless, I acquired a certain personal power with him. When he chastened me, I noticed that he blushed redder than I did.

In short, Flavin's fluorescent light pieces, insofar as they're literary, arise from the manner of early life common to most of us, and their ...what shall I say...weirdness must be entirely adult. That's a compliment; made-up intellectual art is ultimately better art (if not entertainment) than personal, sweaty, visceral ethnic-funk stuff. Mozart *is* better than Roy Acuff or Leadbelly. Flavin, according to the catalog, also produced considerable art incredibly typical of a young artist in the time when there were no hippies but lots of beatniks: poems embellished with watercolor late at night, collages with affectionate/enigmatic inscriptions, and the odd figurative notebook drawing. Most of it, if one can judge (if not, why illustrate catalogues?), is hardly precocious; thus the arrangements of light fixtures aren't merely the latest refinements of a superlative natural decorative talent. That's another compliment. Flavin faced the terrible risk that art depends more on *coming up with something* – God knows how you do it – than on honing down the performance of native ability. There is, in this compendium of reproductions, a seeming link between the early Flavin and the maker of two similar light works in Ace Gallery – small, monochrome paintings with bulbs attached – which might make the *traversement* from object art to peculiarly elusive "proposals" more or less reasonable. For me, however, it's still a mysterious, fascinating business, and I don't want to be around when that inevitable graduate student writes the monograph on "Flavin: Object Into Light."

It's tempting to say that the two pieces are nearly identical. They are physical matches: two vertical eight-foot fluorescent fixtures six feet on either side of a corner; these are crossed by two horizontal equivalents, one on the floor, and the other about two and a half feet higher. All bulbs face inward, to the wall. In the first (facing the wall, at whose ends the things are located) the left-hand vertical bulb glows pink, the right-hand yellow, while the crossbars are blue. In the second, the crossbars are yellow, while the left-hand vertical is pink, the right-hand blue. In other words, the second piece switches the colors of the crossbars and right-hand vertical of the first, and, by examining specific effects maybe we can see why. 1) The vertical members shine their light perpendicular to the one to which they're attached *i.e.*, left-hand pink bulb shines pink on right-hand wall of corner; 2) the three-dimensional quality of the corner is obviated, *i.e.*, due to the light and, in small part, to the obscuring of the floor-wall seam by the crossbars, the two walls come together as simultaneous color planes; 3) the above effect is more intense with the blue crossbars than the yellow; 4) the corner-flattening gradually lessens toward the ceiling, as the light returns to "normal" light grays; 5) the horizontal color "spills" onto the white floor; 6) there is a ninety-degree sector "stain" cast on the white ceiling, most intense (yellow) in the first place, and, most intriguingly, the illumination of the pieces ends, not in dark, but in white. Flavin does quite a bit with very little, and he sticks to his non-technological austerity. It all works out niftily, but Flavin, I suspect, regards himself as anything but a post-Albers superformalist. What the art has to do, however, with that upstate *Dear Theo* stuff is for sharper minds than mine to figure out.

Artforum, Volume 10, Number 3, November 1971, pp. 83–84. [excerpt]

Flavin Exhibit at Albright-Knox Casts New Light on Sculpture
Jean Reeves

One of the most "difficult" artists on the contemporary scene – difficult in an esthetic sense – is Dan Flavin.

An American sculptor with a world-wide reputation, Flavin works with light. His medium for translating it into "art" is that rather ugly, or as he calls it "vulgar" object, the fluorescent tube.

A standard, commercially-produced item, the fluorescent tube customarily is intended to see by rather than to be seen.

Flavin makes us look at is as, if not an art object, at least an object of sight.

Fluorescent lights have seemed particularly repelling object to me when I've thought about them, which I haven't much.

But I'm mending my thoughts after seeing how Dan Flavin has "lighted up" the Albright-Knox Art Gallery.

The soft-spoken, portly artist has installed what he calls "an exposition," rather than an exhibition, at the gallery. It is to be unveiled this evening at Gallery Gala II, a dinner-dance in celebration of the 10th anniversary of the new building, and I'm sure some of the black ties will be more mystified by it than most expositions.

In two corners of the stairwell leading from the new building to the old gallery, Flavin has installed circular fluorescent tubes from floor to ceiling.

There are 25 of these lights and they stretch upward in a row. (Flavin thinks the word column is too "loaded" to describe them) more than 26 feet into the air.

Then, with the steps behind, the viewer finds himself in the upper-landing-gallery, where two additional rows of circular tubes march up the corners, 14 in each row.

We're not usually aware of colors in fluorescent "white" tubes. So look closely. Flavin has alternated "warm white" tubes with "cool daylight whites" in these tall installations.

Flavin described the effect well when he said to me that "the circular light seems to have an obsessive attraction to it; it's compelling, that is, it compels one to want to reject it, in a role like that. We see not only the 'O' of the light but the 'O' of the fixtures that supply the light."

I was not completely won over by these white lights but I was by the other half of Flavin's exposition at the east end of the old building a marvellous, glowing, visual puzzle.

I might say that to speak of Flavin's installing a piece of his light sculpture is a figure of speech. He never mounts a ladder, wields a hammer or turns a screw.

"There's always someone who can do it better than you," he said, "and they need the paycheck. I like to sit at a desk and think."

His structures have been mounted at Albright by John Kushner of the building staff who just may be, Flavin thinks, the best technician he has ever encountered.

With the kind of pink fluorescent light that butchers use to make the meat look pinker (you see the things you can learn from an artist) Flavin has dreamed up in the east gallery a beautiful thing, a kind of paintings in light. What happens to them, too, is something he certainly doesn't understand, but neither do the experts at General Electric.

Three near-square structures of the high-ceilinged gallery, 8 feet high span three corners lighted with blue and pink tubes which do not cast what you would think would be the proper shade of light.

What occurs is a transference of colored light. The blue light crosses over to the right, and the pink light crosses over to the left.

A triangular glow of colored light is formed, too, over the actual fluorescent structure and the color reversal is maintained in it.

What Flavin has done is create something that can be pared to a "painting" in light in these structures. It is an ingenious and exhilarating performance.

The fluorescents supply all the light in the gallery, and it is amazing how powerful are their beams.

The artist has been working with fluorescent light for about 12 years. He chose it because it was "a common modern equipment that hadn't been used" in an art context.

After 12 years of concentration of fluorescent light as a medium he now feels it would be "nice to feed it back where it came from," that is, to put it into public places.

"I'd try to maintain the artifice of art," he said. "That's one of the paradoxes that occurs a lot in art – I think you can do something that maintains the artist's artifice and still is something useful."

He hopes to light the new subway under construction in Hanover, Germany, and to get a public works commission in Rotterdam – a bicycle and pedestrian underpass located beneath a river.

As an artist Flavin sees no reason he shouldn't be paid for his work as well as anybody else.

"If an artist puts on a show in a museum, he should be paid," he said. "Otherwise he's exploited in a very rude manner. Gallery economics are harsh for the artist. The better off the gallery, the harder the bargain it drives."

So, here as elsewhere, Flavin insisted on a cash fee. And he got it.

When I asked him finally the key question, whether it bothers him that people can't see his light works as art, he replied with grace and honesty.

"If they don't single it out as art," he said, "it doesn't bother me. But it seems to me you can't miss it. You may not call it art, but you sure know it's there...

"I like also to use the idea of participant, rather than viewer. Viewer is considerate and apart, studying and contemplating. I don't like that kind of attitude.

"I think what I do is for fairly fast recognition. I don't want to see them (the people) stopped. First impressions are nice. This fits in with all the rapidities of present-day living, the whole society of the road, life behind the wheel of a car, full of instant implications.

"Art," he said, "is not separate from concept. They're one. The experience is better than the attempt to analyze it."

Previewers this evening also will see three new acquisitions of the gallery, all gifts of the Members Council.

They are a silk screen print by Roy Lichtenstein of Pop art fame; a color-field painting by the young American Peter Young, and a 1963 wood sculpture by the American sculptor Carl Andre.

The Flavin show will continue through June 23.

Buffalo Evening News, May 13, 1972.

The Prosaic Fluorescent Light Turns On As Astonishing Art

Mary King

It's not painting, it's not sculpture and it's not architecture, but Dan Flavin's work with colored and white fluorescent lamps partakes of all three. In a stunning show in the special exhibition galleries at the St. Louis Art Museum, there are individual works, but the installation as a whole is so related, so balanced, flowing and harmonious, with interior reversals, rhythms and repetitions, that it is itself one grand cumulative work.

Flavin, a self-taught artist whose exhibitions have attracted wide attention in this country and abroad, lives in the Hudson River valley. During military duty in Korea he was with the meteorological service, and this with a well cultivated knowledge of American and European glass contributed to his perceptions of space, light and color. The St. Louis show runs through March 11.

Flavin uses standard domestic or industrial fixtures and lamps for an art that explores the phenomenology of light and the color that is its inevitable correlative.

It is most related to painting in this regard but also in its frequent use of a framing device, or structure, the consideration of planes, the effect of color adjacencies and the by-products of wash, mottling and shading. Colored light is not only a more extreme intensification of color than is possible in paint, but it sprays and mixes itself and has no physical substance. (Flavin dislikes any association with the "cosmic cosmetics" of Olitski but one can be reminded of one artist, in a useless sort of way, in the other's wide sprays of luscious sweet color. But then Barnett Newman's mystical vertical bands might also flicker to mind.)

The different qualities of light that Flavin achieves – hard, soft, saturated, diffused, chameleon-like, and much more, are parallel to but in excess of the different possibilities with paint. Light as thrust, probe, fountain, and the use of physical fixtures and spatial placements, are all sculptural aspects. *Corners, Barriers and Corridors* (the title of the show), are everyday functions and experiences of light, which Flavin has re-invented, re-used and re-freshened. The indivisibility of the light pieces and their present installation, and the disruption and arrangement of actual space, are ample indication of the architectural element.

Flavin's treatment of light and color, and how being drenched in one color affects our appreciation of the another, his manipulation of the mysterious effects light can have in and on space, will doubtless have implications and repercussions on city planners, architects and interior designers.

The tours de force are the twin exhibits in the rear galleries on either side of the main gallery. They are the same only reversed and are intensely structured channels for movement, light and the experience of light, not only by itself but its relativity.

In each gallery are two tunnels, side by side, of the same dimensions (dictated in part by fire laws). Along the corners of one tunnel or corridor are long tubes of white light, successively daylight, cool white, warm and soft white. Each white has a different color which is emphasized by this context.

The tunnel next to it is neatly contrary. The flow of space is interrupted midway by a wall of vertical fixtures shining bright green in one direction and yellow in the other. One fixture is left out at one end and the colors meet and mingle there like prisoners holding hands through a visiting fence. This wall of light functions not just as the cool slice of a terminating plane but as a gradually, then dramatically dense spatial climax.

As one looks in to the glowing green space, the yellow leaking around through the opening gradually turns a deep orange as the green itself turns white. A glance at the white next door, and it has turned rose. This striking phenomenon does not seem to occur on the yellow side.

In each corner of the entrance gallery are single horizontal eight-foot fixtures spanning the corner at about eye level. Facing out are long light blue tubes, and behind them facing the wall are three colored lamps, alternately pink-yellow-green, green-yellow-pink around the room. Diagonal corners are identical and each fixture shares the end color with the one next to it, making for continuity and integration of the room. The diamond-shape spillage of softly washed color above and below creates a form out of light and elusive color. Without being tricky, these pieces have the elemental fascination associated with fire and water, even the magnetic effect of magic.

In the main gallery are two tall parallel zigzag walls (like Newman's *Tzim Tzum*) with circular fluorescent "daylight" (bluish) lamps along the top from end to end. At the base of the walls along the interior passageway are straight tubes of "cool white" (warmer, more beige than the daylight) facing up. Light spills like mist over the straight rigid, angled walls, the light sources somehow accentuate but at the same time cancel the structure. It becomes an uncontaining channel of light, with fugitive glazings of subtle white, and some stray spillage of colors from the other side of the walls.

(From the balcony above this gallery one gets a more structural view of the installation walls and controlled light sources. From here too one can see the wedges of color in the three outside corners.)

These three outside corner pieces in the main gallery were not conceived only for this show but work superbly with it. They are each made up of "frames" of two horizontal lamps facing in toward the corner. One, *Wheeling Peachblow* washes the walls with a luxuriant mixture of pink and gold, obliterating the corner in a glowing column. In the other two, the wall catches the color adjacent to it, bounces it, and spreads it across the opposite wall – a cross-projection of color waves that splash intact on the wall opposite the source, accentuating the corner as abutment of two planes.

The two galleries to the immediate left and right of the entrance are also related. On the right is a barrier or "fence" with oblong fixtures of red and light blue tubes in identically repeated formation. The room is bathed in lavender light.

In the opposite gallery a similar barrier of all pink lamps fills the room with ever-changing shades of this color. It echoes the lavender but is premixed.

In all cases, the pieces have a relationship with each other, and an effect on each other.

Flavin explores the medium of light in much the same way as the painters of the 1950s explored the qualities of paint, and the sculptors of the sixties got down to the basics of sculpture.

His art is both distant and embracing, austere and sensuous, hard and soft, concrete and mystical, mechanical and ineffably poetic. The sources are clear, the limits indeterminate. He alternately defines and denies structure with light and fills space far beyond physically doing so. It is as much about the relativity of the seeing process as the relativity of color. It has mystery, majesty and surprise.

The exhibition is supplemented by two displays of the artist's drawings, both in Sculpture Hall. One consists of diagrams from this particular installation; the other is simply selected drawings, as well as diagrams for other pieces.

St. Louis Post, January 28, 1973.

Dan Flavin
Germano Celant

The tautological assertions of Dan Flavin, from 1961 to today, have referred to electrical and fluorescent light and the absent and anonymous object, the presence of which differentiates the perception of the spatial and object structures.

His work on the visual imperative of electrical (1961–1963) and fluorescent (1963–1973) light has the unique goal of putting the spectator in front of the light-entity (commonly considered an instrument associating or dissociating the perception) to underline it as an "iconic" and visual affirmation.

Realised without any inventive or fantastical participation and able to manipulate the entity itself, this assertion concerns the analysis of the isolated and isolatable phenomenon of light.

In the years between 1961 and 1963, the light is used as an (anonymous and inglorious) icon that is presented on coloured masonite, or laminated plastic cubes, and assumes the condition of a technological emblem with psychological references (*the heart, the mystery*). A series of electric light icons that Flavin defines this way: "My icons differ from Byzantine Christ held in majesty; they are as mute and undistinguished as the run of our architecture. My icons do note raise up the Blessed saviour in elaborate cathedrals. They are constructed concentrations celebrating barren rooms. They bring a limited light".

These constructions comprised a series that referred to Flavin's first attempt to look for a chromatic relationship between light and structure. The colour-colour and colour-light relation is obvious in *icon IV (the pure land) (to David John Flavin, 1933–1962)* exhibited at the Green Gallery, where Flavin presents the minimum contrast between daylight fluorescent light and, the frontal white of the cube, the whole referring to the use of white in Chinese funerals (the construction of *icon IV* coincides with the death of the brother and is dedicated to him).

From 1963, the icon becomes a technological totem, it liberates itself from its colour-material support and presents itself as fluorescent light. On May the 25th 1963 Dan Flavin chose and exhibited on the wall of his studio a fluorescent tube, 8 feet long, angled at 45 degrees. The colour of the tube entitled *the diagonal of May 25, 1963 (to Robert Rosenblum)* varies according to the commercially available colour gamut. The position of the tube is also subject to variation. Originally Flavin choose the tube of fluorescent golden light and placed it on the wall diagonally, since the luminous diagonal does not possess artistic implications, but displays itself as presence, in a way that "a common lamp becomes a common industrial fetish, as utterly reproducible as ever but somehow strikingly unfamiliar now...".

The diagonal was initially dedicated to Constantin Brancusi. The influence of Brancusi's *Endless Column* in this work is in fact obvious, as it is on the parallel production of Andre and Judd. Brancusi's column is a mythological totem that raises itself outside of time and of space. The fluorescent tube is a technological totem that, using the fluorescent light normally available in the whole world, puts itself in the same condition of a-temporality and a-spatiality.

With this "categorical" affirmation, fluorescent light presents itself through its most elementary and least informative example, the fluorescent light tube. The disposition is elementary, in a way that no visual "noise" comes to disturb the elementary state of the fluorescent light at the infancy stage of its technology.

The tube lives in an autonomous way, like unsigned and un-iconic elements, the only sign resulting from the emitted light that varies according to the gamut of fluorescent lights samples. The informational importance therefore becomes the discovery of light as information in its pure state (McLuhan), with its elementary organisation. The whole of Flavin's work consists in this case of visual analysis and the development of combinations and diagrams of fluorescent light. The variations and combinations are naturally innumerable, thereby Flavin initially, always using tubes of industrial dimensions and colours (2,4,6 or 8 feet – colours pink, gold, cool white, daylight, red,...) associates the light to two to three to four lights put side by side vertically, to demonstrate conceptually the unlimited extension of the association. The ensembles referred to daylight fluorescent lights, simple and banal elements that create interrelations between each other only for their being consolidated to two, three, four identical elements. Then, in 1964, different whites (cool white and daylight) or diverging colour associations, like red and gold. The chromatic variations accompany the spatial mutations. *The nominal three (to William of Ockham)* determines its position in reference to the appointed space in receiving it, so that the score of the existing spaces varies between the single, double and triple cool fluorescent light. From this moment, Dan Flavin's arguments multiply. As Donald Judd emphasised, the work of Flavin concerns the fluorescent tubes employed as luminous sources, the light of different colour diffused in the space and nearby surfaces and the disposition of the tubes on the surfaces. In particular, from 1964 Flavin began to research the installation relationship and position the fluorescent lights in crucial points in space: see *Pink out of the corner (to Jasper Johns)*, 1963–64.

The possibilities of combinations of colour, space and dimension thus become the focus of Flavin's operation, that begins to present combinations of lights of different colours and dimensions until they form geometric images, like *A primary picture*, 1964, which produces a rectangular illuminated area made of primary colours (red, gold, blue).

A tendency to form that, in referencing the figures of Russian constructivism, declares itself in a series of *monuments for V. Tatlin* that, begun in 1964/65, continue today. These pseudo-monuments (the prefix pseudo is used by Flavin to recall the ephemeral and temporal state of the tubes, the light of which extinguishes after 200 hours) referring to the image of the *Monument to the Third International*, with its stratification, are realised in cool white fluorescent light and become themselves a monument to the provisional and communicational structure of light.

A monumental anxiety that leads Flavin, in 1965, to integrate space and fill it with light, is instituted thus in osmosis with the ambient, like in *monument 4 for those who have been killed in ambush (to P.K. who reminded me about death)*, 1966, a multidimensional structure composed of 4 tubes (8 feet long), put in a corner a few centimetres above eye level, capable to transform the square space of the room into a vector convergent in the corner. In *untitled (for the "innovator" of Wheeling Peachblow)*, a square of fluorescent light, gold pink and daylight is positioned at the intersection of the corner and creates a "frame" of light that alters the dimensions of the space, thereby reducing it. Having abandoned the two-dimensionality of the wall and being penetrated three-dimensionally by space, these works begin to display themselves not only as entities, but as light shapes, creators of light spaces.

So in 1966 the fluorescent light is not content with an "side" role anymore, cornered and walled, but it invades the space, it conditions the passages, the actions and movements, the routes of the spectator. It makes itself a cumbersome presence that invades the space that is destined to receive it, like the work realised for the Van Abbe Museum of Eindhoven *greens crossing greens (to Piet Mondrian who lacked green)*, 1966. The fluorescent light thus acquires a multiple existence owing to its diverse properties and spatial conditions. The light exists as a value in itself, as tube light, the light reflects on to the walls, on the combined and nearby lights, on the totality of the environmental whole, the light creates shapes and spaces because of the dispositions and the colours used.

The light installations thus consolidate the space, both integrating it and to denying it. In this sense, *untitled (To Dorothy and Roy Lichtenstein on not seeing anyone in the room)*, 1968, presented at the Dwan Gallery, virtually denies the spectator entry to the adjacent room, whereas *an artificial barrier of blue red and blue fluorescent light (to Flavin Starbuck Judd)*, 1968, at the Gemeentemuseum of the Hague, separates the space into two sections of light.

From 1969, after the large retrospective at the National Gallery of Canada in Ottawa, Flavin's luminous environments assume an ever increasing spatial scale, until they "occupy" entire museums or until they create, like on the occasion of the opening of the Walker Art Centre in Minneapolis, particularly luminous spaces and routes, such as corridors of fluorescent light.

The relationship between light and space in installation obviously brings Flavin's attention the architectural angles and the spatial points of intersection, so that corners continue to appear as the favourite focuses for his light interventions; so much so that, in his recent installation at the Museum of Rice University in Houston, Flavin had a system of walled corners built, in which he placed a series of *cornered fluorescent lights*.

In the empty space of the museum, Flavin (commissioned by the Menil Foundation Collection,) in fact realised a "structural proposal about these vibrant instruments", the fluorescent lights. The Rice Museum was thus subdivided in four areas designed to form together 16 corners. Works were inserted in each corner. On four external corners, Flavin has put green, blue, yellow and pink fluorescent light, one colour becoming frontal and the others indirectly visible. With these works Flavin intended to activate the walls with a series of variations and chromatic-luminous measures. In the four central corners, Flavin mounted a series of circles in contrasting colours, daylight and cool white, so that the perception of the space results from white lights surrounded by coloured lights. On four other intermediate corners, he put a series of squares instead, *untitled*, where colours function as intermediate state.

In a separate room, four *"monuments" for V. Tatlin*, "pseudo-monuments of only temporary illumination", concluded the exhibition, which in the two polarities of his use of fluorescent light, from figural and monumental form to spatial entity, become emblematic of all of Flavin's work.

Domus, Number 519, February 1973, p.44.

Translation from Italian: Alessandra Santarelli

Rays of Hope, Particles of Doubt
Peter Plagens

The problem with art made more or less directly from light (usually electric, indoor) is that the work seems to *look back at you*. It was disturbing enough when self-consciously abstract art, by giving up the conventional ruse of versimilitude, reinforced the "otherness" of the art object and made the viewer almost painfully aware of the gap (in Sartrean terms, "the secretion of 'nothingness'") between himself and the whole world. But the insistent rays of an irradiant work of art deprive the spectator of even his sure ground as the seer by rendering him, too, as a possible object.

> The visible can thus fill me and occupy me only because I who see it do not see it from the depths of nothingness, but from the midst of itself; I the seer am also visible.
>
> Maurice Merleau-Ponty, *The Visible and the Invisible*, p. 113.

The naïve conception that only "light" makes things visible at all and, therefore, art might eliminate the middleman (art object) and deal directly with "light" has always been undercut by the near-impossibility of controlling the aggressive, atavistic sense of "other" which fairly leaps from any source of original light.

> If there is an other, he is never in my eyes a For-Itself, in the precise and given sense that I am, for myself. Even if our relationship leads me to admit or even to experience that "he too" thinks that "he too" has a private landscape, I am not that thought as I am my own, I do not have that private landscape as I have my own. What I say of it is always derived from what I know of myself by myself: I concede that *if I inhabited* that

body I should have another solitude, comparable to that
which I have, and always divergent perspectively from it.
Ibid, p. 78.

Until recently, artists have chosen either to deal with light as raw
spectacle (e.g. the lasers in *Art and Technology* gave you the same esthetic
experience as Niagara Falls), confine it to trinkets (light boxes, etc.),
or drive media machinery with it (movies, photographs, videotapes).
Lately, relatively "pure" light has found itself confined to various rooms,
chambers, or spaces in diluted or deprived character, as if enveloping
desaturation were the only way to domesticate it. Compared to a West
Coast artist working with light like James Turrell, it's taken Dan Flavin
a while to get around to dealing directly with atmospherically lighted
space. Heretofore Flavin has worked out of a Constructivist tradition
(which, with its aura of art history, penetrates most New York sculpture
like *Liquid Wrench*), making "glowing objects," even in roomsize installations in Chicago, Kassel, or wherever. West Coast artists like Turrell
or Michael Asher have, on the other hand, jumped right in if they felt
static, seizable objects were futile and wanted to work directly in
activated (light, wind, emptiness) space, without worrying about the
homages they left behind. Flavin – from his drawings, titles, allusions
to other artists, writing, and art – has a romantic sense of academic
responsibility, of carrying the flame, which has until most recently
restricted him with a powerful, residual feeling of *skulp'char*. (What
does a Flavin look like? A *configuration* of store-bought fluorescent light
fixtures.) But the West Coast's historic inability to sustain its homegrown
styles (San Francisco Abstract Expressionism 1946–50, Assemblage in
the early '60s, Bay Area figurative painting 1957–64, the "L.A. Look"
1962–67) into regeneration is apparently a bugaboo again, and five
years after Turrell's "light painting" show at the Pasadena Art Museum,
here comes Dan Flavin, shedding most of his object references, to take the
play away. Flavin's St. Louis Museum installation is the best exhibition

I've seen in at least five years.

The show comprises "corners" (horizontal or rectangular pieces set diagonally across a corner), "barriers" (roomsize fences), and "corridors" (wide hallways containing floor or ceiling lengthwise rows of fixtures, sometimes with a verifiable wall of vertical lights at the end). The corners are reprises of standard commercial gallery pieces; the barriers are more difficult, energizing/surprising/threatening as they do whole tinted rooms at a time; and the corridors, where we are free at last of things, are simply beautiful. Flavin does allow us individually brilliant, almost painterly "passages": the witty, red green reversals in the horizontal corner works, the sickly overwhelming pink of the untitled ("to Alexandra") barrier, the juicy, almost tactile crunch of Kool-Aid red vs. white in the other barrier ("to Flavin Starbuck Judd"), and the shattering, relentless glow of a corridor terminus ("to Jan and Ron Greenberg"). Flavin supplies a stunning visual vignette at every turn in the odyssey: the quiet pun on a corner (neutralizing it or turning it backwards); strangely shadowed white walls holding the odd silhouette of a museum guard (I am sure Flavin plans for practically everything), a whole room turned blue gray by the color force of a barrier; a luscious Hofmannesque "composition" of colored wall fragments, raw lights and impossible viridian recesses; hallucinations of white squeezed between the vertical yellow tubes at the end of a wall; a "relaxed" rear view through the zigzag corridor toward the entrance, in which the walls far across the museum are altered by context into odd, semiphosphorescent off-whites (this was pointed out to me by a guard); and the very air of a room turned *dark pink*.

But Flavin's achievement is revealed most fully in the total installation, a superbly orchestrated megawork which transcends the individual pieces. (According to the catalogue, Flavin has perpetrated more than 31 one-man museum shows. It sounds like a lot until you realize that for Flavin – as for Turrell, Asher, or Robert Irwin of late – the exhibition *is* the work. Then it still sounds like a lot.) The St. Louis

Museum is a grandiose mid-American culture palace, constructed with repressive tons of masonry in the middle of a vast midwestern acreage (a park in the middle of a hard-case city – now I know why Sonny Liston turned out the way he did – in turn in the middle of a greater midwest terra-fertility) to commemorate a fair, a grain barron's guilt, a *Grand Tour* idea of culture, or all of the above. It's one of those buildings which make schoolchildren hate art the way the smell of rubbing alcohol makes them hate the doctor. It's seemingly the worst ambience for a Flavin show, unless, you think, the strategy is to obliterate completely the surroundings with dry-wall and white paint, or to mount a collection of fluorescent icons on the walls.

The solution as it stands is an ingenious synthesis of individual work(s), environmental work(s), and reciprocity with the architecture – "nonsequential" galleries, odd proportions, doorways, moldings, everything. The installation is symmetrical: a foyer of sorts with corner pieces packed by a "grand hall" occupied by the most advanced and puzzling work of all – a zigzag, roofless corridor topped with side rows of circular white fixtures (shades of Greyhound station restrooms), sheltering more corner pieces on its reverse sides. To either side of the foyer is a large room holding a barrier; moving back along the barriers, you encounter the corridors placed at diagonals. I chose to go counterclockwise: foyer corners to red/white barrier, to a corridor, then down through the zigzag corridor and around the outside for more corners, through the other corridor, and past the second (pink) barrier. For once, a press release is emphatically accurate:

> Moving from the redefinition of the familiar space of a corner the viewer becomes involved with the transformation of an entire gallery by a barrier of fluorescent lights. Next the viewer confronts the more narrow confinement and resulting greater intensity of barred corridors through which passage is inhibited or others through which one passes. Utilizing the second floor

balcony around the large central gallery allows to viewer to look down on the exposition (and on the zigzag rows of circular fixtures).

While I was in the show I found, delightfully, I couldn't think like a critic; I couldn't make art-historical or art world connections, or glue any language to what I saw. Flavin has succeeded via this show in freeing art – from the bogeys of history, formalism, elitism, art-language squabbles, decoration, and the pretensions of institutionalized culture – to a degree unrealized by all those hysterical, add-magazine-coverage-and-stir, dialectical pimples of failed art: post-Minimalism, body art, and Conceptualism. Flavin succeeds because the work prevails on both public and parochial planes:

Esoteric (art world)

Deals successfully with an "issue" in sculpture: the fate of the object in refinement of the Constructivist tradition.

Didactically connects artists on both coasts and points toward a joint further development.

A comment, via "ordinary" hardware, on the preciousness of "high art" objects and the pompousness of "technological" art.

Hip in its involvement with custom-made works, the jet-plane artist, and copious documentation.

Exoteric (public)

Pretty.

Educates a general audience to a few basics via an accessible lyricism. (A group of junior high school girls went by me chattering about the cause of after images.)

Readily available. (I know a couple people who've made their own "Flavins.")

A reciprocally pleasant and educational community project.

With the Flavin St. Louis exhibition there is now a fully realized art in light – diffuse enough to be liberated from the object, yet palpable enough to manifest a poetic statement (as opposed to the hyper-clean, laboratory austerity obtaining on the West Coast); convincing enough in its particulars (specific works) to contain its own history, yet contiguous enough in general (installation) to make (by comparison) new demands on the wholeness of future exhibitions (Flavin's and everybody else's).

Flavin's drawings are another matter, and they raise questions about both the artist's overall style and the focus of curatorial attention on his art. Flavin doesn't draw for show, he draws for his own information; he carries around a tiny ring-binder notebook and, whenever he's got a moment and/or an idea pops up, he makes an unglamorous ballpoint pen notation. Other types of drawings included in a satellite exhibition "before" the entrance to the fluorescent light show include: more orthodox (bigger, more illustrative) pencil depictions of pieces with varying combinations of titles, inscriptions, and signatures; formal schema (ruled white lines representing fluorescent tubes on black paper); and finished plans on graph paper ("made by Sonja Flavin from the artist's original plan and with his guidance"). The last of these are pretty, but the others, frankly, aren't much. In spite of attempted shoring-up through inclusion of 1963 melancholia on Edvard Munch, a studio interior, a snowfall in Williamsburgh, and (I must quote to avoid slander) "one of a group of drawings of plants and still-lifes done for sale in a small mid-Manhattan prints and drawings shop" (1964), Flavin's merit as a draftsman is negligible.

I have come to understand that, for me, drawing and diagramming are mainly what little it takes to keep a record of thought however to whatever use whenever. Within my reciprocating system for fluorescent light such continuous retention is constantly required. One never knows when former notations will become reassumed as relatively pertinent. The system is as active as I can think within and for it. Now, I am satisfied with my understanding.

Dan Flavin, statement in *drawings and diagrams 1963–72 by Dan Flavin*.

The drawings function as a record of Flavin's thinking – before, during and after stations in his oeuvre of fluorescent light; he frequently writes all over the page (since the drawings are notations you might say he draws pictures in his notes), and such inscriptions are dutifully recorded in the catalogue:

Centered lamp 66' finally/ rejected as being awkward/ architecturally; c.l. to r., 6'6"/8'/8' + yellow/ green/ verticals/ yellow centered lamp/ green pink pink/ horizontals/ yellow; high gap; 10'6"; two/ narrow/ flush/ service doors/ required/ 8' ; b.l. to r., for Walker Art Center opening; 12' wall; 6 5 4 3 2 1 2 3 4 5 6/ etc ; wall; gap at about 4" width 3 9 71 6

The recitations of inscriptions are followed by curatorial comment on each drawing (in this case that it was an "early proposal" for the Walker opening, ultimately rejected as being difficult to service). Succeeding entries record further approaches to the Walker "problem," including the "sloping corridor" which prevailed.

Crudely put, Flavin is an inveterate name-dropper. From the catalogue we learn what his tastes are (American glass, cf. Wheeling Peachblow), what artists he admires (Vladmir Tatlin, Barnett Newman, Cy Twombly, Piet Mondrian, Henri Matisse – some whose images are designed into previous shows' posters, themselves in this exhibition), what his politics are (sympathy for those ambushed in Vietnam, Cambodia, Kent State, and Jackson, Mississippi, and affirmation for Senator McGovern), how close he is with other artists and curators ("to Flavin Starbuck Judd," "to Emily," "to Alexandra"), that he has art friends in St. Louis ("to Jan and Ron Greenberg"), and what pedagogies attract him ("to William of Ockham"). That the suspicion pretension is heightened by his particular literary style ("to a man, George McGovern" is a little too folksy-sentimental) can be discounted as personal (e.g. I'm sadly embittered at McGovern for setting the reactionaries ahead ten years with the flattest, most inept presidential campaign since Wendell Willkie). All in all, the drawings are esthetically unrevealing, but they provide a steady stream of the minutae curators are required to caress as scholarly authorities on their subject artists, and a steady stream of proper nouns assuring us that this is *real* business, with *real* importance, accomplished in the *real* world. Oddly, that stuff performs an important esoteric function: it demonstrates to the general public that Flavin is not merely some "far out" guy who blew into town with the outlandish idea of making a show from light fixtures; it demonstrates that Flavin is a serious, ever-evolving artistic temperament *like the others* represented in St. Louis' halls by marble sculpture and carved frames. For this reason alone (because Flavin's art bravely transcends the hermeticism of the art world) the inclusion of an exhibition of bad drawings is okay.

The question is: are these semiprecious liberal art jewels necessary? For the understanding of the specific fluorescent light pieces in the exhibition, no. For the understanding that Flavin is not a holdover of '60s cool technology dispassionately expanding the mechanical boundaries of art in the greater art world game, yes. Dan Flavin is the American artist who at the moment really deserves the tired adjective "important," for he is liberating art from its objects, its elitism, and its hermeticism. For this, we must we willing to forgive a multitude of venal sins.

Artforum, Volume 11, Number 10, June 1973, pp. 32–35.

Art in Relation to Architecture/Architecture in Relation to Art
Dan Graham

While American Pop art of the early 1960s referred to the surrounding media world for a framework, Minimal art of the mid- through late 1960s would seem to refer to the gallery's interior cube as the ultimate contextual frame of reference for the work. This reference was only compositional; in place of an internal compositional reading, the art's formal structure would appear in relation to the gallery's interior architectural structure. That the work was equated to the architectural container tended to literalize it. Both the architectural container and the work it contained were meant to be seen as nonillusionistic, neutral and objectively factual – that is, simply as material. The gallery functioned literally as part of the art. One artist's work of this period (although not always his later work) examined how *specific*, functional architectural elements of the gallery interior prescribed meaning and determined specific readings for the art defined within its architectural frame: Dan Flavin's fluorescent light installations.

The lighting – even light fixtures – within the architectural setting of the gallery are normally disregarded, or considered merely functional or minor interior decoration. As gallery space is meant to appear neutral, the lighting, which creates this neutrality as much as the white walls, and at the same time is used to highlight and center attention on the art work on the wall or floor, is kept inconspicuous. While the background in general makes the artworks visible, the lighting *literally* makes the works visible. The lighting system, within which the specific light fixtures of a gallery arrangement function, is both part of the gallery apparatus and part of the larger, existing (non-art) system of electric lighting in general use: "I believe that the changing standard lighting system should support my idea within it."[1] Flavin's installations make use of this double functioning (inside and outside the gallery/art context) as well as the double connotation of lighting as minor decoration and the anonymously functional creator of the gallery's neutrality: "I believe that art is shedding its vaunted mystery for a common sense of keenly realized decoration. Symbolizing is dwindling – becoming slight. We are pressing downward toward no art – a mutual sense of psychologically indifferent decoration – a neutral pleasure of seeing known to everyone."[2]

Flavin's arrangements of light fixtures in a gallery depend contextually for significance upon the function of the gallery, and the socially determined architectural use of electric lighting. Electric light is related to a specific time in history. Flavin has observed that when the existing system of electric lighting ceases to exist, his art will no longer function. Made of standardized, replaceable units that, in Flavin's words, "can be bought in any hardware store," his arrangements of fluorescent tubes within the interior (or adjacent exterior) architectural frame of the exhibition space function only in situ and upon completion of the exhibition cease to function artistically. Unlike the self-defined or conceptual artwork, for example Duchamp's "found objects,"[3] they take on meaning by being placed in relation to other works of art or specific architectural features in an exhibition space; being part of the architecture/lighting of the gallery, they tend to underscore both the function of the space and other art's dependence upon the standard illumination of the gallery setting. Placed within a group of other paintings and sculpture, Flavin's lights radically disturb the other art's functioning, for it is then unable to rely on the neutral white ground of the gallery walls. The fluorescent illumination plays on the surfaces of paintings, highlighting or creating shadows that disturb their illusionary planes, undercutting (and so revealing) the latent illusionism employed in their construction. Similarly, the space in which the spectator stands is highlighted and dramatized. The effect is both constructivist and expressionist. In one installation, the use of all green lights plunged the interior space into lurid green, while turning the view from outside, defined pictorially by the windows of the gallery, into its after-image, a lavender-purple. The effect can be read ironically, as reversed illusionism, or, literally, as (physical) light and the obverse of the illusionary illumination radiating from the conventional painting.

Systematically, Flavin has investigated this gallery architecture by placing his arrangements of fluorescent tubes:

a) on the wall in either vertical, horizontal and diagonal bands;
b) in the corners of the room;
c) on the floor;
d) relative to exterior light-sources (near windows, open doors);
e) as partially visible/partially invisible, behind columns, architectural supports, or in niches;
f) in the hallway before the spectator enters the gallery, thus altering the spectator's perception when he enters to view the work;
g) in outside space, which serves as an entranceway or antechamber to the gallery/museum itself.

Just as art is internalized within society, the architecture which displays it is defined by the needs of society at large, and by art as an institutional internal need. Art as an institution produces ideological meanings and positions that regulate and contain the subjective experiences of the people placed inside its boundaries. Daniel Buren's work and writing focus on the specific architectural/cultural function of the gallery in producing art's institutional meaning. In general, all institutional space provides a background having the function of inversely defining what it places in the foreground. Since the Enlightenment, public interiors have been largely unornamented, geometrical, utilitarian and idealized. Thus they provide a seamless, clinical, recessive, white ground to set off Man's enlarged activities. The art gallery is an aristocratic relative of this conventional white cube. Its major task is to place the art object, and the spectator's focused consciousness of it, at eye-level center in the interior, and, in so doing, to conceal from the spectator any awareness of its own presence and function. So:

> Nothing which is not the work (of art) manages to distract the eye…. A work is thus dramatized or emphasized (against its will or by request) by the so-called neutral architecture, or indeed the work turns up its nose at any external influence and attempts, despite everything, to attract the eye regardless of the context…In most normal artistic settings, which we have seen in the majority of cases are white cubes, the problems set by the architecture attempt to conceal themselves, in order to support (artificially) the triumph of a bourgeois art, which thus given value can assert itself "freely," within the soft shelter which receives it.[4]

The Modern Movement in architecture is the history of two conflicting conceptions of the role of the architect. On one hand, the architect is seen as an engineer, on the other, as an artist. Functionalism, from the Russian Constructivists through Le Corbusier, culminating in the Bauhaus School of Gropius, can be seen as a method of resolving this conflict as well as the contradictions between two bourgeois value systems: humanism and technological operationalism. The solution, as envisaged by the Bauhaus, lay in subjecting the architectural work and men's needs to a "scientific" analysis in order to produce a functional system.

Man's needs were seen as social needs and were to be incorporated into a unified (total) formal (esthetic) program. An abstract language composed "scientifically," like the basic elements of physics, would be used to produce a materialist architecture built from a language of elemental, ideal forms. Based on a total, reductive analysis of esthetic form, social needs and technical requirements, this approach enabled science and technology to be wedded to esthetics in the interests of social progress. Art/architecture was to be constructed of democratic, recomposible, open modular units (in opposition to totalitarian blocks). Art/architecture, as pure technology, came to be identified with the earlier notion of "art for art's sake," as the Bauhaus architects saw the function of their architecture as the creation of a language of "its" own. This language was liberalist – antirhetorical, antisymbolic and (supposedly) free from ideological contamination, a utopian language of pure function and pure materiality.

Because in the functionalist building symbolic form – ornament – is (apparently) eliminated from the building (form and content being merged), there is no distinction between the form and its material structure; that is, the form represents nothing more or less *than* the material; second, a form or structure is seen to represent only its contained function, the building's structural and functional efficiency being equated with its real utility for those who use it. Esthetically, this idea is expressed in the formula: *efficient form is beautiful and beautiful form is efficient*. This has a "moral" dimension; "efficient" connotes a pragmatically "scientific" approach seemingly uncontaminated by "ideology," which has (capitalistic) use value ("efficiency" is how well a building contributes to the operations of the company housed within it).

One can examine the later buildings of Mies van der Rohe, especially his corporate office buildings. These use transparent glass "curtain walls" to eliminate the distinction – and contradiction – between outside and inside. Glass and steel are used as "pure" materials, for the sake of their materiality. Until recently, these Bauhaus-derived buildings were sheathed in transparent glass. They read from inside out, making evident their functional construction. The function of the building is expressed in terms of the structural, evident materiality of the glass and steel that are exposed directly to view, as are the human activities within the building. The *social* function of building is subsumed into its formal disclosure of its technical, material and formal (self) construction. The neutrality of the surface, its "objectivity," focuses the viewer's gaze only on the surface material/structural qualities, deflecting it from the building's meaning/use in the social system's hierarchy. The glass gives the viewer the illusion that what is seen is seen exactly as it is. Through it one sees the technical workings of the company and the technical engineering of the building's structure. Yet the glass's literal transparency not only falsely objectifies reality; it is a paradoxical camouflage: for while the actual function of the corporation may be to concentrate its self-contained power and to control by secreting information, its architectural façade gives the impression of absolute openness. The transparency is visual only: glass separates the visual from the verbal, insulating outsiders from the locus of decision-making and from the invisible, but real, links between company operations and society.[5]

In attempting to eliminate the disparity between the façade (which conventionally mediates it relation to the outside environment) and its private, institutional function, this type of architecture appears to eliminate the distinction between outer form and inner function. The self-contained, transparent glass building denies that it has an outside and that it participates as an element in the language of the surrounding buildings in the environment. Rather than coming to terms, within its formal statement, with the social language of the surrounding commercially built environment of which it forms a part, the classic modernist building is aloof and noncommunicative. It does not acknowledge that it, too, is usually a commercial proposition. The building's functionalism conceals its less apparent ideological function, justifying the use of technology or technocratic bureaucracy by large corporations or government to impart their particular version of order upon society. Where other buildings have conventional signs of their function oriented toward public scrutiny, the glass building's façade is invisible and unrhetorical. The esthetic purity of the glass building, standing apart from the common environment, is transformed by its owner into social alibi for the institution it houses. The building claims esthetic autonomy over the environment (through its formal self-containment), yet it evinces transparent "openness" to the environment (it *incorporates* the natural environment). This rhetorical ploy effectively legitimizes/naturalizes the corporate institution's claim to autonomy ("The World of General Motors"); the building builds the corporate myth. A building with glass on four sides seems open to visual inspection; in fact, the "interior" is lost to the architectural generality, to the apparent materiality of the outward form, or to "Nature" (light, sun, sky or the landscape glimpsed through the building on the other side.) Thus, the building stands apart from any language but its own.

Esthetic formalism and Functionalism in architecture are philosophically similar. By the same token, Functionalist architecture and Minimal art have in common an underlying belief in the Kantian notion of artistic form as a perceptual/mental "thing-in-itself," which presumes that art objects are the only category of objects "not for use," objects in which the spectator takes pleasure without interest. Minimal art and post-Bauhaus architecture also compare in their abstract materialism and their formally reductive methodology. They share a belief in "objective" form and in an internal self-articulation of the formal structure in apparent isolation from symbolic (and representational) codes of meaning. Both Minimal art and Functionalist architecture deny connotative, social meanings and the context of other, surrounding art or architecture.

By the end of the war, three Bauhaus architects, Gropius, Mies van der Rohe and Breuer, had emigrated to the United States and established themselves as influential teachers in large university architecture departments. There, as advocates of the Modern Movement, they trained a new generation of American architects. The architects as well as the architecture produced by them and their former Bauhaus teachers were given the name "International Style" by the architectural historians Henry-Russell Hitchcock and Philip Johnson. Mies' classicist glass office towers and apartment buildings became the new standard of American technology, especially as this style was easily exported to other areas of the world by American big business. Mies' classicism was based on an apparent trueness to materials (materials being seen for what they were, instead of disguised by the use of ornamentation) wedded to an idealized, "universal," and highly abstract, notion of space. These modernist structures soon became popular packages for international (multinational) corporate branch offices in the capitals of the "Free World." Used as an overseas branch office, the International Style building functions ideologically as a neutral and objectified rationale for U.S. export capitalism, although it would like to be taken as merely an abstract (not symbolic) form. Karl Beveridge and Ian Burn have indicated this symbolic rationale, which America had for its activities and which the form of its corporate architecture (and art) reflected during the postwar period:

> ...a technology which is democratic because it is good, neutral, and progressive, a technology which is equally available to everyone – the means for a better life, and free from ideological bias. The American artists of the sixties and seventies have reproduced this pattern, becoming the cultural engineers of "International art."[6]

Not that some American artists and architects have been unaware of the dilemma of their work's possible expropriation, once it is in the public sector, in the interests of the elite "Establishment" and also by the commercialized mass culture. Politically conscious American artists have evolved two basic esthetic strategies to deal with this twofold social expropriation. The first is to avoid having the art product packaged automatically by the media by the simple procedure of having the art package itself. The American Pop artists of the early to middle 1960s equivocated between imitating the cultural clichés prepackaged by the media (in one sense, accepting the popular or vernacular code/ reading) and various formal distancing devices making the "common" and ordinary appear strange (as these devices are formal and artistic method, this also allowed their works to be read as "art for art's sake"). A second strategy was to use popular techniques and subject matter *and at the same time (in the same work)* allow the work to read alternatively from a formal, "high" art perspective. A work by Lichtenstein, for example, can be both "art for art's sake" and something assimilable to popular cultural meanings. Both readings are simultaneously correct. Owing to its seeming ephemerality in terms of the popular code, such work cannot immediately be assimilated into the institutions of "higher" culture; conversely, the work cannot be immediately assimilated into the value-system of commercial, popular culture (although it speaks the same language) because of its anchorage in "high" art. The aspect of two equivalent, total/complete readings allows a work to question the position for the spectator which either one of these two readings poses and it also permits a questioning of both "popular" and "high" art's formal assumptions. As Lichtenstein told Gene Swenson:

I think that my work is different from comic strips – but I wouldn't call it transformation; I don't think that whatever is meant by it is important to art. What I do is form, whereas the comic strip is not formed in the sense I'm using the word; the comics have shapes but there has been no effort to make them intensely unified. The purpose is different, one intends to depict and I intend to unify... The heroes depicted in comic books are fascist types, but I don't take them seriously in these paintings – maybe there is a point in not taking them seriously, a political point. I use them for purely formal reasons, and that's not what those heroes were invented for. Pop art has very immediate and of-the-moment meanings which will vanish – that kind of thing is ephemeral – and Pop takes advantage of this "meaning" which is not supposed to last, to distract you from its formal content. I think the formal statement in my work will become clearer in time.[7]

Lichtenstein's choice of indirect, and ultimately artistically self-referring, esthetic "political" strategies is a typical one for "progressive" artists of the '60s, who believed that, at best, the radicality of their art activities could "trickle down" to society at large, despite the fact that the art might utilize mass media – popular clichés – for its "content." But Lichtenstein's work, whether reproduced ("second-hand") in the mass media or viewed in art galleries, did allow for such a dual reading. Lichtenstein is ambivalent about whether he wants to consider his work political. In American culture to define a work as ostensibly "political" automatically categorizes it as academic or "high" art; mass culture will have little interest in it, because it assumes what for the mass public is a patronizing attitude. As a category, "the political" is negatively coded: it means, "no fun." Andy Warhol's films, his Brillo boxes presented as sculptures, "Mary Hartman, Mary Hartman,"[8] and the rock group "The Ramones" are various examples of self-conscious works placed in the public media and capable of dual readings as both "high" and "low" cultural forms, but, ironically, neither one or the other.

It is easy to condemn this approach from a rationalist Marxist perspective because the work appears to equivocate in its attitudes toward commercial, vulgarized mass culture, even adopting some of its conventions and sentiments. Instead of negating (and proposing an alternative to) degraded American popular culture, it seems either passively to reflect or actively to celebrate it. European "leftist" archi-tectural critics unconsciously equate mass culture with Fascist irrational-ism, seeing rationalist socialism as both a "negation" of "degraded" mass culture and as the *only* "constructive" solution to the problems it confronts. They see present-day American society in terms of Europe of the 1930s. Similarly, in their critique of the use to which American International Style architecture is put, they use an idealist and historical model as an implicit standard. "Revolutionary" art for them is identified, for historical reasons, with the Russian Constructivist period. In fact, the work of Russian art and architecture after the Revolution was contextualized to real conditions and needs at that time; architects wished to purge personally symbolic (aristocratic – "art-for-art's-sake") elements from the architectural language to functionalize and socialize the means of artistic/architectural production. El Lissitzky summarized this approach:

(1) The negation of art as mere emotional, individualistic, and romantic affair.
(2) 'Objective' work, undertaken with the silent hope that the end product will be regarded as a work of art.
(3) Consciously goal-directed work in architecture, which will have a concise artistic effect on the basis of well-prepared objective-scientific criteria.
Such an architecture will actively raise the general standard of living.[9]

The difficulty with applying Constructivist standards to present-day architectural/social problems is that they impose a blinder on reality as it exists at present. The neo-Constructivist theoretician wishes to remake this reality in accord with "revolutionary" (in fact highly elitist) solutions "from above" and only in terms of his own specialist and theoretical language.

Like International Style Functionalist architecture, Minimal and Conceptual art of the 1960s seemed to claim autonomy from the surrounding social environment. It represented only itself, as a factual, structurally self-referring language. It deliberately sought to suppress both interior (illusionistic) and exterior (representational) relationships to achieve a zero degree of signification. Beveridge and Burn point out that when this type of art is used by big business, the government or the cultural Establishment, either domestically or as a cultural export, it functions perhaps contrarily to the artist's intentions – to affirm America's apolitical, technocratic ideology. For: "to reproduce a form of art which denied political or social content...in fact provides a cultural rationalization for just such a denial."

In rejecting the reductivism and utopianism of modernist architectural doctrine, Robert Venturi and his collaborators propose an architecture that accepts the actual conditions, social realities and given economics of a particular situation. This means, for commercial buildings in a capitalist society, taking the syntax of the commercial vernacular seriously, including the building's relation to the surrounding built environment, the program of the client on whose behalf it was built, and the public's reading and cultural appropriation of the building. A Venturi and Rauch building relies on both popular taste and specialist codes. By displaying its rhetoric and (social) function openly, and by using contradictory conventional codes in the same building, Venturi opts for a realist (conventional) and multivalent architecture, one whose structure is conventional (semiotic) rather than abstract or materialistic, and whose aim is basically communicative. Venturi and Rauch's unbuilt 1967 project for the National Football Hall of Fame is an example of combining architectural allusion with communicative devices taken from the commercial vernacular.

Unlike modern "masters" who advocate unconventional solutions, Venturi advocates using known conventions, even humdrum ones. In dispensing with the myth of the "heroic and original" building, which in its search for new forms and expressive use of materials has simply fueled the surplus economy of late capitalism and helped to provide large corporations with the alibi of "high culture," Venturi and his associates' approach implies a critique of post-Bauhaus ideology. The Bauhaus had associated efficiency and the notion of technical/formal innovation: "revolutionary" design would be efficient design. Today "efficient" design is more symbolic than real; it symbolizes not cost efficiency, but the corporation that has built the structure's hegemonic power (possibly due to its efficient use of social technology). Although the building's structure may read as "revolutionary" (in an esthetic sense), its function (in a social sense) is more often than not reactionary. Venturi prefers to take the ideological or symbolic assumptions of a cultural vernacular at their face value in determining his program. "Democracy" and pragmatic "pluralism" as given ideological values and cultural conventions of the local vernacular can be assumed to be part of the architectural object and, as they are taken into consideration, are free to emerge in terms of the building's rhetoric with alternative meanings/readings.

Venturi and Rauch's advocacy of conventional forms and techniques has an economic dimension. In public building it is usually more (cost) efficient, in both capitalist and Bauhaus formal terms, to build conventionally. If "good design" costs twice as much, then "good design" is not realistic and needs redefinition. And, as Denise Scott Brown notes, in practice Bauhaus-style total design, usually advocated by governmental planning boards, is often "used to betray rather than support the social concerns from which...it sprang." [10]

The question that the work of the American and British Pop artists and Venturi raise is the relation and socio-political effect of art and architecture to its *immediate* environment. Actually, this issue is implicit, merely on a daily, pragmatic basis, in all architectural work. What Venturi appropriates from the Pop artists is the understanding that not only can the internal structure of the architectural work be seen in terms of a relation of signs, but that the entire built (cultural) environment with which the building is inflected is constructed from signs. Pop art acknowledges a common code of schematic signs, conventionalized meanings and symbols which link vernacular, environmental signs to artistic/architectural signs. Abstract art's opposition to representational realism denies that an abstract work speaks the same language as its surrounding environment. The ideology of abstract art equates realism with representational art and, in turn, with an illusionism that can be manipulated to convey univalent, ideologically reactionary information to the masses, who might only understand the older convention (an often cited example is the Socialist Realism of Stalinist Russia). Modernist art has been committed to a purge of illusionist/connotative meaning in order to forge a purely formal, abstract and functional language. For the modernist, realism is identified not only with representational art, but with a morally pejorative pragmatism. If both the cultural and the "real" environment are seen in terms of a culturally connected semiotic coding, and if in practice an abstract work also functions, symbolically, in relation to other cultural signs, then a "new realism" whose basis is the function of the sign in the environment is necessary.

Signs in architecture can either be denotative, *architectural* signs, referring to building itself; or connotative, representing what is to be found within the building (literally or metaphorically), or to alternative – perhaps contradictory – meanings elsewhere. Both types of architectural sign connect with the codified sign system of which they are a part and to all other signs in the cultural environment.

Unlike the buildings of Mies and his followers, whose idealistic purism veils a corporation's less than pristine business practices, Venturi and Rauch buildings incorporate the "commercial" in their code, which allows them, ironically, to comment upon the predominant capitalist commercial environment of the American built landscape. This is also an acknowledgment that meanings in architecture are not inherent to or exclusively framed within the work of architecture itself, but already exist as part of the environment in which the building is placed. A good example is the Guild House where, instead of idealizing or sugar-coating the realities of the lives of the elderly, or of the rather banal environment surrounding the building, or its institutional nature, the building simply tries to make evident what those assumptions are. This is done by building a clearly standard, cheap building and by expressing an ideology (shown in the building's aspirations to elegance) that suggests alternative symbolic meanings. Thus Venturi and Rauch build conventionally, but use this "conventionality" unconventionally to express human conditions in a realistic, discursive manner.

In this anti-utopian, anti-introspective merging of realism and irony, the approach parallels that of Pop art. For Roy Lichtenstein Pop art assumes

> an involvement with what I think to be the most brazen and threatening characteristics of our culture, things which are also powerful in their impingement on us. I think art since Cézanne has become extremely romantic and unrealistic, feeding on art; it is utopian. It has had less to do with the world, it looks inward-neo-Zen and all that. This is not so much a criticism as an obvious observation. Outside is the world; it's there. Pop art looks out into the world; it appears to accept its environment, which is not good or bad but different – another state of mind.[11]

Venturi specifically acknowledges the influence of Pop art as well as "popular" culture.[12] Venturi prefers to make a building's symbolic function apparent by emphasizing it; this is done in a code which is understood not only in the architectural world, but also in the vernacular. An example is the proposal for a Town Hall, part of a larger city plan, for Canton, Ohio, from 1965,

> whose front is more important than its back....The change in size and scale in the front of the town hall is analogous...to

the false fronts of western towns, and for the same reasons:
to acknowledge the urban spatial demands of the street...The
front screen wall...is faced with very thin white marble slabs
to reemphasize the contrast between the front and the back....
The enormous flag is perpendicular to the street so that it
reads up the street like a commercial sign.[13]

The flag displayed on a building emotively signifies, in a code under-
standable to all Americans, at least two related readings: the pride of
American citizens in their country and, especially when the flag is
displayed on a commercial building, the confusion of capitalism with
the American system (of government).

It is interesting to compare Venturi's use of a symbolic, heraldic flag
on a public building to recent works of Daniel Buren using flaglike
hangings in his conventional vertical-strip patter. *In the Wind: A
Displacement*, done in 1978 as part of the exhibition "Europe in the
Seventies: Aspects of Recent Art" at the Hirshhorn Museum, Washington,
D.C., featured eight flags hung from flagpoles in the museum's central
courtyard (an area that reads as interior when viewed from the inner
windows of the museum but which is exterior from the point of view
of people outside the museum, as it is an extension of the entrance
courtyard). The flags hang perpendicular to the building with their
flagpoles titles slightly upward; in other words, the vertical stripes read
the same relative to spectator and to the ground as do conventionally
displayed American flags. The flags were arranged in a circular sequence;
so if the first flag is blue and white, the second is black and white, the
third is orange and white, the sixth is black and white, the seventh is
yellow and white, and the eighth is black and white. While Venturi
and Rauch's project ironically acknowledges the symbolic potency of
the U.S. flag, Buren's work neutralizes any connotational reading for
the work, allowing it to refer back to its architectural positioning and
to help render the architecture's/art's assumptions and functions

more apparent. Buren's work is designed to negate its own potential appropriation as either "high" art or symbolic content. For instance, the use of alternate black-and-white-striped flags between each of the colored flags is a way to cancel the presence of rival symbolic content which the work (a sum of flags) might take in relation to the symbolic function of (other) flags.

Unlike the Functionalist building and unlike the neutrality of Buren's material means, Venturi's architecture acknowledges the same communicative codes that vernacular architecture exploits (usually to sell products). In *Learning from Las Vegas* Venturi, Brown and Izenor criticize the new Boston City Hall (and modernist megastructures in general) for not overtly acknowledging its symbolic assumptions of, or aspirations to, monumentality. They observe that it would have been cheaper (more efficient) for the architects to have built a conventional building to satisfy the Hall's functional requirements topped by a large sign: "The Boston City Hall and its urban complex are the archetype of enlightened urban renewal. The profusion of symbolic forms....and the revival of the medieval piazza and its *palazzo pubblico* are in the end a bore. It is too architectural. A conventional loft would accommodate a bureaucracy better, perhaps with a blinking sign on top saying I AM A MONUMENT."[14]

As Venturi and Rauch's buildings admit more than one linguistic code, they can sometimes express conflicting present-day values rather than being tied to a "higher" language of unified form. Venturi, Brown and Izenor criticize upper-middle-class American architects for their rejection of the forms and symbolic importance of architecture of their own vernacular:

> They understand the symbolism of Levittown and do not like it, nor are they prepared to suspend judgment on it in order to learn and, by learning, to make subsequent judgment more sensitive to the content of the symbols....Architects who find

middle-class social aspirations distasteful and like uncluttered architectural form see only too well the symbolism in the sub-urban residential landscape....They recognize the symbolization; but they do not accept it. To them the symbolic decoration of the split-level suburban sheds represents the debased, materi-alistic values of a consumer economy where people are brain-washed by mass marketing and have no choice but to move to the ticky-tacky, with its vulgar violations of the nature of materials and its visual pollution of architectural sensibilities.... They build for Man rather than for people – this means, to suit themselves, that is, to suit their own particular upper-middle-class values, which they assign to everyone.... Another obvious point is that "visual pollution" (usually someone else's house or business) is not the same order of phenomenon as air or water pollution. You can like billboards without approving strip mining.[15]

Similarly, "beautification" substitutes for serious ecological planning and is aggressively promoted by Lady Bird Johnson, big land developers and Exxon; it clearly serves the ideological interests of those who have the most to lose if the idea of American dependence upon a consumer economy and overuse of energy is seriously challenged.

Venturi and Rauch will mix the "low" commercial code with the "high" architectural code, so that the commercial look of one of their buildings tends to subvert its reading as "high"-value architecture. And in a reverse fashion, the specific historical-architectural references in their buildings tend to question, to put into historical perspective, the usually immediate, unexamined assumptions communicated through commercial, popular codes. This commercial code has evolved to merge the interests of middle-class desires. The code of "high" architecture is a coalition of upper-middle-class "cultured" values, upper-echelon Establishment "taste," with values of the architectural profession as institution. The International Style unifies upper-middle-class and upper-class values in the interest of corporate business and government; at the same time, it looks down upon the "blight" and "visual pollution" it discerns in the complex diversity of smaller, less organized and lower-class codes, all representing alternative value-systems.

Venturi uses irony as a way to acknowledge contradictory political realities, rather than to suppress or to resolve them in a (false) transcendence, employing it to make certain assumptions of a building's given program overt. This use of irony as a "distancing" device suggests Brecht's notion of the self-aware style of acting (as found in classical Chinese theatre): "The Chinese performer limits himself to simply quoting the character played....The performer's self-observation, an artful and artistic art of self-alienation, stops the spectator from losing himself in the character completely....Yet the spectator's empathy is not entirely rejected....The artist's object is to appear strange and surprising to the audience....Everyday things are thereby raised above the level of the obvious and automatic."[16]

In the commercial environment "pure" architectural forms are often modified or violated by applied verbal signs. This is common, as Walter Benjamin and Roland Barthes have both noted, for communications media in general:

> Today, at the level of mass communications it appears that the linguistic message is present and independent in every image: as title, caption, accompanying press article, film dialogue, comic strip balloon. [17]

> Picture magazines begin to put up signposts for him [the viewer], right ones or wrong ones, no matter. For the first time, captions have become obligatory. And it is clear that they have an altogether different character than the title of a painting. The directives which the captions give to those looking at

pictures in illustrated magazines become even more explicit and more imperative in the film where the meaning of each simple picture appears to be prescribed by the sequence of all preceding ones.[18]

Venturi and Rauch facades often function as linguistic modifiers of the building to which they are attached. For example, beneath the quartz-light fixture that illuminates the large painted number "4" at the top of the Fire Station 4 in Columbia, Indiana (1965), itself a verbal and heraldic sign, two black bricks are set into the white brickwork that constitutes the façade to underline the light fixture; the line functions as literary irony and in the decorative/architectural modes simultaneously.

Walking along Main Street or driving in an automobile one sees a row of signs in sequence. Each sign stands out from the signs preceding and following it, having a prescribed, separate meaning in relation to the other signs that surround (and define) it in terms of its position. For a sign to convey meaning, it must conform to the general code shared by the surrounding signs and distinguish itself from – establish its position relative to – other signs. Each sign depends ultimately for its meaning upon its position in relation to the others. Signs change (and react to change in other signs) relative to their function, to general changes within the code of signs, and to shifts in the sequence of signs of which they are a part. Functions of buildings change (a real-estate office might become a medical clinic and then a used-car showroom or an art gallery), which is reflected in their representation in the sign-system.

By the early 1970s this notion of art as continual innovation came to be seriously questioned. Ecological concerns had generated a new cultural ethos that did not accept an idea of progress with its imperative to experiment with nature in order to create an ever-new future. Conservation of natural resources went along with conservation of the past. These changes in social perspective were reflected culturally in the 1970s fashion for "historical" re-creations of past decades, in the "new nostalgia," as well as in the neo-Colonial look of the facades/decor of vernacular architectural forms.

The historically eclectic, domestic (national, indigenous, vernacular and "homespun" as opposed to International Style) and "rustic" aspects of this style owed something to the "high" architecture of the late 1960s post-modernists (Venturi, Charles Moore and others), but used these influences for its own ideological purposes. It is possible that revivalism, in its nostalgic aspect, doesn't intend to clarify, but is meant to veil an accurate reading of the recent past: the connection between "the way we were" and the position we are in now. In place of integrity, postwar history to the present is broken into a confusion of delimited, self-contained decades, as first the '30s, then the '50s, and now the '60s are revived. The public's access to these "magic" eras is further confused with personal nostalgia: history as "memory": memory associated by media with the time when we "grew up." Like the cultural form of the western, the culturally mediated memory of coming of age in one of these recently past decades mythically stands for America's Past. In media representations the present appears confused with the particular "past" time being revived. In films and in television series, such as "Happy Days," "Laverne and Shirley" and "The Waltons," one sees the projection of present-day, largely middle-class "problems," represented by lower-middle-class characters (possibly "our" family forebears, one generation removed) situated back in the half-accurately depicted, half-nostalgically recalled decades of the '50s, the '30s, the '40s or the '60s.

The problem of the authenticity of historical reconstructions is now seen to be crucial, not only in the "new nostalgia" of popular culture, but in the recent, clearly parallel, interest of architecture in the nature of historical syntax: What makes a building real or fake? And what constitutes an architectural tradition?

Consider...[these] buildings, the restored Raleigh Tavern in Colonial Williamsburg, and the 1970s gas station called "Williamsburg." If the claim for authenticity is that they must actually have been built in the 18th century, or as an exact replica of the same, then, alas, the gas station and the conjecturally reconstructed parts of Williamsburg must be called fake. And even the use of indoor plumbing and electricity in Gunston Hall would have to be viewed as a compromise. Clearly, such an unrealistic definition of authenticity presumes that architectural tradition cannot change over time without losing validity or collapsing altogether....

An architectural tradition is composed both of references to an ideal type and of accommodations to particular circumstances. Viewed in this way, the Colonial tradition is more than just a set of 18th-century buildings or latter-day replicas. In other words, the Colonial tradition is a collection of architectural elements to be used in contemporary buildings to evoke to the modern eye (and in the modern heart) both the shapes and the size and, finally, the feel of 18th century America.[19]

The historical, in the form of an architectural allusion, signifies an ideal; but its specific meaning only has relevance in its relation to surrounding, present-day meanings, expressed by surrounding signs in the environment. And this is never neutral, but an active, present representation of one ideological view's explanation of the past in relation to present reality. The past is symbolic, never "factual." In architecture a sign of the past signifies a myth larger than the mere architectural function. "History" is a highly deceptive concept, as there are only histories, each serving some specific present-day ideological need.

Venturi and Rauch's 1968 restoration for the Saint Francis de Sales Church in Philadelphia heuristically overlaps present and past. It was constructed because the newly introduced (actually revived ancient) liturgical practice of the Catholic Church required a free-standing altar to replace the traditional one against the wall. Instead of destroying the old sanctuary, Venturi and Rauch left it as it was and installed an electric cathode light tube (since removed) suspended on a wire, ten feet high, parallel to the ground and just above the eye-level of seated parishioners. The electric line defined an ellipsoidal semicircle inflected inward, and followed the perspective of the parishoners' line of sight, as well as the line of the old altar. It ran from just behind the new altar, following the curve of the apse behind it, to define a boundary that separated the old, rear altar from the new altar whose activities its light functionally illuminated. Here the light tube functioned only as a sign (replacing nothing), a two-dimensional graphic indicator, drawing a (mental) line through the old altar (thus leaving it in relative darkness) without physically destroying it. It literally illuminated/delineated the new area and so juxtaposed the old and the new, placing them in an historical, or archeological, relation to each other. Venturi proposed the word "hybrids" for such works that combine two contradictory or mutually exclusive categories of meaning/description: "I like elements which are hybrid rather than 'pure'....ambiguous rather than 'articu-lated'....I include the non sequitur and proclaim the duality....I prefer 'both-and' to 'either-or' black and white, and sometimes gray, to black and white." [20] Again: "Our scheme for the F.D.R. Memorial was architec-ture and landscape; our foundation for the Philadelphia Fairmount Park Commission was architecture and sculpture; our design for Copley Plaza, architecture and urban design....[while that for] the National Football Hall of Fame is a building and a billboard." [21]

The task of the work of art or architecture is not the resolution of social or ideological conflict in a beautiful artwork, and not the construction of a new ideological counter-content; instead the artwork directs attention to the seams in various ideological representations (revealing the conflicting variety of ideological readings). [22] To do this the work uses a hybrid form, one which partakes of both the popular code of mass media and the "high" code of art/architecture, of both the popular code of entertainment and a theoretically based political analysis of form, and of both the code of information and of the esthetically formal.

1   Dan Flavin, "Some Remarks…; …Excerpts from a Spleenish Journal," *Artforum*, December 1966.

2   Flavin, "Some Other Comments," *Artforum*, December 1967.

3   People tend to compare Flavin's fluorescents to Duchamp's readymades. It is important to make a distinction. Duchamp took an object produced as a commodity from the non-art sector and introduced it into the art gallery in apparent contradiction of both the usual function of the gallery (which is to designate certain objects "art" and to exclude others) and of other "non-contaminated" art objects within the gallery. This would seem to question, on the level of abstract or logical truth, the aristocratic function of art and of the art gallery as institution. In fact, Duchamp's critique is only on the conceptual/philosophical level and was immediately integrated back into the art institution's definitions of what constitutes (the function of) art without directing the spectator's attention to the specific details/practice of the functioning of the gallery or of art in relation to society at a specific historical moment. Duchamp's work resolves the contradiction between gallery art and art in relation to society into a totalizing abstraction; further, it is ahistorical: the condition of "art" is seen as neither social nor as subject to change. By contrast, Flavin's fluorescents only "work" through specific situation installation, either through necessity or esthetic calculation. *Artforum*, Volume 17, Number 6, February 1979, pp.22–23.

4   Daniel Buren, "Notes on Work in Connection with the Places Where It is Situated, Taken Between 1967 and 1975," *Studio International*, September-October 1975.

5   In recent years the transparent glass style has been inverted with the glass façade being replaced by use of reflective (or semireflective, one-way) mirror-glass. Unlike the earlier transparent glass structures, which openly revealed their structural framework, the glass building now presents the viewer on the outside with a purely abstract form (from the inside it allows the corporate worker a concealed vantage point) – a cube, hexagon, trapezoid, or pyramid.

6   Karl Beveridge and Ian Burn, "Don Judd," *The Fox*, No. 2, 1975, pp. 129–42, esp. p. 138.

7   Roy Lichtenstein, as interviewed by G.R. Swenson, *Art News*, November 1965.

8   The American television series "Mary Hartman, Mary Hartman" functioned in a way not dissimilar to

Lichtenstein's art. On one level it could be read as "soap opera." It was impossible for the viewer to know if it was one or the other. Its adherence to principles of identification with characters in a narrative format, its emotional directness, and other conventions of "soap opera," allowed it to be a believable "soap." In "Mary Hartman, Mary Hartman" the validity of the satire itself was continually undercut by the emotional "reality" of the characters' problems, which, in fact, resembled those of most Americans. Because the show was conceived in this fashion as a form of both "high" and "vernacular" art, the writers and actors on the show never deluded themselves into thinking that the program was a "higher" form of art, nor did they take themselves totally seriously as "stars" or media-manipulators.

9 El Lissitzky, "Ideological Superstructure," (Moscow, 1929) in *Russia: An Architecture for World Revolution*, tr. Eric Dluhosch, Cambridge, Mass., 1970, pp. 70–71.

10 Denise Scott Brown, "An Alternative Proposal That Builds on the Character and Population of South Philadelphia," *Architectural Forum*, October 1971.

11 Lichtenstein, interview (note 7).

12 Robert Venturi, Denise Scott Brown and Steve Izenor, *Learning from Las Vegas*, Cambridge, Mass., 1972.

13 Robert Venturi, *Complexity and Contradiction in Architecture* (Museum of Modern Art Papers on Architecture I), New York, 1966.

14 Venturi, Brown and Izenor, *Learning* (note 12).

15 *Ibid.*

16 Bertol Brecht, "Alienation Effects in Chinese Acting," in *Brecht on Theatre*, trans. and ed. John Willett, New York, 1964, pp. 91–99.

17 Roland Barthes, "The Rhetoric of the Image," in *Image-Music-Text*, trans. and ed. Stephen Heath, London, 1977, pp. 32–51.

18 Walter Benjamin, "The Work of Art in the Age of Mechanical Reproduction," in his *Illuminations*, ed. Hannah Arendt, trans. Harry Zohn, New York, 1969, pp. 217–42.

19 Richard Oliver and Nancy Ferguson, "The Environment is a Diary," *Architectural Record*, February 1978.

20 Venturi, *Complexity* (note 13), p. 23.

21 Robert Venturi, quoted in Robert Maxwell, "The Venturi Effect," in *Venturi and Rauch: The Public Buildings*, New York, 1978.

22 This runs parallel in French semiotic theory to Julia Kristeva's critique of unitary text based on "the construction of a single identity (with its own consistent identity)." She advocates instead a plurivocal text "where (various) discourses confront each other...in opposition" and which is "an apparatus for exposing and exhausting ideologies in their confrontation." Julia Kristeva, "The Ruin of a Poetics," *20ᵗʰ-Century Studies*, 7/8, 1972.

Artforum, Volume 17, Number 6, February 1979, pp. 22–29.

Dan Flavin at Castelli
Carter Ratcliff

At its most severe, Minimalism exchanges ready-made objects for pre-conceived forms, as with Robert Morris's cubes and Sol LeWitt's three-dimensional grids. Dan Flavin produces hardcore Minimalist clarities, yet he is a Duchampian as well as a geometer, since the fluorescent tubes and circles he uses are store-bought, as everyone knows. This recent show was confined to tubes. It didn't offer much in the way of development. The earliest work on view, from 1963, was an untitled piece consisting of a single 8-foot-high green tube. The most recent works, from 1975, were the two versions of *Untitled (monument for V. Tatlin)*, each 10 feet high and consisting of eight cool white tubes. The dates could just as easily have been reversed. This kind of consistency, if taken along with Carl Andre's stasis during the 1970s, might prompt the reflection that some Minimalists simply don't change much, even if others do. One could leave the matter there if it weren't for the fact that Andre and Flavin are not strictly speaking comparable. The former's most interesting work came out of a mid-'60s phase of quick change. His '70s have looked like a respite becoming a way of life, whereas Flavin has never shown much development – at least not after he arrived at his mature style (or device). This resistance to the pressures of time has made Flavin central to Minimalism in a very odd way.

By making ready-made objects double as preconceived geometrical forms, his art carries off one of Minimalism's major coups. But note that one can make this claim by talking of Flavin's light fixtures solely as lines and circles and commercial products. Neither Flavin's geometric proccupations nor his Duchampian concerns require one to pay any attention to the light his sculptures shed. The moment one does, questions of Flavin's stylistic and historical tactics fade a bit. They don't dissolve entirely, yet all such secular concerns are obscured by the relentlessly pretty haloes that surround his works. Flavin's religious background is routinely mentioned, though it isn't brought to bear on much beyond the fervently spiritual tone of his wordier titles. I don't think Flavin's biography can be made to elucidate specific meanings of his art. Still, for all the good timing of his innovations, it seems clear that he yearns to make a transcendental leap outside of history. Thus the stasis of his mature work is intentional, not a sign that invention has flagged.

Flavin would no more change his art than an acolyte would presume to change a ritual. Of course, from a worldy, form-obsessed point of view, the circular lights were a change from the tube. For Flavin, however, they seem to have been something slightly different: a way of elaborating the implications of the straight-line tubes and, at the same time, of keeping tubes and circles alike from taking on independent formal significance. In Flavin's art, form takes on meaning insofar as it denies itself (dissolves into light), denying simultaneously the straight lines, circularities and zigzags of history. In this show, the shock of the earliest date soon wore off. Flavin wants to defeat time with his art. He can't succeed, of course, for he carries on the project with undeniably Minimalist tactics – the aura of the mid-'60s was strong here. And yet he never utterly fails, for his transcendent intention is by its nature indefatigable.

Art in America, Volume 68, Number 1, January 1980, pp. 108–109.

New York Reviews
Jane Bell

It's been 20 years since Flavin decided to become a practicing artist.
It's been 15 since his show at New York's Green Gallery: the legendary
occasion when Flavin first marched off to explore the apparently
limitless esthetic possibilities of commercial fluorescent tubing. Flavin
has since nudged those possibilities to extreme limits, most recently in
permanent installations at Grand Central Station and at the Hudson
River Museum. Throughout the late '60s and '70s he maintained the
rigor and elegance of his work, seemingly untouched by the coming
of an era in which informality held sway – and elegance was rarely
seen.

This canny "survey" of Flavin's work, covering the early '60s to the
near present, bore eloquent, even chilling testimony to this. Billing the
show as a survey was misleading: it was in fact a slim reprise which
included a mere six pieces, the first (*A primary picture*) completed in
1964, the last two (both called *untitled: monument to V. Tatlin*) bearing
the inverted dates 1975–71. It was a deliciously safe show, harboring
no awkward art historical surprises: the pieces were all vintage Flavin,
each installation a classic.

Flavin has been labeled everything from a "luminist" to a "minimalist exponent of light art." Certainly he has used light as his primary
material, lustily singing its praises: "Nothing, no storm or flood, must
be allowed to interfere with our demand for light," he once said,
"always more and stronger light." But it's not only the intensity of
light that makes or breaks an individual piece. It's the solid balance
that Flavin achieves between the physical object (whether starkly
clinical or radiantly lush) and the space in which it lives. In spite of its
connotations (industrial, commercial or quasi-Pop), Flavin's fluorescent
light engages in rich interaction with its surroundings: wall, floor

and ceiling become full and equal partners in the creation of the work, as important as the tubes and their metal supports. Flavin likes to combine certain traditional elements of painting, sculpture and architecture into a tight ensemble – not, however, an environment – and to impose his own exquisite order upon it. The fluorescent light with its supporting pan becomes a precision instrument, fine-tuning the space in which it exists.

There's no question that these six pieces come off as orderly, as sleek, as defined as ever. But they have lost their iconic presence over the years. Now Flavin's pieces seem intimate, even humble. *A primary picture*, a rectangular frame of multicoloured fluorescent tubes with one asymmetrical element on the left, radiates a modest glow. *Puerto Rican Light (to Jeanie Blake)* and an untitled crosslike structure of red and blue hugged their respective walls without dominating them. The one cornered piece, *untitled (to Donna)*, was a simple painterly mix: an assembly of blue, pink, yellow and white tubing that cast shadows solid enough to give the illusion of a thin wash of pastel color on the corner walls. In this piece, completed in 1971, Flavin only began to hint at the highly lit theatricality of his lusher and later installations.

But Flavin comes closest to fulfilling his own command for "more and stronger light" in one of the two *monuments (to V. Tatlin)*, a difficult and forceful series of lamp assemblies hung on the wall. Flavin has tuned up the chaste neon glow into a steady glare. The four vertical tubes stop just short of soaring. At once harsh and graceful this is indeed a monument, shot through with a wild and Byzantine force that shows Flavin at the height of his aggressive power.

Art News, Vol. 79, No. 1, January 1980, pp. 159–160. [excerpt]

The Strange Case of the Fluorescent Tube
Michael Francis Gibson

Thou canst read nothing except through appetite.

Hart Crame

I

I met Dan Flavin in May this year.

This essay is not going to be specifically about Flavin, though, but about whether art refers to something beyond itself – or to itself alone. Flavin's work seems to be based on the second assumption, so I shall be referring to our meeting and also to what Marcel Duchamp and Mark Rothko had to say on the subject.

Before coming into contact with Flavin, I was above all curious about where he stood. I knew he worked with fluorescent tubes, and also that he got upset if people referred to them as neon. In France, where I happen to live and where I met Flavin, people make no distinction between the two. When they say, "I must change the neon tube in the bathroom," they mean "the fluorescent tube," of course. I wondered why Flavin was so touchy about this terminology as a member of a minority group might be about the word chosen to designate him. I was told it was because "fluorescent" is an industrial product that can only be used as it is. This is the whole point of his choice, which is dictated, he believes, by the demands of simplicity. Neon, on the other hand, can be twisted into any desired shape. But why, I wondered, this imperative about simplicity?

"In everything I've been involved with since 1963," Flavin said, "I've been at my most effective when simple in the extreme. So simple that it's an affront – or that people regard it as an affront." He says this sort of thing matter-of-factly, as though it were a situation he had not actually chosen. On senses that these works, which may well strike one as irredeemably tautological, are produced by a man who is walking a tightrope. On the one hand there is the banality of his means, on the other his claim to relevance in terms of art. "It's very direct, very simple," he repeats. "We're making a simple proposition that is to the point and has no values away from itself."

"A sort of A equals A statement, then, in terms of logic?" I ventured. "A rose is a rose is a rose?"

Flavin smiled and intoned in a folksy sing-song; "It is what it is and it ain't nothin' else." "Don Judd," he continued, "made a remark to the effect that what exists exists and has everything on its side."

"But your point of view still implies a philosophy, doesn't it?" I urged.

"I suppose so."

"You can't get away from that, can you?"

"I always thought," Flavin countered, "that I would never, as an artist, be an intellectual. So matters of philosophy evade me."

Flavin has, in that respect, both an ambiguous attitude to why he does things as an artist, and an ambiguous cultural heritage, though the latter naturally cannot be said to shine through his work. Both his Irish father ("a failed seminarian," he calls him) and his schooling in a seminary in Brooklyn acquainted him with the philosophy of a Catholic faith with which he has since parted. But he also seems to have been swayed to some degree by the populist suspicion that the realm of ideas is not "for real."

"Everything is clearly, openly, plainly delivered," he insists. "There is no hidden psychology, no overwhelming spirituality you are supposed to come into contact with. I like my use of light to be openly situational in the sense that there is no invitation to meditate, to contemplate. It's in a sense a "get-in-get-out" situation. And it is very easy to understand. One might not think of light as a matter of fact, but I do. And it is, as I said, as plain and open and direct an art as you will ever find." He paused, concluded with an "Amen" and underscored his mock piety with a laugh.

The Catholic past emerges here, as in the speech of Joyce's sceptic, "Stately, plump Buck Mulligan." Like him, Flavin, when he feels at ease, will yield to the urge to burble snatches of mass Latin and to bless the world that lies on the far side of the luncheon table.

"The meaning of the world," said that scrupulous logician Ludwig Wittgenstein, "must lie outside the world. Inside the world everything is as it is and happens as it happens; there is no value in it – and if there were one, then it would be value-less" (*Tractatus Logico-philosophicus*, 6.41).

Wittgenstein is here giving a doubtful expression to both the classical Platonist belief in a "realm of Ideas" and the basic Christian assumption, pervasively present in his own native Austria, which places God in "heaven" – in a "beyond" that is generally attained only after death – or in a "kingdom of heaven" that is "within." These realms are perceived as the realms of meaning. But what if there is no "outside the world" as Wittgenstein calls it? Where could meaning be found in such a case? And, to bring up a related question, to what, in that case, could art refer outside itself? This is perhaps the central problem that has vexed most art of this century, and which is tersely expressed in Marcel Duchamp's dictum: "there is no solution because there is no problem." He is, of course, referring to the standard deathbed question of B-movies: "What does it all mean?"

Now Duchamp, as the French art historian Jean Clair has pointed out, grew up in the climate of sublimity and of frenzied, nostalgic idealism that was the mark of so much Symbolist art. He read the poems of Stéphane Mallarmé and Jules Lafarge and was steeped in the erotic reveries that run through the latter's poetry – dreams, for instance, concerning the well-guarded and sexually unaware teenage girls who could be glimpsed, playing the piano, quite beyond reach behind the fence, the lilac and the half-closed window in the house next door.

And Duchamp's history as an artist begins with a disillusionment. But, interestingly enough, it is not primarily a metaphysical or a religious disillusionment, but an erotic one, a rejection of erotic sub-limity (or sublimated eroticism) which finds its most violent expression in another painful aphorism: *On n'a que: pour femelle, la pissotière, et on en vit* – which can be roughly rendered: "One's only female is the *pissotière*, and that's what one lives by." Duchamp's *pissotière*, incidentally, is not the urinal but the foul-smelling, stand-up construction that until recently allowed the male population of Paris relief in times of need.

Duchamp's gross and provocative derision is connected with the idea that had taken root in his mind: since there is no meaning *in* the world – and since there is no "outside the world" where such meaning might be found, everything, including the fundamental relationship between men and women itself, is devoid of meaning and "there is no solution."

II

Curiously enough, it is the radical scepticism that runs through all Duchamp's thoughts and work which gives even greater value to another statement he made and which, at first sight, might seem to run counter to everything one had come to expect of him: "An artist," he declared, "cannot know what he is doing."

I was naturally tempted to try this out on Flavin. The response was mitigated.

"That's a philosophical question at best," he said, "and nonsense at worst." He smiled and concluded: "I'd rather take it at its best. My own position, which has taken time to evolve, is different from his. I really have an art that serves, you know. It's not a kind of gamesmanship, it's not elitist, it's really very easy to deal with. I don't need museums and galleries or my name on it even. It really seems to function in a remarkable and, let's say, an agreeable way without any context. You don't have to put a label on the light at all and you don't need an art-identifying situation for it. Marcel Duchamp is an inside artist, he plays inside games. I'm not denigrating him, it's just that we have different senses of artistic position."

Then, almost instantly, he felt impelled to add: "He was helpful to me when I was young. He got me a foundation grant in 1964 and would take no thanks for it. I tried to thank him personally and it was 'No-no-no-no-no...' I remember a stream of 'nos'."

Flavin, at the time, had no money to speak of, his son had just been born, and knowing that Duchamp was on the board of the Cassandra Foundation, he asked the older artist to visit an exhibition of his and then to get him a grant.

"So I was in the gallery one day," Flavin continued, "a small gallery just below Washington Square, when he came in with a cap and over-coat on, humming to himself – He went around the room – I think he gave it all of fifteen minutes, during which I had some trouble keeping the gallery owner away from him. I didn't want anybody to disturb him! Then I got a letter saying: 'I hope you can wait until the fall when the grants are made'."

But let's get back to Duchamp's statement: "an artist cannot know what he is doing," and look at how he expands on this. This ignorance, he argues, is all to the good because, to the extent that the artist accepts this form of "blindness," he may also hope that he will manage to produce something that is independent of his will, intelligence or senses. And Duchamp winds up with the astonishing assertion that artistic creation "is something *much* deeper than the unconscious" (in conversation with Georges Charbonnier on Radio France-Culture in Paris, December 1960).

Now it could seem easy enough to dismiss this sort of statement as careless hyperbole – were it not that Duchamp was always extremely careful about the way he phrased things.

So what are we to make of it?

And what could conceivably lie "deeper than the unconscious?"

III

Mark Rothko, in a short essay written in the forties, declared that in earlier civilizations "which were more practical than our own...the urgency of transcendent experience was understood" and that "elements from the familiar world" could be used as representations of the transcendental. "With us," he added, "the disguise must be complete. The familiar identity of things has to be pulverized in order to destroy the finite associations with which our society increasingly enshrouds every aspect of our environment" (reprinted in the catalogues of the Rothko exhibition presented in Rotterdam, Zurich and Paris in 1971).

Here again the same question arises: what are we to make of that?

Rothko once declared that he was "unreligious," partly because this was the case, but also in order to discourage an interpretation of his art in terms of religious stereotypes. So we may assume that he was not referring to some sort of religious experience. But in that case, to what *was* he referring?

This recalls Wittgenstein's assertion that "the meaning of the world must lie *outside* the world" – which may provide us with a further clue as to what the work of art might refer to beyond itself.

According to a widespread view traditionally held in the Western world, a view to which Flavin and the *first* Duchamp ("there is no solution...") are opposed for one set of reasons, and Wittgenstein (it would seem), the second Duchamp and Rothko for another, the supernatural realm lies *beyond* the world of nature, outside universe, so to speak, and beyond the merely natural within man himself. This realm, to put things into simple and rather naïve words, is both infinitely near and infinitely inaccessible and is the realm of God whose intention alone, both in creating the world in the first place and in subsequently redeeming mankind, gives human life and the very existence of the world its meaning. For, as Chesterton rightly remarked, "there can be no meaning where there is no person."

This "intention," "person" or "supernatural order" was, in the traditional view of things, the realm "outside" the world where meaning (as Wittgenstein puts it) might conceivably reside; the realm to which the "question" was addressed – a question whose relevance and existence Duchamp denied; the realm of transcendence beyond all finite associations to which Rothko refers; the realm of things deeper than the unconscious alluded to by Duchamp. The realm, finally, whose very existence is denied by all the persons I have just quoted.

But if this is so, what are these people talking about? What *is* this region so much deeper than the unconscious, this transcendence, this beyond – if it is not, as Flavin implies "at worst," merely nonsense.

IV

Let me present a few more clues, and then try to put the pieces together. "Culture," says Clifford Geertz, "is the fabric of meaning in terms of which human beings interpret their experience and guide their actions." This is not the usual definition of culture that you will find in everyday speech and in the language of officials talking about "culture." It is a valuable statement, however, because it establishes the link between meaning and culture at a time when the art world is deeply, aggressively (or occasionally frivolously) preoccupied with the issue of meaninglessness and the deconstruction of meaning. It also suggests the function of what we loosely term "cultural activities" – though that function naturally remains impossible to circumscribe, being entirely open-ended.

Now the meaning with which we are concerned (the problem and solution Duchamp denied – the "value-beyond-the-work-of-art" which the work designates and which Flavin denies), to the extent that it hinges upon qualities that are still undefined, not only points beyond "daily life" but also to the future whose prospect gives each one of us the motivation to accomplish his chosen tasks. And this future, together with the unending "dance" of culture is, I suggest, the "beyond" or the "transcendent" (but *not* supernatural) realm to which Wittgenstein or Rothko refers.

It is to this dance that the artist surrenders himself in the creative moment. And in doing so he accomplishes two things: he makes the normally invisible dance of our culture visible for all to see and, more important still, points it in a new, as yet unpredictable and, we may hope, more human direction.

So Duchamp, I suggest, was right when he said that artistic creation is something "*far* deeper than the unconscious." But he was also right, up to a point, when he declared that "there is no solution because there is no problem." This needs to be qualified of course: Duchamp's statement is true only to the extent that this problem, although it *does* exist, is relevant neither to logic nor to reason. Yet it is always insistently present as that "deep desire" to which Nietzsche refers, as a dissatisfaction which does not find comfort in what is to hand and whose formulation is: "what am I really looking for?"

This sort of question is, as I said, unanswerable in logic. And so, in logic, no doubt, it does not exist. But this does not mean that it is utterly irrelevant, that it does not exist *at all* and that it is not answerable in other ways. It does exist as an endless ferment in life, bred by a dissatisfaction with things as they are, and it refers to this "beyond" the world (Wittgenstein), this "transcendental experience" (Rothko), this "authentic future" or this "deeper than the unconscious" (Duchamp) whose peculiar function and dynamics we are beginning to recognize as we gradually take stock, not only of the experience of our own culture, but also of other cultures in various parts of the world.

V

When visiting *Documenta* in Kassel this summer, I fell into conversation with a woman friend who runs an art gallery and who challenged me to explain my preferences. After I'd given a quick overview of the ideas I have set down here, she seemed disturbed: "This is just something you made up, isn't it?" she objected. "You can't prove it, can you?"

That depends, of course, on what is demanded as proof. I believe it can be argued and verified. It calls for amplification but in time it may be accepted. Yet I can understand why she was disturbed, for this conception is quite removed from the ideas and methods that currently dominate the art world.

It obviously goes counter to what Flavin said in his playful tone: "It is what it is and it ain't nothin' else."

For if I am right, then the opposite is true. Nothing "is really what it is" because everything is constantly a-building.

Significantly enough, my conversation with this friend took place as we were waiting for one of the most successful events of Documenta to begin: the presentation of Tadeusz Kantor's Cricot Theatre. This production made brilliant use of the contemporary idiom, but instead of limiting itself to dreary reiterations, tautologies and simplistic conundrums, it managed to suggest a "beyond" and a content in which the public found an echo of its real and primarily existential and emotional preoccupations. It was as though the works assembled for Documenta, which lay spread out in the museums and across the plain of the Karlsaue like the dry bones of Ezekiel's vision, were suddenly assembled before us and endowed with breath, organic coherence and life. Kantor's production was triumphantly acclaimed and an extra performance had to be squeezed in on a Sunday afternoon to placate those who had been turned away and had stood hammering at the door when the show began. Kantor's tremendous effectiveness is probably due to the fact that his show generates a body of references by accumulation and repetition which give it a much greater degree of complexity than that which any single work can hope to achieve. This may account for the fact that Kantor's paintings or assemblages, which he occasionally shows in art galleries, while they have merit, are only a pale echo of what he manages to bring about on a stage.

But Kantor's brilliant lesson is not universally acknowledged or understood. And the current avant-garde is no doubt inhibited and even crippled by a number of notions which are now fashionable among theoreticians of art and in academic circles. These erudite people make use of reduction and deconstruction. This may be valid enough when dealing with mere ideological discourse, but it cannot be applied in the same way to the substance of a living culture. This is so because from the day we became human we emerged out of the world of nature and moved into a world of cultural representations which cannot be dispensed with – except at the cost of our own humanity.

A woman, for instance, is not a female. Why? Because a "female" is a biological datum, whereas a "woman" is, and must be, a cultural construction. A woman (like a man) is defined by the way each society behaves towards her (or him). This behavior, at its best, defines and enhances her femininity (or his virility) and facilitates relations between men and women. "A man plus a woman equals a culture," the French anthropologist Christian Gros told me But when the narrative structure of a culture suffers a momentary breakdown, as has been the case in our century for a number of reasons, then the relationship between men and women is also disrupted, the passage between them becomes more arduous and you get the problematical situations presented by Duchamp in his work (in *The Big Glass*, for instance, or *Etant Donnés*) and in his aphorisms (like the one about the *pissotière*). These same situations are reflected in the silly macho statements that appear in Marinetti's Futurist manifestos or in the shrill anguish of much feminist rhetoric.

No society can work without a "beyond" of sorts – because no society can survive without goals – and the most distant, most important and as yet undefined of these goals can only be designated by means of symbolic forms. This means that Gertrude Stein's rose, in terms of art, is always more than a rose – or, in terms of logic, and to paraphrase the German Marxist philosopher, Ernst Bloch, that "A is not yet A."

This is not to say that artists like Flavin are "wrong" or that their work is "irrelevant." Their dance, like Duchamp's or Warhol's, gives visible shape to the crucial dilemma of the age. And this implies that Flavin, contrary to his own conviction, cannot know what he is doing because he *cannot* encompass the dance to which he yields himself.

This also implies that there is a region in us that is still sunless and lives only in the intimations of the dawn. We cannot know what shapes the morning will reveal there. But just as unknown quantities in mathematics are expressed by symbols, so too the symbols of our cultural language speak of the unknown *qualities* over which our dissatisfaction and our yearnings brood. These symbols stand for all that has as yet no face or name in this natural world, though countless supernatural names have, in the past, crowned it with implausible glory.

A German shepherd puppy I owned many years ago, wagged her tail at her own image in home movies, sniffed up all four-legged sculptures and barked at portraits until she grew up and learned to distinguish between living creatures and their representation. After that she studiedly ignored the movie screen and never looked at a painting again, though sculptures were always sniffed, just to make sure. It was as though she was embarrassed at having been fooled: she never glanced at the animated screen in the darkened room, as she might at any other luminous and moving object, but turned her back to it, lying on the floor and, rejecting every solicitation with a friendly thump of the tail, she could not be induced to lift her eyes towards it, even for a moment. She had discovered that images are unreal – they *look* like dogs and people, but a critical nose can tell the difference – so she chose to ignore them. In this she behaved as a true cynic should – which was appropriate enough, considering she was a dog.

But things are different with us. Because we are human, we are irresistibly drawn to the screen that stands before us. But, also, because we are human, we can very well look at it without being afraid of confusing the image with a real being, unless we choose to do so. If the meaning and power of persuasion of all signs and symbols have, as I believe, their foundations within the human mind, we may inquire into where they lead us. It may be that, understood correctly, they don't speed us downhill and backwards to a wasteland of illusion – that the charm of beauty and the power once designated by the supernatural, refer us forward to a natural fulfilment of great scope. If this is so, Flavin's austerity is not inevitable in terms of the specific logic of culture.

Kantor defines his theatre as "a transition that is *in no way venerable* from the other world to our own – the ford at which this transition becomes perceptible." Such a conception offers an alternative – as the demanding professional public that applauded him at Kassel well realized – to the sterile bones, the *disjecta membra* that lay around the plain outside. This alternative is not devoid of the searing irony which is such an important part of our contemporary lucidity.

We may, if this is so, admit that the work of art, the metaphorical rose whose import Gertrude Stein and Flavin both denied, the "object of lowest rank" that Kantor likes to use, can, if rightly handled, stand not for its uninteresting self but for all that lies "beyond" – beyond the banal and frequently grim ironies of the present – and which radiate the barely definable promise of a meaning that always appears to glow on the further horizon of our world. Indeed, its only possible value must lie "away from itself."

Art International, Number 1, Autumn 1987, pp. 105–110.
Revised by the author, March 2004

Dan Flavin at 65 Thompson
Holland Cotter

When a full consideration of light-as-symbol in American art after 1950 is written, Dan Flavin's sculpture will surely earn extended notice. The idea of turning electric illumination into a sculptural material was not, of course, his invention; El Lissitzky planned to experiment with the possibility; Moholy-Nagy and later, dramatically, Fontana produced work with artificial light as a primary component. By comparison with the explorations of these artists, however, Flavin's "found" fluorescence seems uninflected and literal: it neither supplements sculptural work nor functions atmospherically. Indeed, its suffused environmental glow itself becomes a blank, intangible "primary structure," obliterating architectural lines and accomplishing that desideratum of all art: it changes the viewer. If pink is the color Flavin has chosen for a piece, for instance, you can be sure you will look very much pinker in its vicinity – and that you will perceive the world as green for some moments after you leave its rosy glow.

Critical reservations about Flavin's work have often centered on questions of versatility. His formal means are, after all, restricted and probably not of limitless interest in terms of the configurations into which they can be recast. But for that very reason one is struck by the complexities he nonetheless extracts from his materials. This particular success has in part to do with the fact that although historically a Minimalist, Flavin has always had strong affiliations with Pop art. His hardware and colors may bear the badge of stripped-down technology, but they also come out of the candy-colored '60s. Every Flavin installation suggests, however faintly, a hybrid of salesroom, shrine and disco, and his light is never far from the artificially sweetened neon palette with which nearly a half century of American life has been advertised and sold.

I think it is exactly the interaction of Minimalist rigor and Pop humanity that accounts for the unexpectedly expressive potential Flavin's work has tapped in the past few years. This was evident in the installation titled *(to Sabine) summer 1989*, shown last fall and winter at 65 Thompson street. One is accustomed to seeing his fluorescent elements dispersed in logical geometric formations or ganged in clusters; here the four components were long separate tubes that were affixed at one end to a diagonal skylight so that much of their lengths passed diagonally down into the otherwise empty gallery space. Their slightly varying angles of projection gave each element a sense of individual presence. Their placement was even, somehow, worrisome: precariously, even aggressively positioned, they might have been lightening bolts pointing sharply earthward. But, with Flavin's title in mind, it was hard not to see in the piece's plangent blend of green, yellow and pink the sort of rainbow colors that typically bring a clouded summer idyll to a benign resolution.

A second installation hovered in a back room, where a sheaf of horizontal tubes near the ceiling cast everything in a deep unambiguous green light. But was this environment intended to evoke the green of the romantic landscape, the conscienceless radiation of technology or the symbolic verdure of hope? Flavin's conceptual agenda, once chilly and measured, seems to have expanded with time to encompass at least the possibility of lyricism at peace with technology, and there is something heroic in that.

Art in America, Volume 78, Number 5, May 1990, pp. 236–237.

...Notes for an Electric Light Art. (Dan Flavin)
Frederik Leen

James Boswell: "Then, Sir, what is poetry?"
Dr Samuel Johnson: "Why, Sir, it is much easier to say what it
is not. We all *know* what light is; but it is not easy to *tell* what
it is." [April 11, 1776][1]

It is a striking fact that all the established departures from
the Newtonian picture have been, in some fundamental way,
associated with the behaviour of light. [Roger Penrose, 1989][2]

The first diagrams and proposals in which Dan Flavin used solitary but
ordinary fluorescent tubes date from 1963. The first installation he
designed consisted of one fluorescent tube. The fitting was mounted
at an angle of 45° from the floor to the wall of Flavin's studio, a large
loft in Williamsburg, Brooklyn, based on a diagram that described the
proposal as *the diagonal of personal ecstasy / 5 25 63* [Cat. Ottawa, 1969,
#73]. In a later autobiographical essay, he named this installation
the diagonal of personal Ecstasy (the diagonal of May 25, 1963).[3] This proposal
was first shown to the public in *Black, White and Grey*, a group exhibition
at the Wadsworth Athenaeum in Hartford in January 1964. In the
accompanying statement for the label, Flavin explained, "The diagonal
of May 25, 1963 is the divulgation of a dynamic plastic image- object.
A common lamp becomes a common industrial fetish, as utterly
reproducible as ever but somehow strikingly unfamiliar now."[4] This
exhibition was an early indication of a still undefined attitude among
artists to differentiate themselves radically from Pop Art and Abstract
Expressionism. Barbara Rose termed this phenomenon "ABC Art"[5] a
year later in 1965; it would eventually be known as minimal art, despite

the objections of the artists involved. Conservative critics quickly lined up to say that Flavin's proposals were not art.[6] Flavin, however, could count on the support of a few people, resulting, among other things, in his involvement in the *Black, White and Grey* exhibition. A month later in March 1964, he was invited to have an individual exhibition at the Kaymar Gallery in New York.[7] Flavin exhibited two groups of works. The first group contained square objects containing one or more light bulbs and/or fluorescent tubes. These were known as "icons." Flavin created eight in total, of which seven were exhibited. The second part of the exhibition consisted of the works with which Flavin would eventually be most associated, specifically proposals or plans for installations using ordinary, commercially available fluorescent tubes.

Some of Dan Flavin's earliest attempts to create art were shown in the *Art Exhibit by Men of Roslyn Air Force Station* in Roslyn, New York, in January 1957. He had already attended art college for a brief period.[8] "Fortunately, I stopped formal instruction in art after four inconclusive sessions at the Hans Hoffmann School in 1956."[9] In 1958–1959, he took a number of general courses in art history and a course in materials and techniques over two semesters at Columbia University. Directly after leaving Columbia, he was overwhelmed by the work of artists such as Robert Motherwell, Franz Kline, Jackson Pollock, Jasper Johns, and the latest trends in *Art News*. Flavin summarised his uncertainty as follows: "My friend, Ward Johnson, used to send me inspirational postcards bearing reproductions of ten year old Motherwell paintings which looked strikingly like my last week's work."[10] From then on, his work varied from Cézanne-esque charcoal drawings, to texts surrounded with watercolour, ink and charcoal pictures,[11] to montages of found materials,[12] often combined with oil, watercolour, acrylic, an charcoal.[13]

From May 1960 to October 1961, Flavin worked as a guard and elevator attendant in the American Museum of Natural History.[14] Together with a sketch book of drawings of exhibits, quick sketches of visitors and the buildings or telephone lines outside the museum,

"I crammed my uniform pockets with notes for an electric light art."[15] Flavin moved to his new studio after October 1961, where he created his first works with electric light. *Icon I (the heart) (to the light of Sean McGovern which blesses everyone)* [Cat. Ottawa, 1969, #50] was the first in a series of eight square or almost square proposals in which one or more electric lamps were used. Created between 1961 and 1963, they were all called "icons", numbered with a Roman numeral and subtitled.[16] According to a drawing dated January 24, 1963, it appears that several were planned but never executed [Cat. Ottawa, 1969, #69]. The drawing's inscription, *To Be and Would Be Icons*, suggests that not all were intended to be executed; some merely looked like (designs for) icons. With the icon, Flavin referred to a "standard yet variable emblem" – specifically, the blank, unmarked square.[17] Although each icon constituted a separate work of art, they could also be combined in larger ensembles. A drawing dated December 12, 1962 [Cat. Ottawa, 1969, #65] clearly shows eight different ways of combining the first four icons. The caption under each combination identifies the icons concerned, while the title of this drawing defines these ensembles as "iconostases". This inscription refers to the screen in Christian Orthodox churches on which the icons are displayed, separating the worldly section from the holy section of the building. However, "... my icons differ from a Byzantine Christ held in majesty; they are dumb – anonymous and inglorious. They are as mute and undistinguished as the run of our architecture. My icons do not raise up the blessed saviour in elaborate cathedrals. They are constricted concentrations celebrating barren rooms...They bring a limited light."[18]

Icon I consisted of a square, flat, box-like construction measuring 63.8 x 63.8 x 11.8 cm., made of pine and masonite painted in cadmium red oil with a base layer of gesso, a red fluorescent tube of the same length (63.8 cm) mounted on top. The overall form of all of the other icons was identical, with approximately the same dimensions, except for *icon IV (the pure land) (to David John Flavin [1933–1962])*, which was significantly larger. Since this work had been destroyed after being damaged in an exhibition at the Green Gallery in 1963, it was the only icon absent from the exhibition *Some Light* at the Kaymar Gallery the following year.[19] Its design, however, was included in the exhibition as a full scale diagram for *icon IV* [Ottawa, 1969, #52]. Dated June 14, 1962, the drawing clearly depicted that the original measurements were the same as those of the other *Icons*. They were altered to avoid the end of the fluorescent tube being flush with the right-hand end of the box.

Flavin was not the first to use light as a material in aesthetic objects.[20] Based on music, colour organs, the first artistic experiments with artificial light, date to the first half of the 18th century. Until well into the 20th century, visual artists were interested in the imitation of light effects, rather than in light itself. Thomas Wilfred's pioneering work with light, from 1919, was still based on the light organ, but with *Lumia*, he tried to separate his light art from music. Despite considerable success, Wilfred's *Lumia* was never taken seriously as an art form. In 1946, Gyula Kosice, a member of the Argentinean group Madí and an acquaintance of Lucio Fontana, created spatial linear neon constructions, *Estructura luminica Madí (Luminous Structure Madí)*.[21] These structures were first exhibited that same year at the *Primero exposición del movimiento de arte Madí* in the Galería Van Riel at the Instituto Francés de Estudos Superiores in Buenos Aires. Following Kosice's experiments, Fontana first used artificial light as a possible material for sculpture, employing ultraviolet light in 1949. The hanging neon linear structure that Fontana installed as an *Ambiente Spaziale* above the entrance steps of the 9th Milan Triennial in 1951 was a spectacular presentation.[22] Because of its enormous public significance, this work marked a decisive shift in the definition of sculpture. The intrinsic artistic value of the work was tarnished, however, as a practical consequence of the mechanism that allowed the art to be switched on or off. Furthermore, due to Fontana's cooperation with the architects Baldessari and Grisotti at the Biennial, critics questioned the status of the neon line as a work of art. Some identified it as a piece of interior design rather than an autonomous work of art. By directly referencing Alexander Rodchenko's *Spatial Constructions* of 1920–1921, similarly suspended from a wire, Fontana argued explicitly against the monumentality of traditional sculpture. There was even a (coincidental?) connection between Fontana's 100 m. long neon *Line* and Rodchenko's pamphlet *The Line*. Rodchenko wrote that "As one of the fundamental moments of construction, the line has managed to illustrate all the possibilities of these elements which are part of painting"[23] Situated somewhere between painting and sculpture, Fontana's gigantic neon doodle prefigures Flavin's decision still to regard his installations in terms of these categories.

In the early '60s, many artists, mainly around Zero (Heinz Mack, Otto Piene, Günther Uecker) in Germany and Group N (Padua) in Italy, were developing an aesthetic practice based on, or consisting solely of, electric light. Light was usually used as a kinetic medium. For the Zero members, their art was linked to social and utopian principles and ideas of emptiness, cleanliness, immateriality and transparency. One of the practical outcomes of their theories was their investigation of optical processes. Since light is the first condition for sight, it was inevitable that some artists should take electric light as the basic element in their aesthetic production. Otto Piene, for example, produced his first work with electric light, the *Lichtballette* in 1959, with torches and stencils. However, apart from the material use of light, these kinetic experiments had little in common with Flavin's work. Zero manipulated light to achieve an animated narrative structure. In so doing, their work related to the experiments of Moholy-Nagy with *Light-Space Modulator* from 1922 onwards. Moholy-Nagy's use of moving, flashing, and reflecting metal dematerialised the sculptural object and offered an alternative to monumental sculpture. The movement of the light in and around the surrounding architecture produced a painterly effect, demonstrating ideas formulated in the chapter on light in his book *Von Material zu Architektur* from 1929.[24] Just like Moholy-Nagy's *Light-Space Modulator*, the designs of the Zero group were conceived more as a replacement for traditional categories of painting and sculpture. Dan Flavin was not interested in replacing these categories or finding alternatives. His proposition was for an art of electric light, regardless of categories like painting and sculpture. Flavin summarised his position as follows: "I feel apart from problems of sculpture and painting but there is no need to re-tag me and my part. I have realised that there need not be a substitute for old orthodoxy anyhow." [25]

In fact, his use of electric light more closely resembled that of three contemporaries of Moholy-Nagy from the 1920s, Gerrit Rietveld, Walter Gropius and Le Corbusier, than any other artist from the early 1960s. All were architects who formulated new directions in the field of architectural and functional design. In 1920, Rietveld was the first to design a lamp whose initial design consisted of four bare, unadorned Philips tubes arranged in horizontal and vertical positions to form a spatial construction which hung from the ceiling by its electric wires.[26] There is no doubt that Gropius's design for the lighting in the Director's Office in the Bauhaus in Weimar in 1923 was inspired by Rietveld's design.[27] Although unequalled in its inventive form for interior lighting, Rietveld's scheme still remained close to traditional central lighting sources. Gropius shifted the boundaries a little further by applying the principles of architecture to lighting. The diffusion of the light was also tailored to the functional needs of the room. As shown in a photograph and diagram, two tube lamps were located inside the structure against the wall.[28] Despite the advanced tube light technology – both economical and in terms of design – even Gropius did not find it easy to completely distance the design from the traditional idea of lighting as an addition to architecture.[29] Here, Le Corbusier's installa-tion of tube light, such as in the *Villa La Roche* (1923–1925) or in the *Pavillon de l'Esprit Nouveau* (1925) may also be of interest.

In May 1963, Flavin decided that he had reached at a point where he could abandon any reference to handcraft in the fabrication, construction and internal organisation of his basic materials. Accordingly, some of the designs in a drawing dated May 17, 1963 were called *last icon* [Cat. Ottawa, 1969, #72]. This drawing includes a striking sketch in which Flavin anticipates his later proposals for whole rooms. The sketch depicts the installation of a band with a single row of circular fluorescent tubes with a cool white light on a dark blue background.[30] This band went around the whole room and was only broken by the door. The caption reads *FLUORESCENT ROOM / black light too / individual switches / this could be elaborated to include floor and ceiling*. Another diagram from this drawing contained a vertical row of standard fluorescent tubes connected to a painted band. Again, the title was *LARGE ICON (CLASSICAL)*, but something else had been added: *a variant would eliminate / painted strip*, with an arrow pointing to the strip. This variant would be the prototype for *continuous icon* and the *endless icon* (c.f. below), both of which pre-dated the *diagonal of May 25, 1963*. In any case, Flavin did not entirely give up on his idea of icons. On June 28, 1963, he drew the plan *for an icon (to Morris Louis)* [Cat. St Louis, 1973, #13], which unmistakeably followed the formal programme of the *icons* he had already created.[31] On the same day, he designed another one: *the continuous icon* [Cat. Ottawa, 1969, #77] alongside a diagram, *three from meditation (for William of Ockham)*. This last proposal contained the basic design of what would eventually become a critical work in Dan Flavin's production: *the nominal three (to William of Ockham)*, first shown in Flavin's individual exhibition at the Green Gallery in November– December 1964.

But first came his involvement in the group exhibition in Hartford in January 1964. The artist Donald Judd knew Flavin since the "icon" series, when they both participated in a group exhibition at the Green Gallery with Robert Morris in January 1963.[32] Incidentally, at this exhibition, Morris showed his seminal work *Card File* for the first time. In his review, Judd described Flavin's Hartford presentation in a clear, straightforward manner: "A single daylight-white tube has been placed at a diagonal on approximately an eleven by eleven wall at the end of a short corridor just off the court. It makes an intelligible area of the whole wall. There is some relation to the diagonals of Morris Louis. The tube is a very different white, in colour and nature, from the painted white of the box which supports it. The box casts a definite shadow along its length. The light is cast widely on the wall. The light is an industrial object, and familiar; it is a means new to art. Art could be made of any number of new objects, materials and techniques."[33] This distinct, unambiguous description was useful for readers, as there were no precedents for this type of aesthetic work. Evidently, the explicit, unambiguous character of the work had made an impression on Judd. At the time, he was refining his own views on the relationship between art, production and the work of art, which would soon appear in the essay "Specific Objects."[34] After reading this text and his other comments on Flavin, one would not be surprised if Judd wrote "Specific Objects" with Flavin's fluorescent tubes in mind.[35]

Both Judd and Lucy Lippard in their respective discussions noted the didactic confrontation between the icons and the installations, or proposals and plans, for fluorescent tubes in Flavin's individual exhibition at the Kaymar Gallery in March 1964.[36] The artist's indecision was revealed not only in the continuation of the *icons* series or in the somewhat vague title of the exhibition, *Some Light*, but primarily also in the strictly equal value placed on the two parts of the exhibition. In fact, it is probable that the exhibition was originally intended to include only the icons. This can be deduced from Kim Levin's "Reviews and Previews" column in *Art News* which only mentioned the icons. In addition, "Work drawings, like blueprints, accompany the constructions, including one drawing of the positions of the screw eyes on the back of a block". Levin almost certainly obtained this information from the artist or, perhaps, though less likely,[37] from the gallery, even before the exhibition opened. Since the article appeared in *Art News* the same month in which the exhibition took place, the text must have been written before the exhibition was ready. In fact, the drawings were never shown.

The exclusive use of single or multiple "readymade" fluorescent tubes was confirmed in the individual exhibition *Fluorescent Light* at the Green Gallery later that year (1964).[38] Flavin exhibited seven works, one of which was *the nominal three (to William of Ockham)* [Ottawa, 1969, #96; ill. of Ottawa installation: #96], consisting of three parts with vertical fluorescent tubes, planned for daylight bulbs, but executed in cool white fluorescent light. This change was necessary due to the colour interference with the light from other installations. The left hand side consisted of one tube, the central section two tubes and the right hand section three. The first sketch for this installation dates from June 28, 1963 [Ottawa, 1969, #78]. Two diagrams entitled *one (to William of Ockham)* [Ottawa, 1969, #75 & 76] representing a single vertical fluorescent tube, were drawn four days before the installation. A fourth element with four tubes can be seen in the installation plans for the exhibition, but it was ultimately installed in three parts. On August 8, 1963, Flavin wrote in his notebook: "With the *nominal three* I will exult primary figures and their dimensions. Here will be the basic counting marks (primitive abstractions) restated long in the daylight glow of common fluorescent tubes."[39] The design clearly referred to elementary mathematical series and to the use of a limited basic unit which could be extended into endless systems, both of which were evident in Flavin's installation for the exhibition *Alternating Pink and 'Gold'* at the Museum of Contemporary Art in Chicago in 1967/1968. Nevertheless, the theoretical implication of the reference to William of Ockham (Lat. Occam) (± 1285 - ± 1350), an English scholar of the Franciscan order of Christian monks, was significant. As a nominalist and defender of dogma-free thinking, Ockham was a rarity in the Middle Ages. He stated that the theological truth could not be understood, it must simply be believed. According to Ockham, the result of this was that theological truth had to be released from science and philosophy.

Ockham is often quoted as the author of the principle of parsimony. This was formulated with the proposition that "entities should not be multiplied unnecessarily", also known as *Ockham's Razor*. It was this quote that Flavin advised Mel Bochner to include in his article on Flavin's work. Unlike Bochner, Flavin was careful enough not to explicitly attribute this to Ockham. Rightly so, since this version of the *Razor* cannot actually be traced back to Ockham, but may well refer to the recurring phrase in his writings that "plurality is not to be posited without necessity" (*"Pluralitas non est ponenda sine necessitate"*).[40] In any case, it is true that Flavin's motto clearly refers to the principle of the economical use of energy, whichever side of the razor is intended.[41] This is reminiscent of the constructivist adage, "Constructivism will lead Man to manage maximum cultural achievements with a minimum of energy expenditure."[42]

After working with the same materials for a few years, the artist had developed a particular skill in dealing with the requirements, demands and possibilities of the new designs in an exhibition context. As he described, "… my own proposal has become mainly an indoor routine of placing strips of fluorescent light."[43] It was not long before Flavin devised a specific system with a limited number of parameters. Two years after the *Fluorescent Light* exhibition at the Green Gallery, he formulated a concise description – "I know now that I can reiterate any part of my fluorescent light system as adequate. Elements of parts of the system simply alter in system installation. They lack the look of history. I sense no stylistic or structural development of any significance within my proposal – only shifts in partitive emphasis – modifying and addable without intrinsic change. All my diagrams, even the oldest, seem applicable again and continually."[44] A year later, he affirmed this conclusion in a letter to Dan Graham on June 22, 1967. "Last year, I became fully conscious that I had been deploying an interchangeable system of diagrams for fluorescent light held for situation installation". In a letter to Elisabeth C. Baker, he summarised this as, "That proposal is whole now and has been so."[45] The material part of the system consisted of the different standard types of industrially produced fluorescent tubes and their limited number of dimensions and colours.

From the beginning, his installations were always indoors,[46] causing him to take into account the floor, the walls and the ceiling. Within these limitations, the different variables were quickly determined and the standards set. As far as I know, there is not one design for an installation with free-hanging lamps.[47] They are usually arranged parallel to the wall, but they can also be placed at an (often 45°) angle, as in the corner installations, or vertically, as in the floor installation *greens crossing greens (to Piet Mondrian who lacked green)* from 1966.

1 BOSWELL, James, *The Life of Samuel Johnson, LL. D. Comprehending an Account of His Studies and Numerous Works, in Chronological Order; a Series of his Epistolary Correspondence and Conversations With Many Eminent Persons; and Various Original Pieces of His Composition, Never Before Published*, London, (1st Ed. 1791), this quotation from the 5 volume edition, published by G. Routledge & Co. London and New York, 1856, Vol. 3, p. 23.

2 PENROSE, Roger, *The Emperor's New Mind. Concerning Computers, Minds and the Laws of the Physics*, Oxford, Oxford University Press, 1989, note 1, p. 285.

3 FLAVIN, Dan, "...in daylight or cool white." *Artforum*, Vol. 4. No. 4. December 1965, p. 24. A French and English version of the text, edited by the author, was published in the exhibition catalogue *fluorescent light, etc. from Dan Flavin*, Ottawa, National Gallery of Canada, 1969 (September 13 – October 19),

pp. 8–22. The exhibition travelled to Vancouver, Vancouver Art Gallery, 1969 (November 12 – December 11) and New York, Jewish Museum, 1970 (January 21 – March 1). This catalogue documents extensively the aesthetic production of Dan Flavin from 1957 up until 1969, providing both visual evidence and ample detail. Since it is impossible to reproduce all the examples within the confines of the article, the indication [Ottawa, 1969, #...] in the main text refers to the illustration that goes with the catalogue number in this publication.

4 Transcription in exh.cat. *Dan Flavin. Installations in Fluorescent Light*, Edinburgh, Scottish Arts Council, 1976 (August 14 – September 12), part 1, p. 4.

5 ROSE, Barbara, "ABC Art," *Art in America*, Vol. 53, No. 5, October– November 1965, pp. 57–69.

6 Hilton Kramer in a review in *The New York Times* of Saturday, January 14, 1967 on Flavin's one-person show at Kornblee Gallery in New York (January 7 – February 2, 1967): "The notion that Mr. Flavin is an artist is one that commands assent among knowledgeable people one respects. But on the basis of the current evidence – white fluorescent tubes arranged in vertical pairs (and that's all) – he seems to me no artist at all. He's simply been given space in an art gallery." Flavin's answer characterizes his approach of criticism: "You [i.e. Kramer] must contain uniquely stupendous information to enable to recognize who is an artist and not, and therefore, what his art may be. But I do not believe this ridiculous conceit of yours. You cannot play omniscient critic to me or anyone else. You must be a damned fool to harbour such drivel." All quotations from: FLAVIN, Dan, "some other comments... more pages from a spleenish journal", in: *Artforum*, Vol. 6, No. 4, Dec, 1967, p. 23.

7 *Some Light*, New York, Kaymar Gallery, 1964 (March 4 – 29). Installation photographs in [Ottawa, 1969, fig.4, p. 124 fig. 7 p. 190 and photograph above, p. 248].

8 Sufficient biographical detail can be found in Flavin's autobiographical account, indeed written with considerable humour: FLAVIN, Dan, "...in daylight or cool white.", Op. Cit., 1965, pp. 21–24.

9 FLAVIN, Dan, "...in daylight or cool white." Op. Cit., 1965,p. 21. In the 1969 edited version of this text, he added to "inconclusive" "(and disenchanting)", Cat. *fluorescent light, etc. from Dan Flavin*, 1969, p. 12. Two years before, Flavin had specified that he had had no contact with Hoffmann himself but that he left the class, discouraged and disappointed with himself but also relieved of the terrible submission of the student role. FLAVIN, "some other comments", Op. Cit., 1967, p. 21.

10 FLAVIN, Dan. "...in daylight or cool white.", Op. Cit., 1965, p. 22.

11 Poems from James Joyce's *Chamber Music*.

12 Mainly crushed tins.

13 Examples in the cat. *fluorescent light, etc. from Dan Flavin*, 1969, Nos. 1–45.

14 Before that, from the spring of 1959 to early 1960, Flavin worked as a guard in the Museum of Modern Art. Robert Ryman was also a guard in MOMA at that time.

15 FLAVIN, Dan, "...in daylight or cool white.", Op. Cit., 1965, p. 22.

16 Plans for icons were drawn until well into 1964, like the fully-drawn icon-like constructions in an untitled drawing, dated May 30, 1964 and in the drawing *New One* of May 31, 1964 demonstrate. [Cat. Ottawa, 1969, p. 196].

17 FLAVIN, Dan, "...in daylight or cool white.", Op. Cit., 1965, p. 24.

18 Dan Flavin, from a journal entry of August 9, 1962, quoted in Barbara ROSE's "ABC Art", op. cit, p. 68, one of

the documentary pages, parallel to the text, with reproductions and quotations of the artists.

19 *New Work: Part I.* New York, Green Gallery, 1963 (January 8 – February 2). The artist's twin brother died while *Icon IV* was being finished. It was then dedicated to him. J.J. [i.e. Jill Johnston], "New Works [Green]", in *Art News*, Vol. 62, No. 1, March 1963, mentioned this work as "Dan Flavin's big box with a white acrylic surface." This *icon* was refabricated and exhibited at the *fluorescent light, etc. from Dan Flavin*, Ottawa, 1969 cf. cat. entry in [Ottawa, 1969, p. 142, # 61: ill. P. 143].

20 See: KLEIN, Adrian Bernard. *Color Light: An Art Medium. Being the Third Edition Enlarged of "Colour-Music"*, London, Technical Press, 1937.

21 Four *Estructuras* are reproduced in exh. cat. *Kosice*, Buenos Aires, Museo Nacional de Bellas artes, 1991 (April–May), p. 28. They measure approximately 70 x 50 cm. Photograph with *Estructura lumínica Madí* installed in an exhibition with other (later) luminous works of Kosice in SQUIRRU, Rafael, *Kosice*, Buenos Aires, Ed. De Arte Gaglianone, 1990, p. 32.

22 CRISPOLTI, Enrico, *Catalogue raisonné des peintures, sculptures et environments spatiaux,* in: *Lucio Fontana,* Brussels, La Connaissance, 1974, Vol.2, p. 210, No. 51 A 1. Four installation shots in: exh. cat. *Lucio Fontana*, Paris, Centre Georges Pompidou, 1987/1988 (October 13 – January 11), pp. 376 – 377.

23 Translation of the text in KHAN-MAGOMEDOV, Selim O., *Rodchenko. The Complete Work.* Ondon, Thames & Hudson, 1986, pp. 292 – 294. Quotation p. 294.

24 PASSUTH, Krisztina, *Moholy-Nagy*, London, Thames & Hudson, 1985, *Light-Space Modulator (The Light Prop)*, 1922 – 1930, cat. Nos 176 – 183.

25 FLAVIN, "some other comments", Op. Cit., 1967, p. 23.

26 Designed for Dr. Hartog's consultation room in the hospital of Maarssen, the Netherlands. Discussed in FILLER, Martin, "De meubels van Gerrit Rietveld. Manifesten voor een nieuwe revolutie", in: exh. cat. *De Stijl 1917–1931*, Amsterdam, Stedelijk Museum and Otterlo, Rijksmuseum Kröller-Müller, 1982, p. 133. Illustr. showing Hartog's cabinet with the lamp: pl. 76, pl 117; Illustr.of 3-lamp version: pl. 92, pl 131.

27 Ibidem, illustr. pl. 77, p. 117 shows the Gropius design in a photograph of the office, taken in 1923.

28 PROBST, Hartmut and Christian SCHÄDLER, *Walter Gropius. Der Architekt und Pedagoge. Werkverzeichnis Teil 2*, Berlin, Ernst & Sohn, 1987, p. 140, No. 201, colour diagram No. 1.

29 NERDINGER, Winfried, *Walter Gropius*, Berlin, Gebr. Mann Verlag, with Bauhaus Archiv, Berlin and Busch-Reisinger Museum, Cambridge, Mass., 1985, illustr. 16 d. p. 80.

30 Colours were suggested in the catalogue entry of the drawing, written by Flavin and Emily S. Rauh, in the exh.

cat. *Drawings and Diagrams 1963–1972 by Dan Flavin*, St. Louis, St. Louis Art Museum, 1973 (January 26 – March 11), No. 3, p. 10.

31 Donald Judd suggested that there was a relationship between Flavin's *diagonal* and the diagonal strips of colour in the last paintings of Morris Louis (who died in 1962). Cf. infra.

32 "...Flavin was the only artist I knew who I thought was trying to do something out of the way. It's surprising, but there wasn't much around. There were Flavin's boxes and nothing else for a couple of years...I knew him before he did the green box. I considered him the only interesting artist. JUDD, Donald and John COPLANS, "An Interview with Don Judd. "I Am Interested in Static Visual Art and Hate Imitation of Movement," in: *Artforum*, Vol.9, No.10, June 1971, p. 44. The group exhibition was *New Work: Part I*, New York, Green Gallery, 1963 (cf. supra). Other artists in the exhibition were Lucas Samaras, Yayoi Kusama, Larry Poons, George Segal and Milet Andrejevic.

33 JUDD, Donald, "Black, White and Grey", in: *Arts Magazine*, Vol. 38, No. 6, March 1964, p. 38. The article was a report on the exhibition *Black, White and Grey*, Hartford, Wadsworth Athenaeum, 1964 (January 9 – February 9). Flavin noted ironically on the idea of using new materials: "The contents of any hardware store could supply enough exhibition material to satisfy the season's needs of the most prosperous commer-

cial gallery". FLAVIN, Dan, "some remarks...excerpts from a Spleenish journal", in: *Artforum*, Vol.5, No.4, December 1966, p. 28.

34 JUDD, Donald, "Specific Objects", in: *Arts Magazine Yearbook*, 1965, republished in JUDD, Donald, *Complete Writings 1959– 1975. Gallery Reviews, Book Reviews, Articles, Letters to the Editor, Reports, Statements, Complaints*, Halifax, The Press of the Novia Scotia College of Art and Design and New York, New York University Press, 1975, pp. 181–189. The article was written almost one year before.

35 Judd himself on this essay: "People talk about it being my work, a manifesto and things like that; but really, I was earning a living as a writer, and it's a report on three-dimensional art." JUDD and COPLANS, Op. Cit., 1971, pp. 43–44.

36 JUDD, Donald, "In the Galleries", in: *Arts Magazine*, Vol. 38, No.7, April 1964, p. 31, and LIPPARD, Lucy R., "New York", in: *Artforum*, Vol.2, No.11, May 1964, p. 54.

37 The published material from letters (sent or not) to Philip Leider and Mel Bochner, substantiate the assumption that Flavin informed critics for articles that they were preparing about an exhibition. For Leider, cf. FLAVIN, Dan, "several more remarks... in Studio International", Vol.177, No.910, April 1969, p. 174. In a letter of November 1, 1966, Flavin went so far as to advise Bochner: "If I were you, I would feature it", *it* being an aphorism called Ockham's

Razor [Cat. Ottawa, 1969, pp. 204–206].
Bochner did so in the article BOCHNER,
Mel. "Serial Art Systems: Solipsism", in:
Arts Magazine, Vol.41, No.8, Summer
1967, p. 42.

38   For an excellent history of this
important gallery and its dealer, Richard
Bellamy, see: GOLDIN, Amy, *Requiem for
a Gallery*, in: *Arts Magazine*, Jan. 1966,
pp. 25–29.

39   Flavin quoted from his unpub-
lished diary in exh. cat. *Art in Process.
The Visual Development of a Structure*,
New York, Finch College Museum of Art
(Contemporary Study Wing), 1966
(May 11– June 30).

40   Also: "What can be explained by
the assumption of fewer things is vain-
ly explained by the assumption of more
things." *("Frustra fit per plura quod potest
fieri per pauciora")*. BOEHNER, Philotheus
(Ed.), *Ockham, Philosophical writings*.
Edinburgh, Nelson, 1957, pp. xx–xxi.

41   This can even be retraced in the
material condition of Flavin's proposals.
Indeed, fluorescent lights emit an
equivalence of light to incandescent
lamps consuming considerably less
electric energy.

42   MEDUNETSKII, Konstantin,
STENBERG, Wladimir and Georgij
STENBERG, *Von den Konstruktivisten an die
Welt,* Moskous, 1921, in: GABNER,
Hubertus and Eckehart GILLEN (Eds.),
*Zwischen Revolutionskunst und
Soczialistischem Realismus. Dokumente und
Kommentare. Kunstdebatten in der
Sowjetunion von 1917 bis 1934,* Cologne,
DuMont, 1979, No. D45, p. 113.

43   FLAVIN, "some remarks", Op. Cit.,
1966, p. 27

44   Idem.

45   Quotation from both letters in:
FLAVIN, "some other comments", Op.
Cit., 1967, p. 23 (to Graham) and p. 21
(to Baker).

46   Later, he expanded them to outdoor
installations.

47   i.e. without direct contact between
the architectural container (walls,
floor, bottom) and the lights or their
fixtures.

Forum International, Volume 3, Number 15, November-December 1992, pp. 71–82.
Revised by the editors, May 2004.

Outrageous in the 1960s but Seeming Serene in the 90's
Pepe Karmel

Standing in the southwest gallery of the Dan Flavin show at the Dia Center for the Arts, you get about as close to finding inner peace as is possible in New York City. Each corner of the room is occupied by a work from Mr. Flavin's series of *European Couples*: square, open frames made from four fluorescent light fixtures, each of them 8 feet long. The horizontal fixtures at the top and bottom of each frame face forward, throwing light into the room; the vertical fixtures at the sides face backward, filling the corner behind each work with color. White light floods downward from a skylight at one side of the room, mingling with the blue, green, pink and amber glows emerging from Mr. Flavin's sculptures. The colors seem to have been extracted from the sunlight, intensified rather than artificially generated by the fluorescent bulbs.

The Dia show and the concurrent exhibition of Mr. Flavin's work at the Guggenheim Museum SoHo offer many moments like this. In the face of such gorgeous serenity, it's hard to remember how raw and outrageous this work seemed back in the 1960's, when it was first exhibited. Light sculpture in itself was no novelty. But to make it from off-the-shelf fixtures available at any hardware store, that took chutzpah. Anyone, it seemed, could have bought the same fluorescent fixtures and screwed them to the wall (or to each other) in the same simple geometric arrangements.

The Dia show, drawn from the center's permanent collection, consists mostly of works done between 1964 and 1972. The Guggenheim exhibition highlights works acquired in the museum's controversial 1990 purchase of Count Giuseppe Panza di Biumo's collection of Minimalist art; these are more or less evenly divided between a chronological series of sculptures executed between 1963 and 1975 and a large group of works from 1987. Together the two shows offer a valuable oversight of Mr. Flavin's development, including several rarely seen works of historic importance.

The result is not, however, a full-fledged retrospective. The most important omission is Mr. Flavin's 1961-63 series of *icons*, square canvases and boxes with light bulbs (both incandescent and fluorescent) attached to their outer edges. These provide a crucial historical link between 1950's Neo-Dada and 1960's Minimalism. They are also a vivid reminder of Mr. Flavin's sternly Roman Catholic upbringing and the latent tension between spirit and matter throughout his oeuvre.

Mr. Flavin's 1963 breakthrough is represented at the Guggenheim by an untitled piece consisting of a single green fluorescent bulb, 8 feet long, affixed vertically to the wall. The long round tube seems like a compressed version of the cast-iron column that rises from the floor nearby. Its soft, unearthly glow highlights the specific character of fluorescent light, quite different from the acid brilliance of neon or the insistent sharpness of incandescent bulbs. Behind the bulb, the white enameled box of the fixture gleams like an upended marble altar.

Obviously, there were a limited number of things you could do with a single fluorescent fixture, and Mr. Flavin quickly began to explore different combinations. *The nominal three (to William of Ockham)*, also from 1963, consists of a series of white vertical bulbs, 6 feet high, arranged in evenly spaced groups of one, two and three fixtures. When at the Guggenheim's uptown building, the three groups seemed to float on the back wall of an alcove, at a distance from both floor and side walls. At the Guggenheim SoHo, they have been installed so they rise directly from the floor, with the first and last groups placed in the corners between back and side walls. The effect is powerful and oppressive, as if the lights were dragging the walls downward and inward.

The nominal three anticipates several themes in Mr. Flavin's subsequent work. It simple mathematical sequence is echoed by the more complex combinations of the *'monument' for V. Tatlin* series dedicated to the

Russian Constructivist whose work inspired many Minimalists. Four examples from this series, created between 1964 and 1968, occupy the central corridor of the Dia exhibition.

In each piece, white bulbs of differing lengths are grouped in symmetrical or inverted patterns around a central axis, as if Mr. Flavin were systematically exploring the mathematical permutations of a fixed set of elements. Similar permutations appear in the contemporary compositions of Philip Glass, with a similarly strange and beautiful effect, as if you were listening to the music of the spheres: perfectly harmonious and yet indifferent to terrestrial ideas of order.

The nominal three also anticipates Mr. Flavin's later interest in combining his light fixtures into extended fencelike "barriers" crossing and dividing the gallery space. The Guggenheim exhibition includes several important examples of this genre. One of these, *greens crossing greens (to Piet Mondrian who lacked green)*, has not been seen since its original installation in the 1966 *Art Light Art* show at the Stedelijk van Abbe Museum in the Netherlands. Determining the exact dimensions and materials of the 1966 installation apparently required a lot of work. Indeed, the reconstruction was not finished in time for the exhibition's opening.

Many of the Minimalists experimented with similar gallery-filling environments. But in Mr. Flavin's case, the goal of intensifying the viewer's awareness of the physical gallery space is subverted by his work' tendency to dematerialize its surroundings by folding them into its envelope of light. Works like the *European Couples* at Dia may have been intended to stress the physical reality of the corners they occupy. But their actual effect is to transform the occluded space into a mystical, otherworldly realm. Their real antecedent, it might be argued, is Bernini's St. Theresa altarpiece, with its flood of golden light amid the darkness, at Santa Maria della Vittoria in Rome.

The creation of an immaterial space is particularly evident in a series of variants on the *European Couples* format in which the space behind the frame lighted with a different color from that of the forward-facing bulbs. Two 1987 versions of this forward/backward frame (each with four uprights and four horizontals) are on view at the Guggenheim. Unfortunately, the remaining 1987 pieces from the Panza Collection are distinctly weaker than these. Too often, Mr. Flavin settles on a format and runs through a predictable series of color variations.

The curator for both exhibitions was Michael Govan, former deputy director of the Guggenheim Museum and current director of Dia. Mr. Govan was also the point man for the Guggenheim's purchase of the Panza Collection, and the Guggenheim exhibition (or at least the first half of it) does much to vindicate the wisdom of that purchase. The impact of Mr. Flavin's work depends to an unusually large extent on its setting, and Mr. Govan's spare, thoughtful installation presents it to maximum advantage, especially in Dia's exquisitely simple spaces.

The New York Times, September 22, 1995, p. C30.

Dan Flavin
James Meyer

The recent exhibitions at the Guggenheim SoHo and Dia together comprised a good overview of Dan Flavin's activity from the early '60s to the late '80s. While Dia's presentation of its Flavin holdings included several remarkable works – numerous versions of his *"monuments" for V. Tatlin*; 1964–68, two rooms of corner works in different hues; and the all-red *monument 4 to those who have been killed in ambush (to P.K. who reminded me about death)*, 1966, that once dominated the back room of Max's Kansas City where Robert Smithson and Andy Warhol held court – the Guggenheim installation, culled from the vast collection of the artist's work purchased some years ago from Count Panza di Buomo, was the best New York show of Flavin in years.

This comes as something of a surprise. Until now, the Guggenheim's exhibits of its Panza holdings, and of Minimal-type work in general, have been disappointing. The 1992 show that inaugurated the museum's SoHo space paired Carl Andres with Vasily Kandinskys, and Constantin Brancusis with Robert Rymans, installations which made little sense. The contemporaneous exhibition of Flavin's work that was installed in the newly renovated uptown Guggenheim was not terribly successful either: during the day, the fluorescent tubes, placed against the walls along the ramp, or suspended from the ceiling in a central shaft of pink, were overwhelmed by the atrium's glaring whiteness. In the downtown Guggenheim show this fall, however, no exposed windows interfered with one's viewing and each piece was allotted sufficient space. The more room a Flavin has and the more controlled the vagaries of its setting, the more luminous the effect – the more *Flavin*. The Guggenheim curators understood this. To move from one dazzling installation to the next was to be truly enveloped in volumes of color.

The potential of Flavin's work to drown the viewer in a febrile fluorescence has been a subject of some controversy. The greatest advocate of this mode of display is, in fact, Panza himself, whose installations of these works at his villa outside Milan were designed to emphasize this quality. (When I last visited there, the Max's Kansas City piece illuminated a shiny white cell with the intensity of a spaceship out of a Spielberg flick.) On the other hand, Rosalind Krauss has argued that the theatrical conditions of viewing introduced by Flavin and other "Minimalists," and exaggerated by Panza's showy displays, paradoxically only serve to enhance the auratic appeal of this sculpture rather than to point to its objecthood. Commenting in the pages of *October* on the Guggenheim's purchase of the Panza collection, Krauss lamented that it was precisely Panza's favored method of display that had seduced the museum's ambitious director, Thomas Krens, into leveraging the museum's collection to finance the acquisition of Minimalist work. Even worse, this new model of perception demanded the kind of installation space exemplified by Krens' own abandoned MASS MoCA and the international circuit of Guggenheim franchises – in short, a late-capitalist, multinational museum/corporation that could mimic the contemporary viewing experience of flashing signs and television screens, otherwise known as the Spectacle. From Krauss' perspective, the luminosity of Flavin's lights ultimately betrays the materialist impulse of his works: the classic Minimalist equation of literal surface and epistemological and social refusal ("What you see is what you see," as Frank Stella put it). Once the Flavin lamp surrounded the viewer in its glow, rendering him or her numb with optical sensation, once it ceased to declare its material self-evidence and became, of all things, a pleasurable experience, it could no longer be considered a critical work. Indeed, thanks to Flavin (Panza's and Krens' Flavin) and other '60s artists, the post-Modern museum could compete with Shinjuku's neon billboards and MTV.

This is a compelling argument – certainly the most convincing of the various materialist critiques Minimal work has elicited in recent years. For unlike most of these accounts, which too easily align this sculpture with structures of domination, Krauss' essay acknowledges the dialectical character of this venture. The use of a pregiven industrial unit or ready-made as a basic vocabulary for formal innovation during the '60s alluded to, from a position of both complicity and criticality, the system of production and consumption from which it was extracted. Moreover Flavin's lamp, a material thing (a fact highlighted by the presence, in many works, of the electric cord and supporting pan) is a luminous thing too: the fluorescent tube gives off a light that exceeds the thing itself, even if it does not entirely dissolve it. Finally, the Guggenheim show demonstrated the profoundly installational nature of Flavin's project: the discovery of fluorescent light was simultaneously the discovery of the gallery itself. At the entrance, a simple green vertical tube, one of his earliest works, declared its material specificity while exposing the wall and the room before it. Further installations – the famous *nominal three (to William of Ockham)*, 1963, or *an artificial barrier of blue, red and blue fluorescent (to Flavin Starbuck Judd)*, 1968 – showed how the expansion of Flavin's system during the '60s from the single lamp to vast, serially organized works would definitively reveal whole rooms. And while one implication of this gesture was the spectacular display perfected by Panza (by which, I must confess, I find myself seduced) another was the exposure of the gallery as ideological and material construct that could lead to institutional critique – the side of Flavin that could admire Tatlin. It is hard to imagine Daniel Buren, Michael Asher, or Mel Bochner exposing the museum wall without this precedent.

Artforum, Volume 34, Number 5, December 1995, p. 86.

Pink, Yellow, Blue, Green and Other Colors in the Work of Dan Flavin
Marianne Stockebrand

Between 1966 and 1971, Dan Flavin created a series of nine works in fluorescent light, each dedicated to a European couple. Eight of these nine works from the Dia Center for the Arts' permanent collection were exhibited in New York from winter of 1995 to summer 1996.

With the exception of ultraviolet, which Flavin has rarely used in his work, all the commercially available colors of fluorescent light have been included in the *European Couples*: daylight, cool white, warm white, yellow, pink, blue, green, red and soft white. Except for soft white, all of these colors were represented at Dia.

This is the palette of an enormous body of work, and Flavin's use of these ten colors has remained unaltered since 1963. But the formal restrictions of the work are even greater, as these colors are only available in lengths of two, four, six and eight feet. In retrospect, it seems almost unbelievable that an oeuvre of such visual richness and diversity is based on so few parts, yet Dan Flavin's entire work consists of a total of forty components. A great variety has been achieved with these components, ranging from small single pieces to large installations for entire rooms. From 1963 until today some 500 works have been realized.

When Flavin began the *European Couples* in 1966, he had been working with fluorescent light for three years. Astonishingly enough, within that time he had already developed innovative and fundamental ways of using this new material. He had executed a number of single pieces, placed on both the wall and the floor, and had made a significant step toward creating his art in direct reference to its surrounding architecture. The first public introduction of this new material was at the Green Gallery in November/December of 1964. This exhibition consisted of several basic configurations, with diagonal, horizontal and vertical arrangements of one or more tubes, in one or more colors, placed on the floor or on a wall. With this initial exhibition, Dan Flavin began to explore the aesthetic potential of illuminated lines of color as a medium for his art.

There were two major developments after the Green Gallery show, in 1965 and 1966. First, reaching out into a space, primarily by constructing barriers; and second, the idea of broadening the illuminated area by projecting light in more than one direction. A combination of these two ideas, the positioning of light in opposing directions and the incorporation of space by cornering the work, is evident in the *European Couples* series.

A drawing dated 1966 shows what is probably the first instance of mounting fixtures with their tubes back to back, so that their light shines in opposite directions. One tube is placed with the light outward, across a corner and close to the floor. A second, shorter tube is fixed vertically in the middle of the first, facing the corner. There are no remarks regarding color. A piece based on this drawing was shown at the Kornblee Gallery in February of 1966. From the same year dates a more fully developed version, *monument on the survival of Mrs. Reppin*, which was exhibited in the recent retrospective at the Guggenheim Museum in SoHo. The horizontal tube is now lifted from floor to eye level, supported by two additional tubes which run against the wall and meet in the corner. The shorter vertical tube remains attached in the middle, as in the previous drawing. This new configuration increases the illuminated area substantially, as the left tube shines to the right, the right shines left, the horizontal span pours into the room and the vertical shines into the corner. The colors are warm white for the horizontals and a vertical red.

Using the corner as a reflection plane was further developed in a series I will refer to as "near-square corner installations". In December of 1966 at the Nicholas Wilder Gallery in Los Angeles, Flavin showed a frame-like piece consisting of four cool white tubes, each eight feet long. It was placed rather traditionally, with equal spacing from floor to ceiling. Flavin's positioning of the tubes is intriguing: the top light shines upward, while at bottom the light projects into the room. The two sides are fastened at their backs flat to the wall. One can clearly understand Flavin's intention to create an area of light as "full" as possible by directing the tubes in different directions; however, in this piece he has not made optimum use of the walls that form the corner. The piece lacks both the clarity and the natural simplicity which he will achieve a little later in more fully developed works from this group.

The next near-square corner installations were signed under the name of Wheeling Peachblow, a reference to pastel colored American glass from the 19th century. A drawing dated 1968 shows the square with a middle division. It is noted: "farthest corner" and "gold gold" (which is the former name for yellow) and "possible pink or green." In a further development, the central post was omitted, as it obscured the corner, and two single, vertical strips were placed at the outside.

Following this, a work was built with pink vertical tubes facing the corner and yellow horizontals projecting out. The vertical tubes were now attached back to back with the horizontals, thus directing more light into the corner. This provided a greater luminosity upon the walls. The piece was now freestanding, instead of hanging on the wall like a painting.

The near-square frame shape provided options for variations of shape and color. Naturally, it must have interested the artist to tint the two walls flanking the corner in different colors, as in the piece *to Donna* from 1972. The drawing gives an idea of how Flavin evaluates the placement of dark and light colors. In a work of 1975, *To Ellen, aware, my surprise*, the two horizontal tubes facing us are pink, the two vertical ones on the left are blue and the four on the right, green. Flavin increased the green, which by nature is the most intense color of all, thus making green occupy a large area of the corner, dominating the blue.

These few examples demonstrate the range of variations for near square corner installations and provide a context for the *European Couples'* series, which is monochromatic. They are the less complicated, the simpler and clearer versions, which provide the opportunity to compare color and observe certain characteristics.

The first room in the Dia exhibition contained pieces in blue, green, yellow and pink. The second room held work in red, warm white, cool white and daylight. Red is an intense color but its reach is short. Conversely, both green and pink project greater distances, blue somewhat less. Yellow radiates even less, but its tubes keep their intense color while green, pink and blue appear pale. The value of these four colors is comparatively similar, while red and the various whites differ remarkably. For this reason white is rarely combined with another color in Flavin's work, it usually remains alone or in combination with another white.

With the remaining four colors – pink, yellow, blue and green – Flavin has developed a most subtle coloration. It is interesting to note that these four colors are often combined in one work and that has been the case from 1964 until today.

The Guggenheim exhibition offered an example of an early work from 1964 dedicated *to Henri Matisse*. It consisted of four tubes placed contiguously, each measuring eight feet. The sequence of colors from left to right is pink, yellow, blue, green. Pink and green on the outer sides, yellow and blue inside. Yellow is next to pink; blue next to green. This exact sequence is repeated in many other works, both in smaller ones as the one dedicated to the Real Dan Hill, also shown at Dia, and in large site-specific installations such as the one realized in the Kunstbau in Munich, an addition to the municipal museum, which was inaugurated in 1994 with a work by Dan Flavin. The work is situated in a long, narrow space – a remainder from the nearby subway station. It is without daylight. Flavin's amazingly simple intervention was to replace the four rows of regular white fluorescent tubes on the ceiling with "his" colors of pink, yellow, blue and green. The effect is breathtaking: the entire space is tinted, including the walls, the ramp, the columns, a circular built-in room and the floor, which also reflects the stripes from the ceiling.

The vast emptiness of the space allows for greater perception of the power of fluorescent light. It is remarkable how far pink reaches: dyeing the length of one wall, it also fills the space up to the row of columns that bisects the space. Yellow appears to have little impact, but it is reflected on the glossy floor. On the opposite side of the columns we enter the blue/green zone and it's interesting to see the difference in function of these colors in relation to the pink and yellow. Closest to the wall is green, reflecting upon the wall and into the space. Yet the blue, placed further from the wall, supersedes its neighboring color and takes possession of the lower section. Green remains in the upper area. From a distance, the stripes of green, pink, green and blue create something new, for which I am lacking a word. It reminds me of painting, of course, but at the same time it is very far away from that.

The four colors pink, yellow, blue and green occur repeatedly in Flavin's work, especially when the intent of the installation is to expand color to a large volume, to have color occupy large areas of wall space. Of these colors, pink has two specific characteristics, which, taken together, separate it from the other three. Like green, pink has the ability to project a great distance. Unlike green, it also has little impact on the human eye. After looking at pink for a while, the eye remains clear and is able to adjust easily to other colors.

Dan Flavin introduced a new aspect to visual art: the pouring, or flooding of color into space. By diffusing in all directions, the light creates a volume of color. Within this volume, however, color becomes visible only when it touches a reflecting plane, such as a wall, a floor, the ceiling, furniture or people. One cannot see the color flowing within a space, as it is not materialized. It is light, colorful light.

There is little which can be compared or even related to this extremely fascinating phenomenon. Perhaps the most obvious comparisons are with stained glass windows in cathedrals, where color awakens when hit by daylight or with the colorful, natural event of a sunset. Here as there is endlessness. Color without boundaries, which Dan Flavin has made his tool in the creation of art.

Flavin's use of color is so new that we are only now beginning to understand its nature. By introducing fluorescent light to art, he also introduced a new type of color to art. It is his innovation. Color and light become one thing in Flavin's work which is the reason for its newness; however, the ground for this new work was paved by a previous generation of artists. Only through their achievements could this new invention be possible.

Jackson Pollock's use of paint was no less new, revolutionary, or free. Allowing paint to drip directly onto the canvas without brushing it, liberated the entire process of producing a painting; and at the same time he freed painting from being a picture, making the subject matter a different thing from what it had been before. Or, to quote Flavin: "I learned eventually to ignore the grisly pictorial distortions of women of Mr. de Kooning for the wildly intense, far better humored drip, dribble, splash, dash painted systematics of Mr. Pollock at his apparently self-assured uttermost. I sensed that they pretended toward infinity, to painting anywhere, ultimately nowhere."

However, I believe the work of two other artists has had a greater impact on Flavin than Pollock: Mark Rothko and Barnett Newman. From early on, Flavin had admired Newman's work and they were friends for many years, seeing each other on a regular basis and being familiar with each other's work and ideas. In 1969 Newman made a special effort to travel to Ottawa and give the opening remarks at Flavin's important exhibition in the National Gallery of Canada. Flavin was naturally wary, at first, of the similarity of Newman's zips to his own stripes, as this does seem to be the most obvious connection between them. In an interview with Flavin, Michael Venezia asked the artist why he positioned the tube diagonally in his very first piece and Flavin answered: so as not to be confused with Barnett Newman. But Newman's groundbreaking achievement, which has to be seen as fundamental for a younger generation of artists, was his emphasis on the physical presence of color. Newman increased both the scale of painting and the quantity of color by the late 40's; as his paintings sought to envelop the spectator as color reached an new expansiveness combined with a directness previously unknown. Even today, when walking through the Museum of Modern Art, Newman's *Vir Heroicus Sublimis* is the one painting whose presence as color is not surpassed by any other painting exhibited. The other important impact of Newman's paintings is their emphasis on one color: at times a single hue covers almost the entire surface. The value which Newman attributed to plain color must have left an indelible impression on other artists with similar concerns. But while Newman had worked within the realm of painting, younger artists like Flavin and Judd turned away from painting toward work which allowed color to expand in three dimensions.

For Flavin, Barnett Newman may have been more influential, yet there are striking similarities with Mark Rothko's work. Fluorescent light creates a soft-bordered area of color, and the diffused colors call to mind the work of Rothko. As I approached a corridor in the Guggenheim show which reflected a large green, a yellow, and a blue installation, I felt I was facing a three dimensional version of a painting by this great artist. Both Newman's and Rothko's paintings attempt to invade other areas beyond their flat surface, and Rothko's murals in particular immerse the viewer in color, as do many of Newman's super-sized paintings. It took another generation and another medium to factually carry color away from the flat surface, into space.

When Dan Flavin installed what he called *the diagonal of personal ecstasy* in May of 1963, he realized the potential of this "buoyant and insistent gaseous image" regarding colored articulations of an entire room. A drawing from 1963 shows that from the beginning he was involved in "the complete fluorescent system" including the wall, floor and ceiling in his work and he became aware that he could, "play on the structure that bounded a room but not yet so involved in the volume of space which is so much more extensive than the room's box. He added: "I knew that the actual space of a room could be disrupted and played with by careful, thorough composition of the illuminating equipment." If a single strip of light had the capacity to generate enough color to dip the surrounding area, how much more interesting must it be to deal with architecture on a larger scale?

For a show at the Kornblee Gallery in 1966, Flavin proposed a work to occupy the entire room. Two bars of green fluorescent light were to run diagonally, crossing each other within the space. Their construction was based on the post-lintel structure. The higher bar was to be built from eight foot long tubes, the shorter one from four feet tubes. Their placement was designed in direct response to the existing architectural data: the higher bar starts in one corner and runs across the room to the window frame while the lower one runs in the opposite direction, starting at one door frame and ending at another.

As the installation was never realized at Kornblee, we have only a drawing and the artist's instructions. Incidentally, I consider the drawing reminiscent of Malevich and Lissitzsky's drawings, and it's coincidental that Flavin's green barrier is the first work of art incorporating an entire space — outside of painting — since Lissitzsky created the Proun Room in 1923. Referring to the Russians, Flavin explained in 1965: "Thus far, I have made a considered attempt to poise silent electric light in crucial concert point by point, line by line and otherwise in the box that is a room. This dramatic decoration has been founded in the young tradition of a plastic revolution which gripped Russian art only forty years ago. My joy is to try to build from that 'incomplete' experience as I see fit." I believe that the results of what he modestly describes as "trying" are Flavin's greatest achievements. The gallery space is structured asymmetrically, dividing the room into unequal areas. Interestingly, attention is given to visitor interaction at the bottom of the sketch where Flavin notes: "a fluorescent room for the Kornblee Gallery, which will inhibit and permit movement of an adult." By creating a slightly precarious situation, Flavin introduced a psychological nuance to the work, an aspect which would later become crucial to Bruce Nauman's work.

The gallery's entrance is marked at the bottom of the drawing; visitors would enter here and have no other choice than to walk to the right, as the left side would be blocked by the lower bar. To the right, however, they would be able to pass underneath the tall bar and enter a small triangular area, but would then be stopped from walking further by the low bar. Although they could see into it, they could not enter the rest of the room. We can only guess what the perception might have been like; however the juxtaposition or retention in a narrow area with a view of a wider one reminds me of Caspar David Friedrich's painting *Mönch am Meer* with the figure looking out onto the sea in front of him and thus eternity. Although I am well aware of the exaggeration, there is clearly an disequilibrium and tension between the tighter back area and the wider front, where the green light could perform uninterrupted.

Although not for the Kornblee Gallery, the barrier was realized later in the same year for the exhibition *Kunst Licht Kunst* (Art Light Art) which took place in the Van Abbemuseum in Eindhoven, The Netherlands. It was the first long barrier ever constructed by Flavin. Its complete title is *greens crossing greens (to Piet Mondrian who lacked green)* and thus seems perfectly suited to be first shown in the native land of this great 20th century artist, much admired by Flavin. It was again reconstructed for the Guggenheim exhibition where unfortunately the booth-like situation could not provide the original sensation of enclosure.

In his next show at Kornblee the following year, Flavin created another holistic installation, again exclusively with green light. Diagonals were attached to every wall, surrounding the room in a sort of frieze. Each diagonal consisted of two parallel lines — the left composed of two 4-foot tubes and the right of four 2-foot tubes. Their positioning was again determined by the given architecture: with each unit leaning away from the entrance door and each upper end touching a corner, a door frame or molding. The angles of each unit were equal, and were determined by the greatest possible angle on the narrowest section of wall.

In his first two architectural installations, the artist followed two rather different concepts: previously, the green barriers occupied the space; later, the diagonals left the space empty. In sketching the barriers, Flavin viewed the gallery as a picture plane, a frame within which to create the work. The lines formed by the tubes invade the room through repetition, the adding of one element to another, thus going beyond strict two-dimensionality. However, the barriers do not create volume, but rather occupy the space.

The diagonals work differently: by remaining on the walls in an empty space, they are two-dimensional lines. But their placement on these walls lends a coherence to the room, tying together the various elements.

These two different concepts highlighted the relationship between art and architecture, and proved to be fundamental to all future installations using whole rooms. A basic principle in Flavin's art is that, no matter what the single works and installations are like, they are always composed of lines. Lines may occupy, clarify, determine, decorate or obstruct a space – but they do not constitute a mass, they don't create a volume. If one had to place Flavin's work in a traditional category of art, it would be drawing, certainly not sculpture. In fact, Flavin has commented in the past on the wrongness of this word when applied to his work.

Naturally, three-dimensionality exists in his works, but I would prefer to call it an extended two-dimensionality. It evolves by adding units in a linear way, as in the barrier of untitled (to Flavin Starbuck Judd) from 1968 or the counterposition of tubes in *monument on the survival of Mrs. Reppin,* — but that is as three-dimensional as Flavin's objects get. The volume of the work is created not by the tubes or the fixtures themselves, but by colored light, expanding in every direction and creating an essentially limitless aura, fading into invisibility.

The green fluorescent room at the Kornblee Gallery stands at the beginning of Flavin's exploration into what he calls "retinal optics." This refers to fluorescent light's impact on the eye. A description of this impact in the Kornblee installation, from Flavin's Ottawa exhibition catalogue, reads: "The phenomenal effect of this exposition was discovered after a few moments in the gallery. Although the room was pervaded by green light, the light providing tubes appeared to be empty of almost all color. When the viewer then looked toward the daylight source outside the gallery, he saw only complementary rose, until his eyes readjusted."

Since the Kornblee installation, Flavin continued to explore the use of this visual "event" in various exhibitions. This event is made up of both the retinal effect on the viewer, and the specific architecture of the space. From the number of outstanding exhibitions over the past two and one half decades, I would like to concentrate on the one realized in Ottawa at the National Gallery of Canada in 1969, because of the striking quality of its installation and the audacity of both the artist and the curator. In addition to one hundred and fourteen items exhibited retrospectively, the exhibition included seven new installations, most of which were site-specific.

Three sets of tangented arcs in daylight and cool white (to Jenny and Ira Licht) occupied a rectangular room with two doors located in the middle of the two smaller walls. The long walls and the floor were covered by three pairs of arcs, their curves determined by the planar dimensions on which they were placed. The catalogue comments: "Although the overall linear ordering of this room with fluorescent lamps could be immediately comprehended by the participant when he stepped into either of the two opposing bays, the system was slightly confounding to him optically, for each arc in a tangentially paired set was lighted in an opposite colour of white. The optical complication became doubly confusing if the participant viewed this installation a second time from the other bay, for he then saw the reverse of his previous colour experience." Subtle refinement characterizes this installation, with its delicate variations in white. It was the only time Flavin used curves in his work.

Another room in Ottawa consisted of *alternating pink and yellow (to Josef Halmy)*. Beginning at the edge of each of the walls in the room, Flavin placed at the walls' alternating pink and yellow lamps, covering the perimeter of the room. From these two colors, orange emerged, flooding the room entirely from floor to ceiling.

This orange room was situated between two others, which, when combined, formed a dramatic layout: in the room preceding *Alternating Pink and Yellow* was a work of white fluorescent light, from which could be perceived a pale orange from the merging colors in the next room. In the following room, accessible only through the orange room, the viewer was confronted with a large green barrier piece. Upon exiting the green room, the character of *alternating pink and yellow* changed: it now appeared as a deep red rose volume, at least until the eyes re-adjusted.

The design of a glowing line along a room's periphery, which I consider one of Flavin's finest ideas because of its simplicity and integral unimposing quality, dates back to yet another proposed installation for the Kornblee Gallery in 1967. A drawing from that year indicates positioning double rows of green fluorescent lights horizontally, just above the baseboard of the room. Flavin eventually dismissed this idea for the Kornblee, but a variation was executed in 1968 in Kassel for Documenta IV. Here, the room was illuminated by ultraviolet lamps running along the floor and the four corners.

A third room in Ottawa was triangular, with walls of different lengths. The installation experimented with the idea of triangularity by the placement of diagonals spanning the entire length of the walls, thus dividing each plane into two, equal triangles. The installation was asymmetric, yet energetic. The ascending lines made the room seem light, and although there were triangles everywhere, their appearance was hardly noticeable. The dynamic shape of the room was matched by a dynamic, linear decor, providing a wholly different spatial sensation: unacademic and cheerful, simple and complex, clear and enigmatic, all at once.

Dan Flavin was 36 at the time of the National Gallery exhibition in Ottawa in the fall of 1969. But the show represented, as Barnett Newman said in his opening speech, "the intensity and mature devotion of a lifetime, even though it's a young lifetime." In this exhibition Flavin proved his great understanding of the properties of colored light of fluorescent tubes, and his ability to modulate it in subtle, as well as conspicuous ways. He not only introduced a new medium into art, but by incorporating the area surrounding the object he also invented a way to use it beyond its actual shape as an object. Flavin freed color from the flat surface, even from its generating source: the lamp. This fluorescent color cannot exist independent of its source, but it can radiate out from it. The ability to create large areas of color without actual application was a fascinating idea and led to the conclusion that "the entire interior spatial container and its components – wall, floor and ceiling, could support a strip of light but would not restrict its act of light except to enfold it." Flavin could now color an entire space and thereby change its appearance. At the same time, the configuration of the illuminated lines retained its clarity, remaining distinct from the surrounding color fields.

Flavin's approach to space was immediate and thorough. His approach towards color in space happened on a larger scale than ever before, as something not just added to the space, but integral to it. Color in his work is less material than a phenomenon, or to quote Don Judd: "color is an immediate sensation."

I have always been captivated by Dan Flavin's work and its colors, and it's hard for me to imagine that others might not share my enthusiasm. The generosity, brightness and intensity of color which bathe the eyes have a constant appeal and are seductive as ever. I was therefore puzzled when I visited the Guggenheim exhibition with a friend, who, after a while, expressed his doubts as to whether the colors used by Flavin were "spiritual" and then asked my opinion.

The question was so unexpected that I didn't know what to say. I believe I nodded, indicating that I certainly thought so, but then realized I had never thought about it. It was not clear to me how my friend could consider Barnett Newman's colors as being spiritual, but not Dan Flavin's. I suspected the reason was the wide use of fluorescent light in commercial and industrial contexts, thereby giving it a vulgar, unrefined, one-dimensional quality, while art was somehow different. I felt trapped: on one hand I require art to be new, on the other hand there was this more utilitarian use of the material. Could material content be good or bad, right or wrong? No. Bronze has been used for both sculpture and weapons; wood for altar pieces and barrels; therefore fluorescent light should not be an unsuitable medium for art.

I began to look at painting again, in the hope of finding whether my friend's judgement bore any truth. I was seeing anew. I looked at Perugino, Rogier van der Weyden, Dürer, Andrea del Sarto, ignoring the symbolic meaning of color I had learned in school, only looking at color as color.

Andrea del Sarto's *Archangel Raphael and Tobias* is composed mainly of two complementary colors, red and green, which are no less bright, audacious or concentrated as a red and green fluorescent work by Dan Flavin.

Other art works are even more striking, for instance Matthias Grünewald's *Isenheimer Altar*, painted in 1512 to 1515. The color configuration of the entire altarpiece is startlingly radical, especially the two panels of *The Annunciation* and *The Resurrection*. In *The Annunciation*, the

Archangel Gabriel is draped in a warm golden-yellow and bluish-red garment to which, on the left side of the panel, a yellowish-red curtain and a yellow window reflection correspond. From foreground to background there are marked gradations of green, filling the entire chapel, coloring the walls and vault.

The Resurrection is even more surreal. A huge aureole dominates the panel with a radiant light yellow at center, darkening outward to deep yellow, orange and red, surrounded by a blue-green circle. Light pours over Christ, whose head appears to be light itself, coloring the robe yellow at top and shading to red below. The light also illuminates both the foreground containing the grave and two soldiers, and the background's large rock and two figures. Yellow-orange dominates and illuminates the three main areas of the painting: the foreground grave, the background rock and the light circle at top. The formal, as well as spiritual link between these three areas is the long drapery which falls from Christ's shoulders and reaches to the grave. It repeats the blue-green and is transformed from darkness in the top to a very light color at bottom.

Grünewald's colors are a bit mysterious and certainly unusual, even if one considers the time in which he painted. Yet the colors are also modern, and could occur in a Versace dress, or in an ice cream parlor. Art history shows that color is often used within given spiritual or liturgical contexts, but it also shows that it may be independent of such themes.

I refer to one last example, The Deposition by Jacopo Pontormo, painted between 1526 and 1528, for the Santa Felicità church in Florence. It is a symphony in light blue, pink, beige-brown and red. Light blue and pink prevail. In terms of color and light, this painting is closer than any other known to me in evoking the work of Dan Flavin. The dynamic movement of the figures fully dramatizes Christ's deposition – and the emotion expressed in the figures' faces is reflected in the posture of their bodies – but it is the efflorescence of luminous, unearthly color that heightens the effect.

In answering historian Benedetto Varchi's question on the predominance of art over nature, Pontormo stresses that the elements of a painting are to be subordinate to the artistic purpose. About the artist, Pontormo said:

> He is overbold, indeed, wishing to imitate with pigments all the things produced by nature, so that they will look real and even to improve them so that his pictures may be rich and full of varied details. He will paint, for instance, wherever they fit his purpose, glares, nights with fires or other lights, the air, clouds, landscapes with towns in the distance or close by, buildings with many varied systems of perspective [...] and a multitude of other things. Sometimes a scene painted by him will include things that nature never produced. Furthermore, as I said above, he will improve the things he depicts and with his art he will give them grace, arrange them and group them where they will look best. [...] But what I said above about the painter being overbold is proved by the presumption to surpass nature in trying to infuse spirit into a figure and make it look alive while painting it on a flat surface. (Pontormo, 1547).

Four hundred years later, Dan Flavin doesn't try to compete with nature; rather, he fully concentrates on what Pontormo alluded to: the manipulation of the artist's materials in order to achieve his intentions.

Dan Flavin has enriched art with a new type of color and thus a new sensation. His colors in the form of fluorescent light have a degree of richness previously unknown in art. His work is thoroughly modern, particularly in its use of a standard, prefabricated material, easily handled and available in any hardware store. Although much has been said about this so-called "Duchampian" aspect of Flavin's work, it doesn't lead to any further understanding of it. His use of a standard manufactured product is very different from Duchamp's "Readymades":

Flavin buys tubes of fluorescent light just as some other artists buy tubes of oil paint; and, like a painter, he transforms his materials and creates something which didn't exist before. On the other hand, little has been said regarding the truly modern, democratic aspect of his work. No craftsmanship is required, no expertise, no special knowledge. Anybody can build the work. One can go to the store, select some tubes, return home and produce a Flavin. This may not be a pleasant idea to art dealers or the artist but it is certainly an inherent aspect in Dan Flavin's work.

Finally, Flavin's work involves a simplicity of form and economy of material, reductive in means and reasonable in cost, composed with a very direct, factual clarity. It is simple, but at the same time includes a complexity of space, relating to its site modestly and unimposingly, visually present but physically unpossessing. It is seductive, refined and delicate; and although its components are factual, their effects are enigmatic, and transcend any language which might attempt to describe it.

[This lecture was given at the Dia Center for the Arts in February of 1996 on the occasion of Dan Flavin's exhibition *European Couples, and Others*. It is published here in an edited version and dedicated to Franz Meyer for making me work harder]

The Chinati Foundation Newsletters, Volume 2, www.chinati.org.

In Another Light
Richard Kalina

Dan Flavin was the subject this season of three major exhibitions in New York, and, with that kind of high-profile exposure, it really should have been Flavin's year. Yet it didn't seem to be. Flavin is, unfortunately, taken a bit for granted. His work is familiar both historically (as a still-unfolding instance of classic Minimalism) and materially (fluorescent bulbs remain irreducibly what they are). But this familiarity is misleading, for familiarity implies a certain stasis, and Flavin's art has evolved – both the work itself and our perception of it. Its forms, means and associations seem to grow richer and more complex as time passes. New meanings accrue, the frame of reference widens.

Of the recent exhibitions, two were museum shows of older work. The Guggenheim Museum SoHo showed 26 pieces dating from 1963 to 1987, while the Dia Center for the Arts exhibited 15 works from 1964 to 1978 in a show titled *European Couples, and Others*. (Dia has also installed in its stairwell the first of a matched pair of permanent site-specific works – a line of blue and green tubes four stories high, visible from the street day and night. An identical piece will be installed on the stairwell's other side.) The third exhibition was a gallery show at PaceWildenstein in SoHo – a carefully modulated series of 12 horizontal wall pieces in colored fluorescents.

What struck me most forcibly after seeing all three shows was the clarity of the work, the inherent logic, order and legibility, all riding in tandem with the most visceral and emotional of effects. Flavin's art seems to comprise four lines of understanding and intention, operating separately but simultaneously. I see these as: appropriation from the outside world, structure, color and architecture.

This multiplicity provides many entrances into the work. It increases accessibility, but it also sets up ambiguous metaphorical situations, readings operating at evocative cross-purposes to each other. The four dominant lines mentioned above all deal in some way with problems of perception, naming and reference – the kind of applied epistemology that Flavin is most comfortable with. But there is another aspect to his investigations, consistently denied by him but hard to ignore – that of the spiritual or transcendent. As time goes by, these more metaphysical associations continue to hover over Flavin's work, giving another dimension to the overtly factual. Are the similarities to Newman's zips or Rothko's floods of suffused color purely incidental? Is the cathedral-like feeling of an installation of the cool white "monuments" for Vladimir Tatlin just intelligently ironic? And what about the sense of blood and mystery in *monument 4 those who have been killed in ambush (to P.K. who reminded me about death)*, a deep-red corner piece looming out at us from the darkness of the Dia installation? The very nature of Flavin's artistic approach ensures he *can* have it both ways. The interpretive arena is wide open, and moreover it is the artist himself who has cleared the field, so to speak, by making art that, while full of ambiguity, has no built-in doubt. The work is always in focus: you can see it clearly at whatever level of attention you want to give it.

By the nature of its materials, Flavin's art invites a reconsideration of the neo-Duchampian readymade, the object that has been plucked from the world and installed in the context of the art gallery. Lately, readymades or their near relatives have been enjoying something of a vogue. On a recent short walk in SoHo I came across exhibitions featuring fire hoses, beds and mattresses, plastic soda bottles, and in one case an entire section of rusted fire-escape cut off a building and hung by cables from the gallery's ceiling. The effects were all very grittily poetic, but such work seems to operate in a quite different esthetic mode from Duchamp's and Flavin's. It feels arbitrary and strained, the object's removal from the world, an underlining not of artfulness or of a presiding indifference, but of its dysfunction, its pathos.

Flavin's borrowings from the quotidian world are of another order. He takes a humble object, all right, but he knows just what he wants. It's only one class of object, the commercially available fluorescent light fixture. There are a set number of colors and a set number of shapes and sizes. There is the circular fixture and the straight tube in 2-, 4-, 6- and 8-foot lengths. Flavin forms these mass-produced utility products into art objects, but they also do what they were meant to do – light up a room. Consequently, Flavin's work is untouched by the sense of profligacy that attends much recent art involving readymades, the feeling that there is an inexhaustible trove of *stuff* out there that one can art up, empty of logic and function, and turn into something that looks tough-minded but is at heart easy and sentimental.

Flavin's tubes carry with them not only the generalized atmosphere of the industrial, but also the quite specific aura of the milieus they most often illuminate – the supermarket, the office, the factory, the hardware store, the lighting shop, the building supply house. Fluorescent lights are cheap, impersonal, replaceable, modular. They are cool, simple in shape, and they radiate virtually without shadow, emitting only a low hum. They are industrial artifacts poised midway between the old idea of a machine and the new one. The classical machine was active, warm, metallic and noisy – a thing of wheels, gears, crankshafts and pistons. The postmechanical device, with its software and microchips, its optical fibres and smooth plastic, is small, silent and boxed in, but capable of the most complex interconnections.

Flavin presents the industrial in a low-keyed, appreciative way, as a condition of modern existence. Fluorescent light fixtures, like International Style skyscrapers, are made of metal and glass. They are opaque and transparent, strong yet fragile. Flavin's approach to material is straightforward in an essentially Miesian manner. Form follows function. Material embellishments are strictly excluded from Flavin's artistic vocabulary: no customizing, no special bending, no timers, no dimmers, no gestural drawing in space, no mixed media, no text.

The second line of Flavin's practice is the structural. Despite the seemingly limited nature of his materials, he has produced art works in a remarkable number of formal permutations. Flavin's work can be freestanding or wall-based. It can bridge corners or nestle into them, be hung from the ceiling or laid out on the floor. The tubes can face forwards or backwards. They can be oriented horizontally, vertically or diagonally, in a grid or not. There can be single tubes or multiple tubes arrayed in varying symmetries or assymmetries. The tubes can also be placed parallel and next to each other to form solid color fields. In addition, Flavin uses color not just perceptually but as a structural variant, a differentiator.

Some of Flavin's pieces have the planar, graphic clarity of a drawing on gridded paper. For example, *untitled (to a man, George McGovern)*, from 1972, is a triangular, wall-hung work made with cool-white, circular tubes. Ten fixtures run up the wall, abutting a corner, and 10 run perpendicularly to the first set, along the same wall and abutting the floor. From each of these two baselines another eight gradually diminishing rows are generated (the second row getting nine fixtures, the third eight and so on) so as to form a right isosceles triangle. The perceptual results, of course, are not at all straightforward, but the structure is. On the other hand, *greens crossing greens (to Piet Mondian who lacked green)* is a freestanding piece of great architectural complexity (and spooky emotional effect). A green post-and-lintel unit is reiterated to form two bridgelike structures, one made of small tubes in square translucent sheathing and the other of bigger ones, that cross each other at an angle, carving up the room's space in ways hard to quantify.

"Hard to quantify" does not, however, mean *impossible*. Look at any Flavin for a while and the plan starts to unfold. His work, like that of many other Minimalists or Conceptualists – Judd, Andre, Stella, Bochner or Smithson – employs simple counting, measuring and distributing strategies. The *'monument' for V. Tatlin* series, for example, begun in the mid-'60s, parallels Frank Stella's various pinstripe series of the same decade. The fluorescent tubes and the stripes function similarly, and the symmetrical external shape is configured by the outcome of a set of logical placement decisions. Flavin's comprehensibility is helped by the modular quality of his materials. Quantities of two, four, six and eight have sets of potentially complicated, but always graspable relationships.

The serial format works particularly well for Flavin. It invites the viewer to compare and contrast. The 12 colorful horizontal sculptures in the PaceWildenstein show are a good example. They are spaced out around the large room at eye level with enough distance between them so that the hues reflected on the wall don't mix. The sculptures all have the same shape – consisting of two 4-foot tubes with a 2-foot tube centered and sandwiched in between them. But you must stop and pay attention before the color structure becomes clear. In six of the works, the short middle tube is red and the bottom tube is green. In the other six, the colors of the bottom two elements are reversed. The top tube is one of six colors: light blue, green, pink, yellow, red and deep ultraviolet, in that order. This six-color progression for the top tubes is the same for both the red-green group and the green-red group. It sounds simple, but it takes a while to see – which is, I believe, part of the point.

Color is an area where Flavin has made a major, but insufficiently understood, contribution. Along with Judd he has used color as a sensual and emotional counterpoint to the austere structural rigor of his enterprise. While Flavin by necessity has a limited palette, in practice the range of colors is enormous. It can wash and mix along the walls, in the corners and on the floor. A corner grid piece such as *untitled (in honor of Leo at the 30th anniversary of his gallery)*, exhibited at the Guggenheim, consists of five 8-foot horizontal tubes in red, pink, yellow, blue and green spanning the corner and facing us directly, and five similar vertical tubes turned the other way, bathing the corner in a ravishing peachy glow. The pieces in the 1966–71 *European Couples* series at Dia are also 8-foot corner squares, with each sculpture done in a single color. The structure, too, is simpler. They are composed of four tubes – two verticals turned to the wall and two horizontals facing the room. The effect is startling. The corner dissolves, the edges are elegantly demarcated, and the square space turns into a subtly modulated, glowing Color Field painting – an Olitski you could walk through. There is something equally painterly going on in the new works at PaceWildenstein. The horizontal format casts soft-edged rectangles of colors both above and below the fixtures, and Mark Rothko's paintings inevitably come to mind.

Flavin puts his color through all its formal paces as well. He takes advantage of advancing and receding hues, of pure and mixed tones, of direct and reflected light, and of sharp contrast and subtle tonal interplay. Also brought into play are more esoteric color properties, such as the phenomenon of afterimage. The tubes – especially when set in banks, as in *untitled (to Jan and Ron Greenberg)*, with its wall of yellow backed by a wall of green – are chromatically intense. If the viewer looks at them for any length of time, shimmering ghosts of their complementary colors appear.

Flavin uses color in a consciously referential way too – the red and white of the *untitled (to the citizens of the Swiss cantons)* series, or the pink, yellow, blue and green of *untitled (to Henri Matisse)* – but his color also has strong emotional and even physiological effects, though it is hard to say how much of this is intended. It is color you just don't look at; it is color you feel – the blood reds, the antiseptic whites, the warm pinks, the sky blues, the eerie science-fiction greens. One night I sat under a big red corner piece (at Max's Kansas City), eating a steak. The food looked weird, and I had an awful headache that seemed to pulse in time to the sculpture's hum. Detached contemplating is not the term I would use to describe the experience.

The movement out into physical and optical space – the architectural side of Flavin's work – is seen to greatest effect in larger-scale installations. (In contrast, the single diagonal tube in the uptown Guggenheim's big abstraction show looked rather forlorn, as it if were fighting a losing battle against the slope of the museum's ramp.) In a big Flavin installation the air seems suffused with light and color, almost as if one could breathe it. You have a sense of anticipation and of being led along as light spills out the doorway of an adjacent room. Shadows cut floors and walls, corners dissolve; forms are blurred and doubled on polished floors; ceiling beams seem spray painted; and small architectural details – the space between two radiator strips, for example – are highlighted with the most complex blend of colors. As you look, the sculptures expand. How big are they, really – their listed dimensions or the area encompassed by their throw of light? Does the room have other sources of illumination? In that case things are different again.

At Dia, the new permanent installation gives a starkly utilitarian stairwell a sense of drama and mystery. Tubes running up the corner (blue on the two lower floors, green on the two upper) turn brick walls craggy and painted walls glassy, functioning as a radiant armature for the turnings of the stairs. In Flavin's installations the entire space that houses them is subtly reconfigured. The modifications feel as permanent as any architectural renovation, but to undo them, all you have to do is throw a switch.

Minimalism has had great staying power. In sculpture, especially, it has been something that artists (and critics) have had to deal with in their practice. You may be for or against it, but it is difficult indeed not to take it into account. The best of classic Minimalism has continued to present a very good case for itself. Dan Flavin's work is in many ways paradigmatic. While remaining true to its principles, it has continued to grow in complexity, both of effect and interpretation. In the process, somehow, it has taken on a richer, almost affective character.

Classic Minimalism depends upon – and, in a sense, embodies – a built-in rigidity, a stubborn insistence on the factual and the phenom-enological. Implicit in this esthetic is a desire for control that has led most Minimalist artists (Stella is an exception) to keep strict rein on their work's formal variables. While this rectitude might seem to be an impediment to long-term development – certainly it would be anathema to Picasso or Matisse – it has for the most part served the Minimalists well. By maintaining a built-in link to formal variation, the Minimalists have preempted temptation, particularly the temptation to devolve to the overtly personal. The result is an unusually firm grasp of the rule, the better (sometimes) to break them. In fact, the analytic quality of Minimalist art, its seeming clarity of method and intention, actually increases its potential for ambiguity. Minimalism's facets have been sharply defined from the outset, and, over time, inherent contradictions and instabilities establish themselves as reliable gener-ators of interpretational and perceptual complexity. Flavin's work continues to have deep resonance. It still "is what it is" – in the proper Minimalist sense – but then "to be" is, after all, a very tricky verb.

Art in America, Volume 84, Number 6, June 1996, pp. 68–73.

Dan Flavin, 63, Sculptor of Fluorescent Light, Dies
Roberta Smith

Dan Flavin, a leading Minimalist sculptor known for working with fluorescent lights, died on Friday at a hospital in Riverhead, L.I. He was 63 and had homes in Wainscott, L.I. and Garrison, N.Y.

The cause was complications from diabetes, said his son, Stephen.

A rotund man whose cheerful, cherubic looks belied a personality both brilliant and caustic, Mr. Flavin belonged to a generation of artists that redefined American sculpture in the wake of the Abstract Expressionists, who had redefined American painting.

His contemporaries included Lee Bontecou, John Chamberlain, Robert Irwin and Donald Judd, all of whom were inspired by the large scale, saturated colors and simple compositions of the Abstract Expressionists. With them, Mr. Flavin moved sculpture away from an implicitly figurative, usually Cubist vocabulary toward a new focus on space itself, often defined by daringly impersonal use of new industrial materials. He helped establish a tradition that continues to proliferate in various forms of installation and environmental art.

The material Mr. Flavin fastened on, the fluorescent light fixture in its many colors and lengths, was at once sensuous and austere, straightforward and celebratory. He was perhaps the first artist to employ electric light in a sustained way, and he remained one of the best. In retrospect, its presence seemed appropriate to a former Catholic altar boy who recalled being "curiously fond of the solemn high funeral Mass, which was so consummately rich in candlelight, music, chant, vestments, processions and incense."

Mr. Flavin arrived at the idea of using fluorescent tubes after several years of painting and drawing Abstract Expressionistic works to which he sometimes added scribbled texts from the Bible or James Joyce. These were followed by a brief period in the late 1950's and early 60's of making boxy wall reliefs in strong monochromatic colors, to which he attached colored light bulbs and fluorescent tubes.

In 1963 Mr. Flavin placed a single gold tube directly on the wall, and came to realize, as he later wrote, that "the actual space of a room could be disrupted and played with by careful, thorough composition of the illuminating equipment." Thereafter he began using the tubes on their own, deploying them in fencelike barriers across rooms or doorways, in vertical arrangements along walls and in various criss-crossing or framelike constructions that spanned corners.

The result was an art brazenly radical and very much in the vein of Marcel Duchamp's ready-mades, yet characterized by profound, even ecstatic beauty that was at once painterly and architectural. This beauty emanated from a combination of the tubes' intense lines of color, the softer glow of their diffuse, spreading light and the geometric arrange-ments of the tubes' metal pans. Mr. Flavin became adept at getting the most out of all three. He might turn the light elements away from the viewer, so that the pans formed dark lines across the glowing color effects, or combine tubes of different colors to create tints of a third.

He was equally at home with almost no color, contrasting the different whites of fluorescent tubes designated daylight, cool white and warm white, and in the early 1970's he began working with circular fluorescent lights.

His pieces could be symphonic, filling entire museums – as they did the rotunda of the Guggenheim in 1971 and again in 1992 – and highlighting their exteriors as well, as at the Staatliche Kunsthalle in Baden-Baden, Germany, in 1989. Or they could strike single chords, as small, portable combinations of short tubes whose compactness recalled his early reliefs.

The emotionalism of Mr. Flavin's early work never disappeared, but was relegated to the elaborate dedication titles with which he acknowl-edged debts and admirations both personal and artistic. He dedicated pieces to friends, colleagues, fellow artists, sometimes to the museum workmen who installed them, even to a beloved golden retriever. In the 1960's, he dedicated a large series of pyramidal wall pieces to the Russian Constructivist Vladimir Tatlin, to whose esthetic he felt closely connected; in 1990, another series was dedicated to the great English potter Lucie Rie, an homage in keeping with Mr. Flavin's avid collecting of Japanese tea bowls and American glass.

But Mr. Flavin could be equally generous with blame and was famous for scathing letters to friends, former friends and editor, written in a slightly ornate style.

Daniel Nicholas Flavin Jr. was born in New York City on April 1, 1933. His parents apparently did not encourage their son's early demonstrations of artistic interest. In 1969, in the catalogue of his first retrospective, at the National Gallery of Canada in Ottawa, he identified his parents as "an ascetic, remotely male, Irish Catholic truant officer, whose junior I am, and a stupid, fleshy tyrant of a woman who had descended from German royalty without a trace of nobility." He had a twin brother who died in 1962.

Mr. Flavin studied art history at the New School for Social Research and Columbia University, but was almost completely self-taught as an artist. He had his first exhibition in 1961 at the Judson Gallery in Greenwich Village and first exhibited his fluorescent works at the Green Gallery on 57th Street in 1964. He was represented by the Leo Castelli Gallery for many years and more recently by the Pace Gallery. Next month, the Danese Gallery on East 57th Street will exhibit works from the Tatlin series, along with drawings by Kasimir Malevich.

Mr. Flavin married Sonia Severdija in 1961; they were divorced in 1979.

In addition to his son, of Los Angeles, he is survived by his wife, Tracy Harris, whom he married in 1992 in the rotunda of the Guggenheim amid an installation of his work.

The New York Times, December 4, 1996, p. D25.

Arranging Light to Make the Most out of Minimalism
Roberta Smith

Dan Flavin's love of light earned him a place in the history of Minimal Art. It was an affection befitting a lapsed Roman Catholic who would later recall being mesmerized by the candles of high mass, and it found its ultimate expression in the fluorescent tubes that Flavin started using in 1963.

These crisp linear structures came in various arrangements, simple to complex, small to environmental. Covering walls, spanning corners, forming "barriers" that progressed across rooms, they were at once flatfootedly literal, seductive and epiphanic. Their lines of intense color released pools of fainter hues into the atmosphere, often achieving an expansive soulfulness that gave the lie to Minimal Art's notorious reductiveness.

Flavin, who died in November at age 65, found his way to the fluorescent-tube pieces through a series of works that he called *Icons*. With titles redolent of religious fervor and parts picked up at hardware stores, they were cobbled together between 1961 and 1963 and exhibited at the Kaymar Gallery on La Guardia Place in 1964 They have rarely been exhibited since, although one or two may be familiar from the pages of old catalogues, like the one for Flavin's retrospective organized at the National Gallery of Canada and seen at the Jewish Museum in Manhattan in 1970.

The Dia Center for the Arts has now reunited seven *Icons* for the first time since 1964, along with Flavin's first fluorescent light tube piece – a single gold diagonal from 1963 – and a big, glorious "barrier" piece from 1970. In shuttling eight-foot squares of red and light blue tubes, it proceeds the length of a large gallery, bathing the space in fire and ice.

Also on permanent display are pieces in blue and green that Flavin designed for Dia's two stairways and that were completed just before his death. Coloring the staircase windows from the bottom to the top of the building, they look best from outside, at night, adding considerable life to the west end of 22nd Street.

The *icons* recalls a great moment in American art, just after 1960, when Abstract Expressionism was on the wane and younger painters were exploring the possibilities of nontraditional materials. Several of them, including Flavin and also Donald Judd, suddenly found that they had edged over into the relatively uncharted territory between painting and sculpture; they were involved with real space, but still dedicated to intense color.

The *icons* show Flavin just encountering this territory, with boxy monochrome reliefs enhanced by incandescent and fluorescent lights. His love of color, light and colored light are just finding themselves, and his Irish sentimentality, expressed in parenthetical dedications, is ripe. The pieces here are dedicated to the musician Blind Lemon Jefferson, the architect Louis Sullivan and various friends of the young artist, including John Reeves, a clairvoyant whom he met while attending Columbia University.

With thickened volumes and bluntly truncated corners, to which Flavin might affix red "flasher" lights, these awkwardly faceted shapes both violate and exaggerate painting's hallowed rectangle. (They are remarkably similar to the reliefs that Judd was making at the same time, although the two did not meet until the time of the Kaymar show, which Judd, then working as a critic, reviewed admiringly.) The lights can seem to add insult to injury, turning each painted form into a kind of pedestal, while also suggesting strange alarm boxes or other industrial elements.

These contrasts may have more profound sources, some of them undoubtedly autobiographical. In continually playing painted color against the electrical kind, the works reflect Flavin's interest in different physical states of color. And these differences can also be read morally, as little tussles between good and evil, or the last vestiges of Flavin's Catholic upbringing.

Icons III, for example, contrasts three very different reds: the sexy cherry red of an incandescent bulb on its top edge, and the true, hot red of a fluorescent tube along its bottom edge, with the relatively wholesome barn red of the box itself. *icon VI (Ireland dying) (to Louis Sullivan)*, is a box painted sharp green whose one flattened corner features a red flasher light, its brightness subdued by a cover of dark green glass. *icon V (Conran's broadway flesh)*, slightly larger than the others, is a box painted pale, fleshy pink whose four sides are lined with clear "candle" lights, a contrast that brings to mind a blank theater marquee while remaining starchily innocent, even liturgical.

Flavin would soon resolve, or bury, these differences in the sophistication of the fluorescent tube pieces with their ever-more-intense and enveloping arrangements of color. But the *icons* come before them, more emotional, dumber and cruder, like Romanesque before Gothic.

The New York Times, September 19, 1997, p. E38.

Dan Flavin's Epiphany
Joachim Pissarro

In May 1963, Dan Flavin (1933–1996) displayed for the first time a neon fixture as a work of art. He hung an ordinary, 8-foot long, cool white fluorescent lighting fixture diagonally on the wall of his studio and gave it the most extraordinary title: *the diagonal of personal ecstasy (the diagonal of May 25, 1963)*. It was an act – an "epiphany"[1] – that would alter the course of his career and indelibly shape his work to come. Flavin had also resorted to the same material in other diagonal light pieces he created at the time: for example, *the diagonal of May 23, 1963 (to Constantin Brancusi)*, whose 8-foot long yellow fluorescent light is likewise installed at a 45° angle, but with its left edge touching the floor.

Flavin's *untitled*, conceived the following year, consists of two parallel pink fluorescent fixtures hung horizontally, the shorter one above the longer one. A recent gift to the Art Gallery – and one of the works featured in the 1998 exhibition *Then and Now* – it prompts a reconsideration of the artist's 1963 epiphany on its thirty-fifth anniversary.

Flavin was aware – and proud – of the significance of his neon piece, not only in general terms for the lower Manhattan art world of the moment, but also for his own artistic and historical position. The personal impact and emotional resonance of the work, its precise date of creation, as well as its definition as a geometric figure, were all conflated in its emphatic title: *the diagonal of personal ecstasy (the diagonal of May 25, 1963)*. Suggesting a point of departure, an important moment in the early days of minimalism,[2] this title was forthright in its literalness.[3] And then again, it was not. It remained elliptical in that it addressed every fact about the piece but one: its medium. That the work was made out of light – or, more accurately, out of a neon tube that projected cool, quivering, fluorescent light – was not mentioned. Instead, by using the term "diagonal" as a substantive, Flavin suggested that this geometric line was ethereal: disembodied, holding on to nothing but its moment of revelation and date of creation, which were absolutely integral to the work's content and meaning.

Flavin's title, together with the impeccably neat engineering diagram that accompanied the piece, also provided hanging instructions: *the diagonal of personal ecstasy* was obviously not meant to be hung horizontally (as neon fixtures usually are). That it was to fixed diagonally instead was clearly intended by the artist to deny the possibility of reading the piece in a functional or instrumental way. Flavin would reverse this denial in *untitled*, which hangs horizontally. He thus playfully insinuated that it *could* be mistaken for an ordinary piece of lighting equipment; only its radiant pink color gives it away. Additionally, *untitled*'s parallel fixtures reinforce the connotation of a regular 1960s office lighting unit – even though here again the top tube, one-quarter the length of the bottom one, disrupts this connotation. *the diagonal of personal ecstasy*, however, would simply "collapse" – at least conceptually, as a work of art – if it were hung vertically or horizontally. Yet despite their differences, both *the diagonal* and Yale's recently acquired *untitled* resort very much to the same system. Flavin, in his laconic style, emphasized the point himself:

> I know now that I can reiterate any part of my fluorescent light system as adequate. Elements or parts of that system simply alter in situation installation. They lack the look of history. I sense no stylistic or structural development of any significance within my proposal – only shifts in partitive emphasis – modifying and addable without intrinsic change.[4]

This brief statement, written three years after Flavin's epiphany, and two years after the Yale piece, requires some explaining. In the artist's mind, no one light piece was structurally different from another. Only modifications to individual parts – what Flavin called "shifts in partitive emphasis" – distinguished them. If one compares *the diagonal of personal ecstasy* to *untitled*, these shifts are quite obvious: one fixture/two fixtures; diagonal/horizontal; cool white light/intense pink light; straight line/parallel lines. But according to Flavin, such variations did not affect the fact that, with *the diagonal of personal ecstasy* and its related group of works in 1963, he created an entire system, not just a few individual works of art. Or rather, he created a system that was itself the work of art. No individual expression of it was more significant than another. In what is surely the ultimate minimalist position, Flavin thereby argued that in creating one work, he created his entire oeuvre, all at once. There was no evolutional program, no progression. Neither *untitled* nor *diagonal (to Constantin Brancusi)* was a step above, away from, or posterior to *the diagonal*. Flavin's art "lack[ed] the look of history."

Such a denial brilliantly challenged the then current critical model of a step-by-step process intrinsic to the creation of art. What is fascinating about Flavin's work is that he reacted not so much against artists – e.g., his elders of the second generation of painterly abstractionists – but against art critics and art historians. One could say that Clement Greenberg and Michael Fried had – negatively – a much greater influence on Flavin than did Willem de Kooning or Jackson Pollock. Flavin's personal gibe against the historicism that so dominated art criticism in the 1960s deserves quotation:

> Impromptu flickers from Billy Who?, lasers through the night, "Lights Canceling Orbits," numbered evenings of inept art on technotivity in the Armory do not inform me about my effort. That proposal is whole now and has been so. It requires no technological embellishment nor must it join the technocratic, "sci-fic," or art-as-progress cult for continuing realization. Moreover, I do not feel compelled to hope for a more wonderful day before the fact in promo-proto-art history. I am not anxious to prefer to speculate against posterity. I like thinking here and now without sententious alibis...[5]

Flavin's creation of *the diagonal of personal ecstasy* constituted a metonymic act. To describe it as an "epiphany," then, hardly overstates the case. It all came to the artist in one fell swoop, one revelation. His use of artificial light, which can be turned on and off with the flick of a switch, is of course a perfect metaphor for such instantaneous creativity. And in recalling as well the biblical moment of creation, it signaled the artist's absolute control as well as his own interest in mystical literature. There was no room for improvisation, accident, intuition, or failure. Nor was there room for the artist's hand. *The diagonal of personal ecstasy* did not need to be fabricated. With his "concept" already in mind, Flavin merely purchased an ordinary neon fixture of the sort used in millions of offices worldwide. Not unlike Duchamp's readymades, the work was there, all at once.

As the full title of *the diagonal of personal ecstasy* might suggest, Flavin granted much attention to dates throughout his career. His frequent references to them were idiosyncratically poetic rather than functional or evolutional, however. Here, for example, is how the artist described himself to the readers of the catalogue of his 1989 restrospective in Baden-Baden:

> I was born a fraternal twin, screaming (as usual), on a rainy, wet and dreary gray Saturday morning of April 1, 1933, in Mary Immaculate Hospital in the outlying Jamaica section of Queens County within New York City of the State of New York, United States of America. Even without much formal education, I have been able to think and to issue various arts for slightly more than 32 years.
> I am still pleased to be.[6]

Flavin's art and his words carry analogous tensions between the obvious – the uselessly obvious, even – and the evasive. Contradiction and opposition are their constitutive ingredients. One could say about

Yale's *untitled* that everything is there, in one's face, glaringly pink – yet one cannot quite grasp it. And at the same time, it wears such a sense of normality that one can almost ignore it. Yet if you stop in front of *untitled* and face it for a few seconds, it wraps you up in its aura of pink light. You become part of the piece. More than thirty years after the artist's initial gesture, *untitled* continues to enrapture.

The author extends his warmest personal thanks to Lesley Baier and Jennifer Ludwig for their contributions to this article.

1   It is with this metaphor that Thomas Crow describes the sudden discovery, or appropriation, of a neon fixture and its use as a medium that became Flavin's signature mark. See Thomas Crow, *The Rise of the Sixties, American and European Art in the Era of Dissent* (New York: Harry N. Abrams, Inc., 1996), 142.

2   The first usage of the term "minimal art" only occurred in 1965. It is usually ascribed to Richard Wollheim's article "Minimal Art" (*Arts Magazine*, January 1965). Referring to Mallarmé's proclaimed fear when facing a blank sheet of paper as he was about to write a poem, Wollheim imagines that Mallarmé could have been a proto-minimalist artist: "...could one imagine anything that was more expressive of...the poet's feelings of inner devastation than the virginal paper? The interest for us of such a gesture is, of course, that it would provide us with an extreme instance of what I call Minimal Art" (reprinted in *Minimal Art: A Critical Anthology*, ed. Gregory Battcock, with an introduction by Anne M. Wagner (Berkeley and Los Angeles: University of California Press, 1995], 388).

3   Before the term "minimalism" was coined, all sorts of sobriquets applied to this group who questioned the very validity of "painterly painting," or to an art in which the artist leaves the mark of what he/she is doing. To name but a few, Michael Fried referred to them as "literalists," Barbara Rose spoke of "ABC Art," and Lawrence Alloway of "Systemic Painting." See Anne M. Wagner, *Reading Minimal Art*, in Battcock, 10–11.

4   Dan Flavin, "Some Remarks," *Artforum* 5 (December 1966): 27.

5   Dan Flavin, "some other comments...," *Artforum* 6 (December 1967): 21; reprinted in Battcock, 402.

6   Neue Anwendungen fluoreszierenden Lichts mit Diagrammen, *Zeichnungen und Drucken von Dan Flavin*, exh. cat. (Baden-Baden: Staatliche Kunsthalle Baden-Baden, 1989), 7.

Yale University Art Gallery Bulletin, 1997–98, pp. 84–87.

Berlin – Dan Flavin
David Anfam

As befits the former premises of a bank, the Deutsche Guggenheim
Berlin on Unter den Linden is basically a bland set of cubic spaces.
Such a setting could well spell death to many kinds of art – including
pre-modern, figurative and especially expressionist works – which
may benefit from a less impersonal ambience. But it would be hard
to imagine a better marriage than that between this simple site and
the literally eye-opening show *Dan Flavin: The Architecture of Light* (closed
13th February). On paper there was no hint that the exhibition was
anything other than a routine curatorial exercise. Its modest tally of
nine items all came from the Guggenheim itself, mostly its Panza collection holdings. Nor was there any special thematic agenda. However,
the unexceptional elements united to a perfect whole. While Flavin's
raw materials – commercial fluorescent light fixtures – are utterly
ordinary, the final experience that they negotiate is not. From his
limited hardware, Flavin extracted illimitable effects.

Encapsulating a quarter of a century of Flavin's career, the nine
pieces in Berlin exemplified most of its key phases. The spectator's course
began in cool whiteness with the daylight lamps of *the nominal three
(to William of Ockham)*. Next came *greens crossing greens (to Piet Mondrian
who lacked green)* (1966) so that, with a quick backward glance, one
seemed to hear an entire new language gathering in the differential
between these two constructions. The change from white voids to
green thoughts, from vertical to horizontal and from a single planar
statement to a barrier-like crossroads presented at once the plainest and
the most arresting of moves. It was like a lesson telling that knowledge
can be reduced to the play of a binary system. In confrontations of this
type – where we must think afresh about building blocks of vision
and meaning – Flavin's work, and indeed minimalism in general,

found some of its finest moments.

The few steps separating the first two rooms also induced perhaps the biggest of surprises as the greenness of the second space inflected (by optical compensation and contrast) that of the erstwhile daylit *nominal three* to a livid pink. Similar phenomenological twists abounded. The blue illumination in *an artificial barrier of blue, red and blue fluorescent light (to Flavin Starbuck Judd)* (1968; Fig.58) caused the red to appear much more darkly saturated. The white wall outside the corridor containing the golden 'recto' side of *untitled (to Jan and Ron Greenberg)* (1972–73) likewise became a complementary violet shade. More subtly, a red tube turned towards the wall covertly modifies the three warm white ones facing forward in *monument on the survival of Mrs. Reppin* (1966) and the conjoined blue and pink lamps of *untitled (to Barbara Nüsse)* (1971) together lend the atmosphere around this imageless icon a penumbral haze. These optical reversals and conceits run against the matter-of-fact grain of Flavin's attitude by injecting a sense of subjectivity and duration into what at first looks forthright, objective or instantaneous.

Neverless, to see Flavin as an Op artist or visual prankster invites the worst of misreadings. Another error would be to take his fields of light for updated versions of the 'abstract sublime' located somewhere between Rothko's lucent mysteries and, say, the spiritual or environmental ambitions of James Turrell or Bill Viola. To be sure, at one level Flavin's work is sheer aura, a gaseous nothingness brightly coloured. On almost every other level it is the antithesis of that strain in Western art – from at least Romanticism onward – that has pursued airy, transcendental realms.

Flavin and his minimalist *confrères* cannot be understood without taking the full measure of their reaction against the ideology of their predecessors, typified by the abstract expressionists. The signs of this rejection populate Flavin's titles, statements and the pragmatism of the things he made. These last are indexed to architecture – most practical of the arts – by being both site-specific (the pieces were often conceived for a particular space) and site-dependent (they are next to nothing without something to illuminate). Even so, they eschew grandeur. Instead, as Flavin said, 'my icons do not raise up the blessed saviour in elaborate cathedrals. They are constructed concentrations celebrating barren rooms. They bring a limited light.' The titles pare down matters still further. Thus the citation of the fourteenth-century nominalist William of Ockham refers to the start of an ongoing philosophical belief in facts or objects rather than universals. Flavin's titles uphold this stance by nominating a single day – for example, *the diagonal of ecstasy (the diagonal of May 25, 1963)* – or person, be it the famous Vladimir Tatlin or the anonymous 'innovator of Wheeling Peachblow'. So too is every component of what Flavin termed his 'situations' meant to deny metaphysical gush. Hence the lights are industrial artefacts, their colours and sizes are standardised and their placement rarely departs from rectilinear or diagonal patterns. A mere flick of a switch will end the whole affair. Throughout, a disturbing tension remains between impalpable radiance and the ever-so basic means that bear it. For Flavin, it might be said that General Electric had ousted the fiat lux of Genesis.

Scholarship has only recently started to trace the full extent of the intellectual shift from the romantic idealism of the 1940s and 50s to the sceptical empiricism of the 60s and 70s that underpinned artists like Flavin, Don Judd, Richard Serra and others of their generation.[1] Possibly for this reason, the otherwise rather glamorous full-colour catalogue to the show appears too summary to explore the diverse issues that Flavin's achievement broaches.[2] It is in any case a mixed bag of entries. Some of them contain real insights such as Jonathan Crary's remark on Flavin's relation to the global de-symbolisation of luminosity in an era when light moves as 'depthless, placeless flows of information'. Other entries offer academic twaddle: 'What is delimited thereby is limitation itself, but without positing the unlimited in any ahistorical sense.' Contrary to this vein of tautology, *Dan Flavin: The Architecture of Light* was in fact notable – its intrinsic merits aside – for also inviting a broader enquiry into context and content.

Among the questions that arise are what was the extent of Flavin's politics? Are parallels between his position and, for example, Ludwig Wittgenstein's logical atomism – both sought to demystify experience into limited propositions while keeping an eye on a domain outside language – coincidental? What might Flavin owe to the pastel neon dazzle of art deco (remember his reverence for Frank Lloyd Wright and the streamlined Guggenheim Museum building)? And do not his pronouncements and titles, like Jules Olitski's, play a riff around the art that recalls the ironies of Pop culture? If one side of Flavin's intentions was to shed a 'limited light' on 'barren rooms', another surely recognised a wider world beyond. As Flavin himself concluded: 'Life in light continues.'

1   See, for example, D. RASKIN: *Donald Judd's Skepticism*, unpublished Ph.D. thesis, University of Texas at Austin [1999].
2   *Dan Flavin: The Architecture of Light*. Essay by J. Fiona Ragheb, with entries by Joseph Kosuth, Frances Colpitt, Michael Govan, Brydon E. Smith, Jonathan Crary, Tiffany Bell and Michael Newman. 96 pp. incld. 29 col. pls. (Guggenheim Museum Publications and Harry N. Abrams, New York, 1999), DM 59. ISBN 0-89207-223-7 (PB) and 0-8109-6926-2 (HB).

The Burlington Magazine, Volume 142, Number 1166, May 2000, pp. 326–327.

Dan Flavin, Posthumously
Tiffany Bell

Shortly before Dan Flavin died on Nov. 29, 1996, he signed off on the plans for three permanent installations of fluorescent light.[1] These projects consisted of interior lighting for Santa Maria in Chiesa Rossa, a church built in the 1930s in Milan, Italy; interior and exterior lighting for Richmond Hall, a supermarket converted to an exhibition space for the Menil Collection in Houston, Tex.; and interior lighting for six barrack buildings that are part of a former military base that Donald Judd made into the Chinati Foundation in Marfa, Tex. Under the direction of Steve Morse, who was Flavin's studio assistant for several years, all three projects have been completed: the church in 1997, Richmond Hall in 1998 and the Chinati buildings in 2000.[2]

Chinati Foundation, Marfa

The Marfa plans had a long gestation. The initial contract for the work to fulfill Judd's conception of a museum of permanently installed work by him, Flavin and John Chamberlain was issued by the Dia Art Foundation in 1979, Flavin traveled to Marfa in the early 1980s, and models of the buildings and meeting notes suggest that he conceived his plans around that time. Nonetheless, he did not disclose his ideas completely until March 1996.[3]

The six buildings are U-shaped structures that have been renovated in the local vernacular architectural style with adobe walls and metal roofs. To accommodate Flavin's installation, all the windows except two at the end of each long wall have been closed over; entrances are on the inside of the U toward the ends of the long sides. Inside, two parallel corridors have been constructed at the bottom of the U, with walls – 86 feet on the outside and 44 feet on the shorter courtyard side – that lean left, making a 76-degree angle with the floor.

Passage through the leaning corridors is blocked by eight back-to-back pairs of 8-foot long fluorescent fixtures that extend from floor to ceiling, parallel to the walls. Gaps the width of the lamps are left between each pair of fixtures, allowing one to see through the color cast by the lamps on the fronts to the different color at the backs.

In three of the buildings, these light barriers are placed at the centers of the corridors' lengths, so that color is largely contained within the leaning walls. In the other three (they alternate from one building to the next), the lights are placed on both ends of the corridors, which allows color to flood into the long arms of the building as well as the inaccessible interiors of the corridors. The first two buildings contain pink and green lamps; in the second two, yellow and blue lamps are similarly place; and the last two have both a pink/green and a yellow/blue corridor.

The repetition of arrangement and color in the Marfa corridors is characteristic of much of Flavin's art. As in the work of other Minimalists, such as Judd, Carl Andre or Sol LeWitt, an inherent systematic order distinguishes his art from the expressionism of the previous generation and takes on relevance with regard to many issues of the early '60s: handmaking versus industrial production, the nature of individuality, the importance of part to whole, and so on. For Flavin, the projection of a system was particularly important because it provided a kind of framework to work with and against. The repetition and regularity of his elements and his arrangements provided a structure within which he employed a strategy of systematic change.[4]

Although Marfa's tilting corridors were a striking new development for Flavin, the use of diagonals and other aspects of the piece derive from earlier works. Flavin's first solely fluorescent piece to be exhibited employed a diagonal element: *the diagonal of May 25, 1963 (to Robert Rosenblum)* was a single 8-foot fixture with a cool-white lamp placed on the wall at a 45-degree angle. The spacing of the parallel lamps at Marfa relates to *untitled (to Dorothy and Roy Lichtenstein on not seeing anyone in the room)*, 1968, a work in which a rank of single cool-white lamps is set vertically into a doorway.[5] In that work, the lamps face away from the viewer, illuminating an empty room while blocking passage into it, like the Marfa works that are barricaded at each end. In both cases, the architecture and lights operate in tension with each other. The walls invite passage but the lamps prevent it; the lights shine forth brilliantly only to be contained and framed by the walls. The Marfa works, however, are neither as blunt nor as austere as the 1968 work, with its cool, colorless light. Also in contrast, the exposed backs of the fixtures in the earlier piece suggest prison bars and give a vaguely political character to the work. At Marfa, the double-sided arrangement and the intensity of the paired, contrasting colors fill and complicate both the existing and constructed space. The physical experience of the work becomes dynamic and visually disorientating.

The Marfa installations in which lamps are midway down the passage recall an earlier corridor, *untitled (to Barry, Mike, Chuck and Leonard)*, 1972–75, a hall 8 feet tall and wide, of a length dependent on the available space,[6] with back-to-back pink and yellow lamps placed floor to ceiling midway down its length. As in Marfa, to see the work completely, the observer is forced to walk around the construction (in Marfa, this means going outside and crossing the courtyard to reenter the building). This experience introduces some surprises, as the color and intensity of the lights change from side to side. The construction of the earlier work set up a square frame that tends to play with notions of perspective; one's gaze travels down the visually converging lines of the walls, much as in Renaissance perspectival painting, to meet a plane of light fixtures.[7] In the Marfa works, the angled walls and fixtures disrupt the expected order of right angles, subverting the sense of architectural proportion and balance. In this regard, they recall a corridor conceived and built around the time Flavin was first thinking about the Marfa works, *untitled (to my dear bitch, Airily)*, 1981, in which diagonally placed blue lamps ran along the walls and ceiling of an 8-foot-high and -wide corridor.[8] The familiar structure encouraged one to pass through; while the lights did not block the passage, their placement warped one's sense of rectilinear order.

The dynamic quality of the installation in Marfa is amplified by color. Though he utilized a limited range of commercially available hues, Flavin combined colored lights to very different effects, both expressive and spatial. In Marfa, he paired bright, contrasting colors: pink/green and blue/yellow. Green is the most luminous and intense of the fluorescent colors; when pink and green are mixed they seem to radiate yellow. As one looks into the corridor toward the green lamps, the color turns white as the eye compensates for the intensity of the green light. This physiological effect strengthens the pink light as seen from the green side. When one walks around to look at this light barrier from the other side, the yellow reflection on the barrack walls is seen to be the result of emanations of soft pink highlighted by green. These subtle transformations play against the predictability of the repeated structures.

Richmond Hall, Houston

Flavin's project for the Menil Collection was also under discussion for many years. Dominique de Menil had a long-standing interest in his work, and the idea for a permanent installation in Houston emerged in the late '70s.[9] It wasn't until 1996, however, that Flavin was commissioned to light Richmond Hall (the building takes its name from the street on which it is located). By this time, poor health prevented him from traveling. Although he had seen the building in the late '80s, the scheme for the lighting was developed largely on the basis of videos of the space and architectural plans.

Flavin was not given any restrictions, but he decided to leave the Richmond Hall structure unchanged. Built in 1930, it has a simple rectangular shape with a storefront and wide-open interior that allowed it to serve the changing neighborhood – first as a grocery store and later as many different bars. Flavin's installation respects the architecture of the building and the partly commercial character of the neighborhood by working in accordance with these conditions and retaining the storefront. Taking advantage of a relatively rare opportunity to work outdoors,[10] Flavin devised a horizontal line of green lights at top of the long sides of the exterior walls. They extend an ornamental frieze on the front and enhance the blank sides of the building while simultaneously illuminating a parking lot and subtly alluding to neon signs on nearby buildings.

The entrance lobby, defined by two diagonal walls converging from the building's front corners, is lit by 16-foot lines of white light running diagonally from bottom left to upper right on both walls. While made specifically to mimic the angle of the walls they are mounted on, these lamps also recall, again, Flavin's first fluorescent-light work, *the diagonal of May 25, 1963*.

The main event is in the large, unbroken interior space, which is 125 feet deep and 50 feet wide. Here, an arrangement of 4-foot fixtures extends along both long walls. A horizontal line about 4 feet above the floor running the length of both long walls consists of two filtered ultraviolet lights facing into the room. Above that line, starting in the front corner and placed at 4-foot intervals, is a succession of vertically oriented single lamps facing the back wall of the room, in a sequence of pink, yellow, green and blue. Below the horizontal line is the same sequence of colors offset slightly from the ones above them and facing toward the front wall. The two walls mirror each other.

Once again, this installation derives from an earlier work. In 1973, Flavin made *untitled (to Saskia, Sixtina, Thordis)* for a room at the Kunsthalle in Cologne measuring 164 by 72 feet. The configuration of lights was the same except that the horizontal band of lamps was blue and the sequence extended from left to right as you faced each wall; therefore, on one side the upper lamps faced the back wall and the lower lamps the front, and the other side was the reverse.

Though the differences between these two works seem minor, their effects are significant. In the earlier work, photos suggest that the abundance of blue light produced a bluish tone throughout the room. In comparison, the ultraviolet tubes in Houston cast very little visible light. They form a subdued, dark-purple line. According to Morse, Flavin's assistant, ultraviolet light was chose for its ability to blend the other colors. The same four colors used in Marfa appear here, but the result is entirely different. Rather than contrasting, they work together, completing the spectrum and producing an overall white light throughout the space. The coloristic effects are localized. Units of color project from the lamps and reflect on the backs of the next fixture along the wall, as well as bouncing faintly onto the ceiling. The light filling the central part of the room is rather disconcerting. One recognizes it as very much like the bright daylight outside, yet it is artificially made. (A small skylight that does not supply a great deal of natural light to the overall space provides a reference point.) The grand scale and decorative array dissolve into the brilliant yet empty interior space.

Santa Maria in Chiesa Rossa, Milan

The invitation to light Santa Maria in Chiesa Rossa, a building by Giovanni Muzio (a prominent figure in Milan's Novecento group, a Fascist-era movement dedicated to reconciling classical tradition with modernism), came in 1996 from the parish priest, Father Giulio Greco. Having seen Flavin's installations in Count Panza di Biumo's villa in the nearby town of Varese, Father Greco asked Flavin to light the church as part of an overall renovation. By restoring the church, he also sought to revitalize the surrounding neighborhood, which lies on the outskirts of Milan and accomodates a range of socioeconomic groups. His plan was realized with assistance from the Dia Center for the Arts and the Fondazione Prada.

Given Flavin's sometimes adamant denial of spirituality in his art in interviews and published letters and his rejection of the Roman

Catholic church in a well-known autobiographical essay, it is surprising that he took on the commission.[11] Nonetheless, as pointed out by Michael Govan, Flavin maintained a constant "dialogue with the profound aspirations of art and religion."[12] He called his earliest works that used light "icons" – in lowercase letters and in quotation marks. They are square, boxlike monochrome constructions with attached incandescent lights – both ordinary and candle-flame bulbs, sometimes colored or blinking – or occasionally fluorescent. Their titles ironically refer to the sacred presence invoked by religious arti-facts while their material presence maintains their status as secular objects. Similarly, Flavin's seminal Minimalist light work *the nominal three (to William of Ockham)*, 1963, alludes to Catholic theology. William of Ockham's Nominalism insisted that reality lies in the experience of real things and that abstract notions, such as God, depend completely on faith. Flavin thus introduces religious thought in a way that prioritizes concrete experience over spirituality.

Flavin at least paid heed to religion when he memorialized a church in a room adjoining a permanent installation of his lights. Commis-sioned by the Dia Art Foundation to restore and renovate a building in Bridgehampton, N.Y., that had formerly been a Baptist church (and a firehouse before that), Flavin retained a stained-glass window, a lectern and a metal cross lit by blue neon. He collected photographs of the congregation and presented all these mementos in a room adjacent to his fluorescent lights. Though primarily an homage to the building and the people who had once used it, the gesture nevertheless denotes a respect for the earlier sacred function of the building, and the pres-ence of the neon cross and the stained-glass window seems to allude ironically to the pairing of light and spirituality, topics regularly raised in discussions of Flavin's work.[13]

The Milan project, then, offered a particular, perhaps quintessential, challenge to the artist. According to Morse and another assistant, Prudence Fairweather, Flavin took the commission because he was impressed by the passion and conviction of Father Greco's written request; he was also interested in Muzio's building.[14]

Typical of Muzio's work, Santa Maria in Chiesa Rossa melds Renaissance proportions with modernist simplicity. It is a large brick structure with a portico in front consisting of substantial columns supporting the pediment, some empty niches and a large arched clear-glass window over the entrance. Inside is a nave surmounted by a generous barrel vault supported by large but simple columns and flanked by side aisles; a transept separates the nave from a central apse behind the altar. With its rather severe design, classic proportions and lack of ornamentation, this building provides a good situation for Flavin's lights.

Declining health kept Flavin from visiting Milan as well, and he relied on photographs, videos and Morse's description to understand the site. One of the few surviving works Flavin designed for a building with a purpose other than the exhibition of art, the installation works in concert with the church's structure and very specific function. It elegantly and dramatically enhances the architecture and respects the purpose of the building.

Again, pink, yellow, blue, green and filtered ultraviolet lights are used in the installation. But here, color is contained in specific areas and remains pure with them. In the nave, along the edge where the columns meet the barrel vault, a horizontal row of 4-foot fixtures holding three lamps each – green and ultraviolet facing up; blue, attached to the side of the fixture, facing the center of the space – stretches from the entrance to the transept and washes the vault with aqua. At the same height, along the near wall of the transept, similar fixtures containing pink, ultraviolet and pink lamps form a line of soft color that reflects against the opposite wall. At both sides of the rounded apse, fixtures containing three lamps – yellow, yellow and ultraviolet – face away from the congregation and make a vertical line from the floor to the height of the other lights.

While the lights articulate architectural features, they also provide a panorama of color enveloping the entire church, that moves from the coolness of the green/blue to the warmth of pink and then yellow. Because of the large front windows and smaller openings along the side aisles and the end walls of the transept, the intensity of light and color is more pronounced at night. Changes in light coming through the windows over the course of the day give other dimensions to the work, linking it to the passage of time and to a specific place.

Serial variation in Marfa, unity of organization in Houston; light in tension with architecture in Marfa, light in harmony with it in Milan; color massed in oddly distorted spaces to intense expressive effect in Marfa, or sparsely disposed in serene, classical spaces in Houston and Milan; taken together, these late works demonstrate both the consistency of Flavin's practice over 33 years and the range of experience elicited by it. The placement of what may be Flavin's least "minimal" work in the context of Judd's serious-minded, coolly beautiful Chinati installations might indicate a bit of humor, while the awesome beauty of the church lights might indeed, despite Flavin's protestations, suggest some kind of spirituality.

1   By "signing off," I mean that Flavin signed the certificates of authenticity for these works. These certificates, which were drawn up for almost all of Flavin's light works, were usually signed after the work was fabricated to document and authenticate the conditions of the work. They list title, date, placement of fixtures, color of lamps, edition number – constructed, uncommissioned works were all made in editions of three or five – and sometimes other information such as exhibitions or where the work was fabricated. In the case of large-scale, commissioned installations, according to Prudence Fairweather and Steve Morse, who worked with Flavin at the time, the certificates were made before the fabrication to be held in escrow until the funds could be raised to make the works.

2   A fourth work, *untitled (for Janet Chamberlain)*, 1995, was also posthumously completed in 1998 for the Hypo-Vereinsbank in Munich. This work dramatically lights an interior floating staircase with lamps placed under each tread.

3   This information comes from discussions in May 2000 with Marianne Stockebrand, director of the Chinati Foundation, and from the records of the project at the Dia Center for the Arts. Though no drawings have been found so far, the notes refer to drawings, and architectural models exist at the Chinati Foundation.

4   In 1996 Flavin wrote: "I know now that I can reiterate any parts of my fluorescent light system as adequate. Elements of parts of that system simply alter in situation installation. They lack the look of a history. I sense no stylistic or structural development of any significance within my proposal – only shifts in partitive emphasis – modifying and addable without intrinsic change. All my diagrams, even the oldest, seem applicable again and continually. It is as though my system synonymizes its past, present and future states without incurring a loss [of] relevance..." Dan Flavin, "some remarks...," in *Dan Flavin: three installations in fluorescent light/Drei installationem in flureszierendem licht*, Cologne, Kunsthalle Köln and Wallraf-Richartz Museums, 1974, p. 90. Originally published in *Artforum* (Los Angeles), December 1966, pp. 27–29.

5   "The parenthetical dedication was a reference to the newly wedded Lichtensteins, through a remembrances of a 1961 Lichtenstein painting, *I can see the whole room...and there's nobody in it.*" Brydon Smith and Dan Flavin, *fluorescent light, etc., from Dan Flavin*, Ottawa, National Gallery of Canada, 1969, p. 240.

6   The first time it was installed, at the Fort Worth Museum, it was 33 feet long. Barry, Mike, Chuck and Leonard were builders and electricians involved in the first installation of the work dedicated to them.

7   For a discussion of Flavin's corridors and their use of perspective, see Jonathan Crary, *untitled (to Jan and Ron Greenberg) 1972–73* in *Dan Flavin: The Architecture of Light*, Berlin, Deutsche Guggenheim Berlin, 1999, pp. 34–35.

8   Airily was the artist's champion golden retriever.

9   From an interview with Paul Winkler, former director of the Menil Collection, Aug. 3, 1999. Drawings from 1977 showing plans for a building to house Flavin light works are reproducecd in *"monuments" for V. Tatlin from Dan Flavin, 1964–1982*, Los Angeles, Museum of Contemporary Art, and Chicago, Donald Young Gallery, 1989, nos. 83–85.

10   Other exterior works include a courtyard in Basel's Kunstmuseum, exterior lighting for a small Dia Foundation building in Bridgehampton, and the entranceway at the Hudson River Museum in Yonkers.

11 Dan Flavin: "Everything is clearly, openly, plainly delivered. There is no hidden psychology, no overwhelming spirituality you are supposed to come into contact with. I like my use of light to be openly situational in the sense that there is no invitation to meditate, to contemplate. It's in a sense a 'get-in-get-out' situation. And it is very easy to understand. One might not think of light as a matter of fact, but I do. And it is, as I said, as plain and open and direct and art as you will ever find." In Michael Gibson, "The Strange Case of the Fluorescent Tube," *Art International* (Paris), autumn 1987, p. 105. Flavin discussed his Catholic upbringing and education in a seminary in dismissive and angry tones in "'...in daylight or cool white' an autobiographical sketch," *Artforum* (Los Angeles), December 1965, pp. 21–24.

12   Michael Govan, "Dan Flavin: Sacred and Profane," lecture at the Dia Center for the Arts, Apr. 30, 1988. To be published in Dia's *Robert Lehman Lectures on Contemporary Art*, vol. 3, forthcoming.

13   In a little-known project completed in the early 1980s but no longer existing, Flavin actually did the lighting for a place of worship. Again, the commission came from the Dia Arts Foundation. The building was a mosque in New York City. It should be noted, however, that when Flavin first agreed to this commission, the building was to be a performance space. Though he completed the commission, even using colors symbolic in the Muslim faith, it was with some reluctance.

14   Steve Morse, conversation with the author, August 1999, and Prudence Fairweather, conversation with the author, May 2000.

Art in America, Volume 88, Number 10, October 2000, pp. 127–132.

Dan Flavin, Chinati Foundation, Marfa, Texas
Libby Lumpkin

The West Texas town of Marfa is a dusty, one-traffic-light, *Last Picture Show* sort of place located sixty miles north of the border on the high plain known as *El Despoblado*: the uninhabited place. After the cavalry abandoned the local fort in the 1940s, few had reason to travel there, at least until Donald Judd settled in Marfa in the early '70s. Inspired by the light-and-space ambience, he established what came to be called the Chinati Foundation as an alternative to New York City's exhibition venues. If you are among the pilgrims who have made the trek to the foundation without benefit of landing your Lear on one of the privately owned airstrips nearby, you have driven at least three and a half hours from El Paso or Midland on a lonely stretch of highway that cuts through expansive fields of tall yellow grass. If you have arrived after dark, typically the consequence of inconvenient flight schedules, you may have parked just outside town at the preferred site for viewing the Marfa Mystery Lights. These unexplained luminescences, first reported by native inhabitants and pioneers in the 1800s, periodically and unpredictably animate the night horizon (I've seen them myself).

Suffice it to say that everything about the setting conspires to encourage the nostalgic and the mystically inclined. As a consequence, the achievement of Dan Flavin's *untitled (Marfa project)*, 1996, permanently installed at the Chinati in October, is doubly impressive. The work, whose design was completed by Flavin shortly before his death in 1996, has no more difficulty cutting through the romantic, Land art-aesthetic fog generated by Marfa's exotic locale than his earliest fluorescent lamp pieces had in dispensing with the 2,000-year-old association of luminescence with mysticism and spirituality. In fact, the monumental size of Flavin's Marfa project, which occupies six buildings and a total of 36,000 square feet, and the peculiarities of its systematic design suggest that the skeptic Flavin took the opportunity at the end of his career to reassert, on a grand, theatrical scale, the resolute secularism with which his career had begun.

Stepping into any of the six identical buildings in which the work is housed, one is immediately captivated by room-saturating, brilliantly colored lights. Double-faced, slanted ranks of 8 or 10 fixtures (336 fluorescent lamps in all) are paired, pink with green in the first two buildings, blue with yellow in the second two. Ranks of both these pairings occur in the two final buildings. The impression is a bit retro-techno, since fluorescent lamps are beginning to look dated, but also lively and seemingly loud, though no sound beyond the low buzz of electrical current is actually heard. Thus, on entering the Marfa project, one abruptly steps out of the rustic, whistle-stop world of the old fort, for which the stuccoed and porticoed buildings once served as barracks, and into the wholly artificial ambience of what appears to be an alternate universe.

In lesser hands, the dramatic surprise of retro-technology hidden in an environment of entropic decline would fall victim to the most adolescent form of sci-fi "narratives of source," the fluorescent lamps coming off as a cache of kryptonite or as tubes in which interplanetary aliens incubate their eggs. In fact, Judd's own nearby installations barely escape this romantic pitfall. Despite their modular designs and rigorously industrial aesthetic, the kilometer-long array of concrete sculptures that stretch across the Chinati's grounds suggests the cosmic alignment of Anasazi ruins. And, housed inside two huge, remodeled artillery sheds, Judd's one hundred "primary structure" mill-aluminum boxes – which constitute one of the great moments of late-twentieth-century art in any setting – subtly evoke incubators birthing genetic permutations of the Minimalist box.

If Flavin's project resists the Marfa fog, it does so by sheer force of will. The ranks of lamps, which vaguely resemble slanted prison bars, block passage from one side of the symmetrical, U-shaped buildings to the other, thereby ingeniously manipulating and theatricalizing the viewer's response. Like moths to a Bug Zapper, one is kept in motion, drawn down long hall after long hall, in building after building, toward the material brilliance of the highly saturated colored lights. The instinctive attempt to reach a center, or at least locate one visually, is repeatedly frustrated, forcing one's retreat. The luminescent feast, created in the four standard, factory-issue hues, resists transcendental allegorization as profoundly as do Henri Matisse's contradictory blue and yellow stained-glass windows in the chapel at Vence. The color pairings are distributed throughout the work without apparent explanation, satisfying only the most basic requirement of variation. Rather than some mythic umbilicus, Flavin's work reads, quite literally, as the middle of nowhere – the least mysterious of lights.

Thus Flavin's Marfa project, at once pleasingly seductive and disconcertingly withholding, leads its pilgrims to the same dead end at which Wittgenstein found himself after years of contemplating color. In his late writings, which inspired the mid-twentieth-century resurgence of the tradition that has come to be called Minimalist philosophy, Wittgenstein concluded that, in most cases, the prospects for a substantial meta-theory are meager. Indeed, Flavin's Marfa project may owe its apparent Bergamot-Chelsea freshness to the renewed interest in Minimalist philosophy as expressed in the colorful secularity of recent abstract painting. Certainly, the interest on the part of younger artists in Flavin and many of his contemporaries, particularly Ellsworth Kelly, Bridget Riley, and Gene Davis, indicates a sea change, both in the present culture and in the reading of '60s abstraction. In short, Flavin's fluorescent lamps hold their own in Marfa by holding onto an antimystical, antispiritual aesthetic – an elegantly decentered, thoroughly secular *despoblado*.

Artforum, Volume 39, Number 4, December 2000, p. 141.
Revised by the author, May 2004.

Minimal?
Michael Govan

Dan Flavin came to reject the idea of 'Minimal art' that he was credited with having helped to invent. As he complained in one of his typically provocative written notes:

> The popularisation of the dubious, facetious, epithetical, proto-historically movemented, art critical stereotypes of "minimal" art and artists has become so nationally pervasive already that one absurdly dilettanted mid-Western woman has tried to advise me that an exposition of mine within The Museum of Contemporary Art of Chicago would have been more appropriately "minimal" if I had restrained my use of color to one hue, yellow – instead of just two.[1]

Flavin joked that he preferred to call it 'maximalism', emphasising his art's bold effect over its economy of means.[1]

In the early 1960s, Flavin's radically simple and systematic application of readymade fluorescent light fixtures put him – along with a few of his American contemporaries including Carl Andre, Donald Judd, Sol LeWitt, and Robert Ryman – at the vanguard of a new art. But it is the nearly limitless expressive results he achieved in light and colour over the next thirty-three years of work that have earned him a place as one of the most important artists of his generation.

The 'Minimal' aspect of Flavin's work might first be evidenced by the fact that between 1963 and his death in 1996 the oeuvre consists almost entirely of light installations made from arrangements of commercially available fluorescent tubes in only ten colours (blue, green, pink, red, yellow, ultraviolet, and four whites) and five shapes (one circular and four straight fixtures of eight, six, four and two-foot lengths). Similarly, 'Minimal' might suggest the work's systematic, geometric configurations; its reliance on a single distinctive material (mass-produced fluorescent fixtures); and the removal of any idea of craft or the 'artist's hand' from its execution.

Arguably any art 'ism' is useful shorthand to capture the affinities among works of a closely related generation of artists. But wasn't 'Minimalism' invented then fifty years earlier in Kasimir Malevich's paintings like *White on White* (1918) or Marcel Duchamp's *readymades*? Indeed, Flavin's palette recalls Piet Mondrian's elementary Modernist vocabulary of rectangles and lines in red, blue, yellow, black, and variations on white and grey – made systematic by the prescribed dimensions and colours of the fixtures. Is it simply that 'Minimal' art takes to extremes a Modernist tendency to reduce and isolate the formal elements of visual experience in articulate abstract design?

Unfortunately the term 'Minimalism' connotes specific characteristics that do not even suggest the true contributions made by Flavin and his colleagues who collectively explored remarkable, and hitherto uncharted, territories of observation and expression. If one desired to generalise about the commonalities of some of the artists who came to prominence in the 1960s and 70s under the label of 'Minimalism', there are more compelling collective achievements than their reductive formal vocabulary. For one thing, the 'Minimalists' were thinking expansively about the entire phenomenal effect of the visual experience, and the entire space of the container within which it is perceived. Andre's walked-on metal floor grids take sculpture off the pedestal, directly implicating the ground plane; Judd's multifarious variations on the box consider not only the nature of the surfaces, but the potential of a work's interior, in space and in logic; LeWitt's wall drawings are a series of instructions and procedures that take visible form only in relation to the physical qualities of the actual wall upon which they are inscribed and realised; and Ryman's 'white paintings' are distinguished not by image but by the arrangement of factual properties of material, size, and installation that define their actual existence in relation to their site. A related group of artists, including Robert Irwin, Maria Nordman, and James Turrell, dispense entirely with the object in favour of pure perceptual experience.

Flavin helped open this field of artistic investigation through his preoccupation with the relationship between his fluorescent lights and their architectural context. In addition to the distinctiveness of the medium, and its specific linear and sculptural arrangements, Flavin's light implicates its entire environment. As he wrote,

> In time, I came to these conclusions about what I had found in fluorescent light, and about what might be done with it plastically: Now the entire special container and its parts, wall, floor, and ceiling could support this strip of light but would not restrict its act of light except to enfold it...[3]

Realising the inadequacy of traditional categories to describe his unique art, Flavin once suggested the term 'situations', and used the word 'proposals' instead of 'works'.

Many of Flavin's most notable later achievements were site-specific installations where art and architecture were inextricably intertwined, including nine works permanently installed in Bridgehampton, New York, in a former Baptist church restored and renovated by the artist with the patronage of the Dia Art Foundation in 1983; a site-specific installation for the entire spiral rotunda of the Frank Lloyd Wright designed Solomon R. Guggenheim Museum in New York City and his last major works, an installation for six barracks in Donald Judd's Chianti Foundation in Marfa, Texas, and the lighting of the 1920s Giovanni Muzio designed Chiesa Rosa in Milan – both posthumously executed.

The enduring quality of the intimate relationship between Flavin's lights and the specifics of their architectural context is evident throughout the oeuvre. And as the site-specific projects relate to a whole container, individual works usually relate to typical elements of architecture, as is demonstrated in this installation at the Serpentine Gallery in London. The classical architecture of the building – punctuated by glass that offers natural light inside and allows Flavin's light to permeate the exterior landscape at night – largely determined the selection and arrangement of works that nearly spans the artist's career, beginning with his first work in pure fluorescent light, a gold, diagonally-mounted eight-foot fixture from 1963, *the diagonal of May 25, 1963 (to Constantin Brancusi)*.

Flavin's proclaimed discovery of fluorescent light and this first work came to him in an instant:

> From a recent diagram, I declared the *diagonal of personal ecstasy (the diagonal of May 25, 1963)*, a common eight-foot strip with fluorescent light of any commercially available color. At first, I chose "gold."
>
> The radiant tube and the shadow cast by its supporting pan seemed ironic enough to hold alone. There was literally no need to compose this system definitively; it seemed to sustain itself directly, dynamically, dramatically in my workroom wall – a buoyant and insistent gaseous image which, through its brilliance, somewhat betrayed its physical presence into approximate invisibility.
>
> (I put the paired lamp and pan in position at an angle forty-five degrees above the horizontal because that seemed to be a suitable situation of resolved equilibrium but any other positioning could have been just as engaging.)
>
> It occurred to me then to compare the new *diagonal* with Constantin Brancusi's past masterpiece, the *Endless Column*. That artificial *Column* was disposed as a regular formal consequence of numerous similar wood wedge-cut segments extended

vertically – a hewn sculpture (at its inception). The *diagonal* in its overt formal simplicity was only the installation of a dimensional or distended luminous line of a standard industrial device. Little artistic craft could be possible.

Both structures had a uniform elementary visual nature, but they were intended to excel their obvious visible limitations of length and their apparent lack of complication. The *Endless Column* was like some imposing archaic mythologic totem risen directly skyward. The diagonal, in the possible extent of its dissemination as common light repeated effulgently across anybody's wall, had potential for becoming a modern technological fetish.[4]

Flavin's interest in the Endless Column's serial and systematic structure is a clue to his own formal intentions. Brancusi, however, is only one relevant reference for the piece. The dynamic placement of the fixture also recalls the essential compositional diagonal of Russian Constructivist art that was an important source for Flavin. Later, when asked why he chose the diagonal orientation, the artist once remarked that he wanted to differentiate his gesture from Barnett Newman's (vertical 'zip').

Furthermore, this seminal work was made as Flavin was finishing a series of works called 'icons'- wall-mounted constructions comprising square, painted boxes elaborated by various kinds of attached light fixtures and bulbs; and while Flavin describes the selection of the gold colour as 'arbitrary', it is hard not to speculate that the diagonal conjures the gold of an 'icon' in his ironic sense:

...my icons differ from a Byzantine Christ held in majesty; they are dumb-anonymous and inglorious. They are as mute and indistinguished as the run of our architecture. My icons do not raise up the blessed savior in elaborate cathedrals.

They are constructed concentrations celebrating barren
rooms. They bring a limited light.[5]

Noting his reference to icons, art critic Betsy Baker distinguished
Flavin's work from other new artists working in light in 1967, 'Flavin
does something for one's idea of light: it is he who makes its mystical
qualities uncompromisingly evident, by the very fact of such stark
presentation.'[6]

And of course, the diagonal's declared 'personal ecstasy' suggests
the moment of artistic inspiration. But, as art historian Anna Chave
notes, 'the rigid glass tube is also plainly phallic. This is literally, a
hot rod, and Flavin coyly referred to the specific angle he poised the
fixture...alluding to the characteristic angle of an erect penis on a
standing man.'[7] The synthesised religious and the sexual connotations
of the artist's revelry might even ironically suggest a holy 'ecstasy', as
illustrated for example in Gianlorenzo Bernini's archetypical *Ecstasy of
St. Theresa* sculpture (1645–52), though in Flavin's case male in gender
and personal to his artistic (not divine) revelation.

In her well-known 1990 article 'Minimalism and the Rhetoric of
Power', Chave reread Minimalism's rigorous serial forms and industrial
materials in terms of male fixations with power complicit with a
corporate-industrial dominated society – specifically comparing it to
Fascist architecture, and discounting readings by 'sympathetic critics'
that Flavin's art embodies 'the potential for transcendental experience...
recognized through light in virtually all spiritual traditions.' While
Chave's interpretation of Flavin's use of electrical power as an obsession
with dominant power does not hold weight in the long run, her
objection to a softer spiritual interpretation (that might draw an easy
historical line from ancient religious art right through Malevich and
Mark Rothko to Flavin) is a critical understanding that runs into some
of the intentional ambiguities in the work. As she noted, 'In Flavin's
mind, his Diagonal was less a reaffirmation of the possibility for

spiritual experience in contemporary society, than "a modern techno-logical fetish".' Despite, or perhaps because of, the artist's education in a Roman Catholic seminary that provided his first in-depth contact with art, Flavin's 'icons', for example, bear out his use of irony as an antidote to a potentially sentimental reading or evangelical mission that might be located in the use of light in the tradition of art.

Flavin's subtle play between the ironic content of his art, and its laconic formal abstraction, is dramatised in one of his earliest and most important works of 1963, made of three groups of vertical eight-foot white light fixtures on a wall – on the left edge one fixture, in the centre two fixtures, and on the right edge three fixtures. An elemental series, a triptych, a factual accounting of the beginning, middle, and end of a wall, Flavin dedicated the piece to William of Ockham, and called it *the nominal three*.

> With *the nominal three* I will exult primary figures and their dimensions. Here will be the basic counting marks (primitive abstractions) restated long in the daylight glow of common fluorescent tubes. Such an elemental system becomes possible (ironic) from the context of my previous work.[8]

The nominal three comprises a rational and variable system that Flavin intended to be extended and rearranged within a specific architectural container. One installation proposal adds a fourth element of four tubes and arranges the individual elements on four separate walls. A later extension of this idea was realised in a work for a staircase that placed one tube on the first floor, two on the second, etc.

The dedication is explained in a note by Flavin to the artist Mel Bochner:

> ...On this sheet, I enclose a lovely tempering aphorism which has been with me for a few years. "Entia non multiplicanda

praeter necessitatem." "Principles (entities) should not be
multiplied unnecessarily." Of course it is "Ockham's Razor."
If I were you, I would feature it. Briefly, my Columbia Viking
Desk Encyclopedia recognized William of Ockham thusly...'
d.c. 1349, English scholastic philosopher, a Franciscan.
Embroiled in a general quarrel with Pope John XXII, he was
imprisoned in Avignon but fled to the protection of Emperor
Louis IV and supported him by attacking the temporal power
of the papacy. Rejecting the doctrines of Thomas Aquinas
he argued that reality exists solely in individual things and
universals are merely abstract signs. This view led him to
exclude questions such as the existence of God from intellectual
knowledge, referring them to faith alone. 'The nominal three'
is my tribute to William...'[9]

Flavin's citation of Ockham's dictum that 'no more entities should
be posited than are necessary' and his philosophy known as 'nominalism' provide a sort of theological underpinning for 'Minimalism'. If
nominalism held that faith in God must be known separately from
any rational deduction from facts of this earth, Flavin's *nominal three*
becomes a touchstone for his art: keeping the question of faith out of
bounds of the discussion of art, which is matter and is, therefore, no
proof of anything spiritual.

Flavin continued to ward off the spiritual interpretation of his work,
writing in 1967 to Betsy Baker in response to her Art News article,
'My fluorescent tubes never "burn out" desiring a god.'[10] And two
decades later, Flavin became more emphatic,

It is what it is, and it ain't nothin' else...Everything is clearly,
openly, plainly delivered. There is no overwhelming spirituality
you are supposed to come into contact with. I like my use of
light to be openly situational in the sense that there is no

invitation to meditate, to contemplate. It's in a sense a "get-in-get-out" situation. And it is very easy to understand. One might not think of light as a matter of fact, but I do. And it is, as I said, as plain and open and direct an art as you will ever find.[11]

Still, Flavin's ironic play with his own curious theological interests serves a purpose. Had Flavin wished to divorce the art from anything other than its abstract form, would he not have dispensed with references and dedications altogether? In fact Flavin placed his work on the edge of the whole spiritual tradition in art, confronting it directly in order to pursue his own concerns. Flavin used his titles and dedications to balance his abstractions with specifics, and employed all-enveloping light and colour to present the phenomenal in lieu of the symbolic.

The practice Flavin developed of dedicating works (in parenthesis), rather than titling them, became a way of grounding his art in a specific context of place, time, or reference – in parallel to its 'untitled' state of pure abstraction. The dedications leave a trail of the artist's ideas, influences, and personal relationships. Several are reserved for artistic greats of the twentieth century, ranging from Flavin's modern precursors to his close contemporaries. Brancusi, Henri Matisse, Vladimir Tatlin, Ad Reinhardt, and Judd are included in dedications in this selection at the Serpentine. Friends and acquaintances, however, far outweigh the more public dedications to the greats. Judd was of course a friend, as was a lesser-known artist, Dan Hill, designated 'the real Dan Hill' by Flavin so as not to be confused with another artist named Dan Hill who was receiving more public attention. The *European Couples*, four of which are represented in this installation, were contemporary art collectors. Heiner Friedrich was one of Flavin's first dealers in Europe and went on to be his most substantial patron over the course of his life, primarily through the acquisitions and commissions of the Dia Art Foundation that Friedrich founded with Philippa de Menil in 1974.

The simple but colourful 1964 work aptly dedicated to Matisse is comprised of a single vertical eight-foot, four-bulb fixture, with the four basic colour lights of Flavin's electric palette (blue, green, pink, and yellow). It serves as a starting point to examine Flavin's lifelong preoccupation with colour. In their close proximity the four colours are each washed out slightly by the others, becoming almost pastel. The overall light emanating from the piece appears white, blended from colours representing different ranges of the light spectrum. But whenever a body or a wall interrupts the even flow of light, its shadow breaks the colours apart like a prism, revealing the slightly diverse origins of light in the adjacent parallel tubes. A later work, dedicated to 'Don Judd, colorist', presents a similar effect, enhanced by larger volumes of light of each colour. (Flavin and Judd shared colour as one of their deepest bonds.)

The work dedicated 'to the real Dan Hill' shows off the exuberant edge of Flavin's concentration, mixing, and contrasting of the same four colours. A two-bulb fixture leaning against the corner holds two eight-foot tubes, green and blue, facing out. Attached to the back is a two-bulb, four-foot fixture holding pink and yellow, facing into the corner. The corner of the room holds the mixed warm yellow-pink, intensifying the complementary cool blue-green washing the walls outward. The blue, green, pink, and yellow light feature in the 'Matisse' and 'Dan Hill' works appear in pairs and combinations throughout Flavin's oeuvre.

Like pigments used in paint, each of the colours of Flavin's commercially available fluorescent light is manufactured with slightly different phosphors and pigments inside a glass tube, and therefore each bulb has different qualities, not only in the colour of the spectrum it emits, but in the quantity and quality of light it throws. Flavin orchestrated both the colour and luminosity of light in space. On the classic painters' colour-wheel, red, blue, and yellow are primary. For the human eye the equivalent primaries in light would be red, blue, and green – a subtle point Flavin makes in the dedication of his first large-scale installation: *greens crossing green (to Piet Mondrian who lacked green)*. Paying homage to Mondrian and at the same time revising his essential Modernist palette with the addition of green, the dedication embodies Flavin's sense of irony and ambition in equal doses.

Commissioned in 1966 for an exhibition at the Stedelijk van Abbemuseum in Eindhoven,[12] the work dedicated to Mondrian consists of two fence-like constructions of green light crossing each other at slightly different heights, physically blocking access to half of the gallery in which it is installed. Made in green light, the most powerful of all the fluorescent colours, the installation takes over the entire gallery environment in light and space. It became the first of a series of so-called 'barrier' constructions that literally divide the room they inhabit. *Untitled (to you, Heiner, with admiration and affection)*, Flavin's most ambitious barrier, was also created in green light. Made for the Kunsthalle in Cologne, Germany, in 1973, and of variable length, it measured four feet high, and 116 feet in length in its original installation. This monumental work is being exhibited for the first time since then (in a shorter configuration) in this Serpentine presentation.

If green light is the most overwhelming of Flavin's colours, the most rare and complex is ultraviolet. Known also as 'black light,' ultraviolet light sits on the edge of the visible spectrum. In a dark room, such as the one Flavin constructed for the *documenta IV* exhibition in Kassel, Germany, the ultraviolet bulbs appear a soft purple, but have spectacular effects on any white or fluorescent materials near them. Flavin used ultraviolet light in combination with other colours for various effects, both visible and invisible. Since it is ultraviolet radiation inside all fluorescent tubes that activates the fluorescent pigments, Flavin may have also used the high frequency ultraviolet light to help enhance and blend the light of other more visibly coloured bulbs. A 1990 series of works in black light were dedicated appropriately to Ad Reinhardt, recalling the artist's black paintings. Shown in a room filled with ambient light, as in the present installation, the black light is nearly invisible; in low ambient light its unique effect is emphasised.

Ambient light, in the form of daylight from exterior windows or light generated from other lamps nearby, affects some colours like ultraviolet and red more than others, but is an important variable in the exhibition of any of Flavin's works. Low ambient light relatively intensifies the light and colour of the featured fluorescent bulbs. Yet the artist rarely showed his work in a completely dark room, preferring instead to respect the natural interaction with any daylight in a given architectural space. In a site-specific installation, Flavin could tune the intensity of his light in relation to the surrounding ambient light. In the case of individual works, he was aware that they would react differently in each situation.

Unlike most other fluorescent colours derived from the combination of ultraviolet radiation and phosphorescent pigments, the deep colour of red bulbs is achieved mainly by coating the interior of the glass tube with opaque red pigment, giving the bulb itself saturated colour, but sharply reducing the quantity of light output and therefore its influence on the space around it. Its physical presence is strong, but its light is subtler. Thus Flavin often employed red as a distinct note in relation to the strong chords emanating from the other colours and whites. A rare work constructed entirely of red bulbs, Flavin's 1966 *monument 4 to those who have been killed in ambush (to P.K. who reminded me about death)*, casts only a small volume of light on its surrounding walls. Conceived as a kind of war memorial, the work achieved special notoriety when it was installed in Max's Kansas City bar and restaurant, the artist's hangout in New York City in the 1960s. Only when isolated from competing ambient light does Flavin's 'monument' reveal the full depth of its haunting blood-red glow from four eight-foot red lamps arranged in a corner.

The use of the corner is a primary theme throughout Flavin's oeuvre:

I knew that the actual space of a room could be broken down and played with by planting illusions of real light (electric light) at crucial junctures in the room's composition. For example, if you press an eight-foot fluorescent lamp into the vertical climb of a corner, you can destroy that corner by glare and doubled shadow. A piece of wall can be visually disentangled from the whole into a separate triangle by plunging a diagonal of light from edge to edge on the wall; that is, side to floor, for instance. [13]

The dark corner could be obliterated by the single fixture facing out from it, or by focusing light into it, as Flavin did in a series of 1966–71 constructions dedicated to *European Couples*: nine works in all the basic fluorescent colours (blue, green, pink, red, yellow and four whites), each consisting of a square of four eight-foot tubes placed across a corner, the vertical sides focused into the corner and the top and bottom facing out. The luminous square reverses the relationship between wall and corner, leaving the wall dim, and exploiting the volume between them. In other works Flavin elaborated on this basic scheme, creating multi-coloured constructions that blended and contrasted colour in the meeting of the square and triangle.

The corner was the 'crucial juncture' that became the starting point for Flavin's lifelong pursuit of the relationship between light and architecture that he summed up (in 1965, only two years after his first work in fluorescent light):

...What has art been for me?

In the past, I have known it (basically) as a sequence of implicit decisions to combine traditions of painting and sculpture in architecture with acts of electric light defining space... [14]

The corner also has deeper resonance for Flavin, highlighting the artist's fascination with the two luminaries of the Russian avant-garde, Malevich and Tatlin. In 1915 Malevich exhibited his *Black Square* painting in the same *First Futurist Exhibition* in Moscow that Tatlin installed a corner construction of metal, wood, and rope. In the Orthodox religion, the corner of a room holds special meaning as the place where an icon is hung. To their audiences Malevich's and Tatlin's gestures were loaded with the meaning of replacing the sacred icon with Modern art. Malevich's 'Suprematism' bordered on a proposal for a new, modern godless religion inspired by man's potential technological and social transformation. Flavin's early works, particularly his 1962 'icons', were imbued with a similarly complex relationship with their religious referent. Yet while the Modern Russians intended their works to *supersede* the icon with their utopian vision; Flavin makes his gesture with irony and at least an ounce of wit. His icons are dedicated not to the collective potential of humanity, but to a few, mostly tragic, specific individuals. And his lines and squares in the corner are intended less to replace the sacred space of the icon than to occupy the dark leftover space of the gallery.

Flavin's most sustained series of work, 'monuments' dedicated to V. Tatlin (1964–82), project a similar pathos, contrasting the Russian Modern artists' utopian aspirations with the facts of their sometimes tragic fates. Flavin's inspiration was Tatlin's design for a spiral tower that functioned both as art and architecture. The proposed *Monument to the Third International* (1919) symbolised the apotheosis of the ideals of the Russian Revolution and the potential for collaboration of artistic, technological, and political energies. Yet Tatlin's Constructivist dreams for achieving a Utopian society through art, including his monument and a da Vinci-like personal flying-machine, went unrealised. Tatlin died tragically, rejected and destitute (as did some other great artists that were the most favoured subjects of Flavin's early dedications)

Monument 7 in cool white fluorescent light memorializes Vladimir Tatlin, the great revolutionary, who dreamed of art as science. It stands, a vibrantly aspiring order, in lieu of his last glider, which never left the ground. [15]

Even the dynamic Constructivist diagonal of his first fluorescent work reflects Flavin's special reverence for his Russian predecessors. Flavin wrote that his early work was:

Founded in the young tradition of a plastic revolution which gripped Russian art only forty years ago. My joy is to try to build from the "incomplete" experience as I see fit.

Yet in his revision of Tatlin's project, Flavin discounts Tatlin's monumental aspirations:

I always use "monuments" in quotes to emphasize the ironic humor of temporary monuments. These "monuments" only survive as long as the light system itself is useful (2,100 hours). [16]

The artist's appropriation of technology is not, like Tatlin's, a proposal for a new order. In place of Tatlin's future Utopia, Flavin proclaims the light fixture's factual ephemeral presence. Nor is Flavin's work, as critic Anna Chave suggested, a celebration of or 'complicit with the corporate-industrial dominated society'. The fluorescent bulb is, rather, the pedestrian utilitarian result of the industrial revolution Tatlin had such transcendental hopes for.

Flavin's gesture is more complex. It is an ironic commentary on the commercial fate of the Modernist ideal, tempered with sympathy for the often-tragic fate of the artist. It substitutes the timeless universal ideal with an ephemeral individual fact, and rejects concepts like God and humanity in favour of specific individual lives. It often prefers the gallery's ancillary corners, floors, and columns to its sacred walls. Like Ockham's nominalist theology, it has a fundamental built-in resistance to making spiritual claims from its material fact.

Call it nominalism., or even Minimalism, the rigorous fundamental formal and philosophical foundations Flavin built for his work – his conscious choice of a restricted and readymade medium of commercially available fluorescent light, and his use of irony, humour and tragedy – limit the oeuvre's potential spiritual, utopian, or heroic ambitions in favour of an even more expansive field of investigation: the present, illusive, environmental, and phenomenal visual effects of light defining space.

1 Dan Flavin, in *Dan Flavin: three installations in fluorescent light*, Cologne: Wallraf-Richartz Museum and the Kunsthalle, 1973-74, p. 108. Flavin's writings in general are as eccentric in form as they are meaningful and insightful in content. Irregularities in grammar and spelling are common, and contribute to the urgency of his sentiments.

2 Conversation with the artist, summer 1992.

3 Cologne, p. 87. From Flavin's most XX autobiographical account, '...in daylight or cool white', which began as part of a lecture in 1964 and was revised several times, notably in the December 1965 issue of *Artforum* and for the Cologne exhibition.

4 Ibid, p. 87, from '...in daylight or cool white'.

5 Ibid, p. 83. The commentary is taken from a 'record' book entry dated 9 August 1962.

6 Baker, Elizabeth C., *Art News*, March 1967, pp. 52–54, 63–67.

7 Chave, Anna, 'Minimalism and the Rhetoric of Power', 1990.

8 Cologne, p. 16.

9 *Dan Flavin: fluorescent light, etc.*, Ottawa: National Gallery of Canada for the Queen's Printer, 1969, p. 206.

10 Cologne, p. 94.

11 Michael Gibson, 'The Strange Case of the Fluorescent Tube', *Art International*, no. 1, Autumn 1987, p. 105.

12 Flavin designed the work for the 'El Lissitzky drawing cabinet' gallery of Stedelijk van Abbemuseum, Eindhoven, for the exhibition *Kunst-Licht-Kunst*, 24 September – 5 December 1966.

13 Cologne, p. 87, from '...in daylight or cool white'.

14 Ibid, p. 87.

15 Quoted from a wall text written by Flavin for the Los Angeles Museum of Contemporary Art's Temporary Contemporary exhibition, *"monuments" to V. Tatlin from Dan Flavin, 1964-1982*, 21 April –17 June 1984, and travelling.

16 Quoted in Suzanne Munchnic, 'Flavin Exhibit: His Artistry Comes to Light', *Los Angeles Times*, 23 April 1984.

Dan Flavin, Serpentine Gallery, London, 2001.

How many artists does it take to change a light bulb?

Jonathan Jones

It is the humblest and most taken-for-granted of lights, burning steadily, unnoticed by passers-by in a corridor or an underground car park. Monotonous, characterless light, lacking atmosphere, opposite of the lights we cherish – those elaborately shaded, delicately directed spots and table lamps. In cities around the world, you see it in the hot night, hung up over street vendors' stalls. Fluorescent light is proletarian light.

In the art of Dan Flavin, the humble is elevated. Commercially produced, fluorescent strip lighting takes on the sacred power of the candle held by Mary Magdalene, as painted in the 17th century in Georges de La Tour's *The Penitent Magdalene*. Flavin's fluorescent light is enduring, tranquil, cool. The very qualities that in other situations make it invisible and unloved – the seamlessness of the glow, the lack of dramatic intensity – become beautiful.

The power of Flavin's installations is that they never let you forget the origins of the light that bathes us in green and red, chills us with funereal white, grants us a rapturous revelation of gold. After wandering through the various rooms of London's Serpentine Gallery, turned into chapels and cupolas of colour, filling your eyes with a fizzing mixture of orange, blue, pink, you may feel drunk. But you are never asked to lose track of material reality. This is an urban, modern light. The tubes are all quite clearly plugged into the wall. There is no magic here, except the electricity system. A couple of tubes flicker, though they are so amply filled with light, like fat cigars of colour (or luminous phalluses, as was said of Flavin's breakthrough work, *the diagonal of May 25, 1963*), that these flutters are absorbed as ripples, confirming the overall strength of the light.

Looking through the windows, you see people walking their dogs, riding bikes, peering in curiously. Except that Kensington Gardens are now pink. Your senses are drugged, you find yourself experiencing a levity, and a confusion about what you are seeing. If the means of his art are prosaic, its effects are disorienting. But, like everything about Flavin's art, this is easily explained. We see an afterglow of "complementary colour" after we are exposed to a more powerful colour, a way of balancing out the way our mind comprehends the visual world. In the cleverest *coup de théâtre* of this installation, Flavin's 1978 work *untitled (to you, Heiner, with admiration and affection)* inhabits a long gallery with windows looking out over the park. The piece is a long, low wall, just over a metre high, of green fluorescent lights, extending the length of the room, filling the space with greenness. Everyone's skin is green. We are elves in an electric, glowing forest.

This is a very American art. To get the exact tone, you have to set it against the American cityscape it reflects, in which artificial light is used with unbounded enthusiasm – pink neon signs over motels, malls washed with gold light. Through American eyes, even in the banal functional device of fluorescent strip lighting, we have created something utterly new and marvellous on the earth, an artificial paradise where we need never be in the dark.

Flavin's art is a celebration of this empire of light. His art isn't afraid of becoming another part of the city's decoration. One of the works here, *monument 4 for those who have been killed in ambush (to PK who reminded me about death)*, was made in 1966 to be part of the décor of Max's Kansas City, the famous New York bar where artists hung out in the 1960s and 1970s. This is an evilly red object, an arrangement of four red fluorescent lights; it is deeply, sumptuously nocturnal. Flavin reveals here that red is the closest light to darkness itself, and you would be excited – and perhaps a bit nervous – drinking after hours in a bar lit by this fiery redness.

He reveals the potential beauty of an electric, modern, urban world, but he does so by limiting how much of this world's complexity he allows into his work. He uses one component (industrially produced fluorescent lighting), and restricts himself to the colours it normally comes in (10 in all). He doesn't exploit the other, more obviously spectacular, resources of modern light – no lasers, writing in neon, strobes, spots. Compared with the play of light you encounter just passing along an American highway, his art is ascetic.

This strategy has a name. Flavin was one of the New York artists who in the 1960s rejected the flamboyant, painterly work of the previous generation of American artists, the abstract expressionists, and sought to make art that was the opposite of the forceful emotionalism of Jackson Pollock, Willem de Kooning, Mark Rothko. Along with Don Judd, Carl Andre and Robert Morris, Flavin was one of the key figures of minimalism.

Dull on paper but glorious in the gallery, Flavin's art uses minimal means to luxurious effect. Concentration is pleasure, and Flavin concentrates everything he loves about art into this game he plays with strip lighting. Minimalist art can be exuberant, we realise, among such positively florid expressions of sensuality as Flavin's electric tulip *untitled (to the real Dan Hill) 1b*, an arrangement of blue, green, pink and yellow tubes that casts a magnificent chromatic glow on the wall. Flavin distils a theory of art into his work. This is neither painting nor sculpture, yet refers to both. His fascination with colour is that of a painter – one early work is dedicated to Matisse – and yet he's interested in forms in space, like a sculptor. He also "draws", arranging his lines of light in space. Then again, he's an architect, transforming spaces: his lights change the feel of the rooms so radically they become structural components of the space rather than decorations. His series of framed spaces defined by classical pillars and pedestals of light dedicated "to European couples" (actually to European art collectors) are little houses of light, like classical follies in a landscaped garden.

This art does not exist without being installed. A strip light only stops being an ordinary strip light when placed in a certain Flavinesque way. More than any of the other early minimalists, Flavin's art takes on new meanings in different locations, against different architecture. This experimentation with site-specific possibilities has continued since his death in 1996, with the opening of posthumous permanent installations, and now this installation at the Serpentine, which plays freely with Flavin's classic works, using the gallery's architecture as part of their effect. The Serpentine show is curated by Michael Govan, director of the Dia Centre in New York, which has been closely involved with Flavin's work since its foundation in 1974.

This posthumous career illuminates Flavin's art. Light has been a symbol of the spiritual and imperishable for centuries in western art. But what happens when light is ubiquitous, when it never fades, when we're constantly immersed in synthesised colour? Flavin is at one level celebrating and enjoying this modern light, but there's anxiety too. Because his palette is so limited, his means so specific and their material nature evident, his art makes us aware of nature as it seems to offer a counter-nature. In the end it is elegiac rather than utopian. His works dedicated to the Bolshevik visionary Vladimir Tatlin are glorious tombs, shining epitaphs to the failure of a dream: Tatlin's proposed monuments to the Russian revolution have become, with time, images of folly and defeat. Flavin called a lot of his works "monuments". And this is what they are – monuments, but weightless, the opposite of grandiose. They are just light, shed by very ordinary devices with a limited lifespan. They are modest, graceful tributes, afterglows. Eventually they will go out.

Everything Flavin made is a monument to the ordinary humble servant, electric light, and to that which has no weight in history, everyday moments, the corners of our lives we don't remember. "I can take the ordinary lamp out of use and into a magic that touches ancient mysteries," Flavin wrote in 1962, hoping that when his lamps no longer worked, when the entire electrical system passed into history, it would be remembered that they once gave light.

The Guardian, August 28, 2001, p. 10.

Conceptual artist with a light touch
Mark Irving

Most people hate fluorescent lights, perhaps because they remind them of chill office lighting: their cold impersonal glow a visible analogy for the all-seeing eye of management. The American artist Dan Flavin, however, did the impossible and spent his whole career turning them into delicately beautiful works of art. The present exhibition of his work at the Serpentine Gallery, London, organised by the Dia Center for the Arts in New York, a supportive collector of and showcase for Flavin's art from the 1970s, is the artist's first significant retrospective in the UK and is a testament to his obsession with the aesthetic potential of fluorescent light.

Flavin switched on to this potential with his seminal work *diagonal of May 25, 1963*, an ordinary 8ft-long lighting fixture with a bright yellow (he called it "gold") tube. Describing it as a "diagonal of personal ecstasy" – fixed to the wall with one end on the floor and the other pitched at an angle of 45 degrees, the piece is suggestively phallic – Flavin changed the fluorescent light from being something that hummed anonymously above you to a dazzling line of light.

While certain neon tubes have been designed to lure houseflies to their death, Flavin's work is kinder. Working with a palette of four different kinds of white tube and six coloured tubes – blue, green, pink, red, yellow, ultraviolet, and using what varied lengths of tube were commercially available (two, four, six and eight foot), Flavin spent decades exploring different compositional arrangements, sometimes placing the tubes together, sometimes apart, in a quest to achieve as reduced and elegant an expressive language as possible.

In common with his American contemporaries Carl Andre, Donald Judd, James Turrell, Sol LeWitt, Robert Ryman (they would come to be known as Minimalists) Flavin's work dispensed with the notion of striving at "being" sculpture (something that stood in the middle of a gallery). His work instead proposes the gradual absorption of architectural space itself as the subject of art. Flavin's series of works dedicated to the monument proposed by Tatlin to celebrate the achievements of the Russian Revolution – the central rotunda of the Serpentine is given over to these angelic columns of white fluorescent lights – is an ironic, if respectful comment on the irreconcilable differences between artistic idealism and the world of *realpolitik*. For Flavin working in the 1960s, art could no longer sustain visions of Utopia.

While there are clear formal comparisons to be drawn from Flavin's work with early 20th century artists such as Malevich, Mondrian and Matisse, his distrust of the monumental owes something to the work of Constantin Brancusi, one of Flaivn's heroes, whose sculptures played on the idea of endlessness, of never-ending chains or columns – in other words, they refuted the concept of the solitary, isolated work of art. For Flavin and his American colleagues, this presented a brilliant model for their practice: by making art that didn't look like art, but looked like the stuff that surrounds us – lights, floors, boxes – it made art as big, as important (if not more so) as the space that contains it. This clever strategy reveals Minimalism (Flavin hated the term) to be a greedy impulse: it is actually about maximising, not reducing the creative canvas. And what greater element could an artist take on as his material than light itself ?

Flavin was a past master at reducing things to their most basic components to achieve a greater effect: by working with light – a substance that inevitably tinges the surfaces of things around it – he colonises the architecture in which these lights are placed, thus incorporating the visual experience of being in these rooms – in other words, your vision – into the work. This may explain why he called the pieces he created from the mid 1960s right up until his death in 1996 "situations" rather than sculptures, since the term implies this collaborative partnership between the work and the spaces in which they are shown. It was this powerful synergy between the two that secured Flavin the commissions for the astonishing Chiesa Rosa in Milan, the rotunda of the Guggenheim Museum in New York and the series of works at Marfa, Texas, the "museum" of contemporary art established by his colleague Judd.

Flavin's expertise in mastering architectural space is impressive: walk into a room occupied by a Flavin piece and you find your true colour soon disappears: whites take on different hues, your retina becomes saturated with colour and views of the landscape of Hyde Park as seen through the windows of the gallery are changed into Martian scenes of pink or sepia.

All this exquisiteness with light has long made Flavin the darling of the chic designer crowd. The striking use of fluorescent lighting around the turbine hall and stairways of Tate Modern, for example, owes everything to Flavin. One of the risks inherent in co-opting standard fluorescent lights (Flavin's preferred brand is now obsolete) as art, and architecture as your accomplice is that, outside the rarefied confines of the art gallery, it can become difficult to distinguish one from the other.

The Financial Times, August 28, 2001, p. 12.

How I found heaven on the tube
Charles Darwent

A wonderful thing – no, sod it, a miraculous thing – happens when you walk from the Serpentine Gallery's rotunda into the room containing Dan Flavin's *untitled (to you, Heiner, with admiration and affection)* (1973). The piece, a wall built from Flavin's trademark neon strip-lights, divides the space in two. On the far of it are the gallery's windows, with a view of Kensington Gardens beyond. All the usual park-ish things are going on in this vista – picnickers picnicking, children wailing, dogs being moodily canine. But something odd has happened. The green of Flavin's neon strips has leached the colour from the scene, so that it looks like a 30-year-old home movie of itself. Inside the gallery, everything is verdant, alive, actual. Outside, mere actuality is reduced to an image: filmic, faded and two-dimensional.

It's heart-stopping. The piece achieves an ambition as old as Plato's cave: it out-reals reality. In Flavin's hands, the world of parks and dogs becomes a has-been, a lick of nostalgia. It is the artist's world, defined by his gently buzzing neon grid, that is the here and now, the living space; the place we want to be.

Miraculous? Well, yes. You feel that you're witnessing not so much a transformation as a transubstantiation; the changing of an element – light – so essential that it can only be altered by an Einsteinian shift of colour and time. Flavin's *to you, Heiner* raises all kinds of questions, one of them being exactly where (and what) it is. Is the piece Flavin's humming neon wall, or the room in which it stands, or the whole world? Its grid is reflected in the gallery's windows, so that it seems to exist outside of them. Does Flavin's artistry lie in that flickering green reflection, or within it or beyond it?

I don't want to sound like a loony here, but it does seem that there's something deeply religious going on. In part, of course, it's coincidence, to do with the ancient associations of glass, light and colour. Like stained glass, Flavin's work asks questions about what we see and how we see it: whether the images we're looking at are things that absorb light or things that emit it. (Just to make this phenomenon more phenomenologically uncertain, the natural light in the Serpentine's rooms is so bright that it's hard to tell whether Flavin's neon bulbs are even switched on. In the case of the black-lite strips in *untitled (for Ad Reinhardt) 2d* (1990), you feel sure they aren't.) If you're minded that way, it's possible to read Flavin's colours – morose blues, minatory reds, sherbert-dab pinks and greens – as having a significance that is almost liturgical. The white of the works in the gallery's rotunda – the various "monuments" for V. Tatlin, made between 1964 and 1975 – is clearly about purity (or, if you prefer, immaculacy), even if it is of a formal rather than a divine kind.

Like all good miracles, there's a moral edge to Flavin's work, too. The point about any transubstantiation – water into wine, wine into blood, base metals into gold – is that the initial commodity must seem unpromising. The is particularly true in the case of Flavin's chosen medium: we tend to associate neon strips with a trashy way of seeing, ignoble light. The artist appears to have been strict about buying his materials off the shelf, as readymades. The colours in his private liturgy were thus also available to strip-club owners in search of a rosy glow or bartenders who wanted to stop people shooting up in lavatories. In rescuing neon from ignominy, Flavin was offering the late 20th-century redemption of a kind.

In the end, though, the wonder of his work is in its perverse emotional power. Neon strips are pointedly anonymous: insofar as Flavin has laid his hands on them, it has been to arrange them in simple geometric shapes. (One, *the diagonal of May 25, 1963 (to Constantin Brancusi)*, is a single yellow strip tilted at 45 degrees.) Flavin's works have personal dedications, but, according to the artist, they're ironic: "I always use 'monuments' in quotes," he said, noting that his own would burn out after 2,100 hours. And yet there's something deeply attached, deeply personal about these works, a quality that goes way beyond handy words like "readymade" or "Minimalism". If you're reading this on Sunday morning, my advice is to skip church and head for the Serpentine Gallery. You'll never get to heaven if you don't.

The Independent on Sunday, September 2, 2001, p. 11.

Dan Flavin
David Batchelor

It is an obvious but often unremarked fact that our experience of colour has been transformed over the past 100 or so years. This revolution, a small but highly visible part of the larger revolutions in industry, electrification and electronics, has meant that colour in the modern city is almost entirely new and completely unnatural. Most of the colour we now see is chemical or electrical; it is plastic or metallic, it is flat, shiny, glowing or flashing (or it is broken, switched off and as if it were never there). It is intense, but also ephemeral; it is vivid, but also con-tingent. And it is ubiquitous: always and everywhere allied to commerce and the street. It is perhaps equally obvious – and also largely unre-marked – that for most of the last century the traditional forms of art fail to acknowledge and respond to this aspect of modernity. With a few important exceptions in Dada and Constructivism, it was not until the late 1950s and early 1960s that a few artists in Europe and the Americas began seriously to enquire into the nature of this colour and its characteristic materials. Among them was Dan Flavin.

Many of us are familiar with Flavin's signature work, which, after 1963, was made exclusively with commercially available fluorescent lights and their fittings. Less well known are the works which imme-diately precede *the diagonal of May 25, 1963 (to Robert Rosenblum)*. I first came across examples from the 'Icon' series when I visited Donald Judd's New York house in 1995, a few months after he had died. I was being escorted around the five-storey SoHo building looking at some of Judd's own work and at pieces he owned by other artists. It was a much less predictable collection than I had imagined: among works by Stella and, I think, Andre, there was a Duchamp snow shovel, a small box by Lucas Samaras, a soft drainpipe by Oldenburg, some African bowls and two flashing, glowing box-like things. I hadn't got a clue what to make of them, and didn't at first recognise them as being by Flavin. They are small, improvised and irregular: not exactly thrown together, but certainly hand-made from a variety of hardware store materials – three different types of lamp and lamp holders, electrical flex, hardboard, plywood, household paint and, in the case of *icon III*, a 24in square section of red linoleum. They are strange – "blunt, awkward, interesting", as Judd put it.

They are paintings of a sort – paintings with problems. The original installation shot, a grainy black and white image of 1964, shows six works placed uncomfortably close together on a short wall in the Kaymar Gallery, New York (one hung a different way up from how I had seen it). Even without being able to discern their brightly coloured surfaces and glowing lights, they look refreshingly unsubtle: a bit disorderly and a bit deviant, like a line of suspects waiting to be interviewed after a disturbance. They are paintings, but only just, and not for much longer. It's easy to know that in retrospect, but much harder to imagine what they must have felt like at the time. These are borderline works, anomalies which don't quite make sense as paintings, but don't yet make much sense as anything else either. They are works with potential, but part of their potential is to be a public embarrassment.

A boxy monochrome painting with a bit of light stuck on its side is either a bit smart or a bit desperate – or a bit of both. A couple of Rauschenberg's 'Combines' incorporate small flashing lights among other things on their large complicated surfaces, but here the collision is more direct, more blunt.

Rauschenberg worked hard to absorb wildly diverse objects and fragments into a more or less unified pictorial field, and a part of his brilliance was in his ability to hold off the moment at which the literal finally ruptured the pictorial. With Flavin it is more like a contest between two incompatible elements, one or other of which was going to have to give way (or that at least is how it appears now).

It may have been as a result of the *icons* that Flavin came to accept –

warily at first, no doubt, and then enthusiastically – that the colours and materials of the street had finally, for him, eclipsed the traditional colours and materials of painting and sculpture. Other artists at the time were beginning to make pieces which were shiny, reflective or transparent, saturated in chemical and highly artificial colours but Flavin's *icons* were the first that glowed, and this remains a scandalously under-rated achievement.

Tate, issue 26, Autumn 2001, p. 18.

Editorial note

Texts included in this volume appear as originally published, unless otherwise stated. Only titles of works have been standardized.

Copyright notices